The Substance of Spinoza

THE SUBSTANCE
OF SPINOZA

Errol E. Harris

HUMANITIES PRESS
NEW JERSEY

First published 1995 by Humanities Press International, Inc.,
Atlantic Highlands, New Jersey 07716.

Library of Congress Cataloging-in-Publication Data

Harris, Errol E.
    The substance of Spinoza / by Errol E. Harris.
      p.   cm.
    Includes bibliographical references and index.
    ISBN 0–391–03827–3
    1. Spinoza, Benedictus de, 1632–1677. I. Title.
B3998.H276 1994
199'.492—dc20   93-3851
                            CIP

A catalog record for this book is available from the British Library.

Printed in the United States of America

Contents

Preface

Since the publication of *Salvation from Despair: A Reappraisal of Spinoza's Philosophy*, I have delivered a number of papers to Spinoza conferences, some of which have been published in their proceedings, and have contributed others to commemorative volumes and journals. All of these papers I have now revised and in some measure rewritten, and they are here collected together with two hitherto unpublished essays under one cover.

Salvation discussed the body of Spinoza's philosophy as it appears in his writings, and although the views of some of the older and better-known commentators were taken into consideration, the later influence of the philosopher was not closely examined, nor were some of the more recent writings about his work. In the essays included in this book various particularly teasing problems that arise out of Spinoza's thought and exposition are discussed and the way in which certain recent and contemporary commentators have addressed them. In Part 3, I have examined the influence exercised by Spinoza's philosophy on some of his successors, and their reactions to it. As the correct interpretation of Spinoza depends on the reading of certain key passages, reference to these crops up again and again in my discussion of the way others have interpreted, and misinterpreted, him. Consequently, some repetition has been unavoidable, but I hope that each new recurrence to the doctrines discussed will serve to throw fresh light on them from a different angle.

The title of the book is deliberately ambiguous. It is appropriate because the subject throughout is, by and large, Spinoza's doctrine of Substance; at the same time, what is discussed does bear upon the substance of Spinoza's philosophy, even if it does not treat of it exhaustively. No attempt, however, has been made to cover the whole range of Spinoza's system in this book, as was done in the previous volume; and a measure of acquaintance with the texts by the reader has been assumed. There are numerous other aspects of Spinoza's work and questions that arise out of it which are not discussed, in part because I have paid some attention to several of them in the earlier book, and have not found occasion to examine them more closely in the interval that has since elapsed. There is certainly plenty of scope for further investigation, and had opportunity served, I should like to have examined more in depth Spinoza's psychology and his ethical theory. His political theory, especially with regard to democracy, freedom of thought and religious tolerance, merits scrutiny and discussion; and I could also wish to have gone more deeply into his views on prophecy, the function and significance of religious ceremonies, miracles, and the distinction between true religion and superstition. But, like everybody else, I am subject to limitations that are not easily overcome, and for which, perhaps, no apology need be made.

In the course of my research into Spinoza's predecessors' writings on the Original Contract, I think I may have made a discovery, not philosophical but literary: namely, that John Milton was the English translator of the 1648 edition of *Vindiciae contra tyrannos*, now attributed to Duplessis Mornay, which was (like many others, including Spinoza's own *Tractatus Theologico-Politicus*) published anonymously. None of the experts whom I have consulted have been able to produce evidence either in favor of or against the assumption, but the evidence which has persuaded me is the similarity both of style and of argument between that translation and Milton's own treatise, *The Tenure of Kings and Magistrates*, which was published only one year later. I should be most interested to discover if there is any more substantial evidence, and where it might be found, either that Milton was indeed the translator, or that it was somebody else. The settlement of this issue, one way or the other, however, has no bearing on the philosophical subject of Chapter 8, below.

A complete bibliography of works by and about Spinoza would fill a volume by itself. For the one at the end of this book I have drawn heavily on those compiled by my friends Jon Wetlesen and Theo van der Werf, but even since they were published further important material has appeared, not all of which has been brought to my notice. I can only hope that what has been offered will prove helpful and at least relatively adequate.

Immediately after Spinoza's death, his bad reputation as an atheist (which in truth he was not) led to a suppression and neglect of his work for more than a century; and in recent years, the reaction against metaphysics, by Logical Positivists, Existentialists, and even some Phenomenologists, has resulted in a decline of interest in Spinoza. But Spinoza studies have always flourished in the Netherlands, where Vereniging het Spinzahuis keeps them alive and up to date. Elsewhere on the continent of Europe also Spinoza studies have not been neglected, and new impetus has been given to them by the resuscitation of an annual journal, *Studia Spinozana*, to replace the long-defunct *Chronicum Spinozanum*. Today there are healthy signs of revival, and the recent formation of a North American Spinoza Society will be heralded by Spinoza enthusiasts with gratification and good hope.

Neglect of so profound a philosopher is hardly to be tolerated, and those who find more in philosophy than a mere intellectual exercise will not lightly forgo the benefit and inspiration to be gained by close study of works in which the deepest insights and most penetrating thought of one of the greatest minds of all time have been concentrated within the comparatively small compass of a handful of volumes.

E. E. H.
HIGH WRAY

Acknowledgments

The publisher gratefully acknowledges permission to use the following material:

In Chapter 1, from "Method and Metaphysics in Spinoza," originally published in *Studia Spinozana*, Vol. 2 (1986).

In Chapter 2, from "Finite and Infinite in Spinoza's System," originally published in *Speculum Spinozanum*, ed. Siegfried Hessing. London, Routledge and Kegan Paul, 1977.

In Chapter 3, from "The Infinity of the Attributes and *idea ideae*," originally published in *Nueu Hefte für Philosophie* (Spinoza 1677–1977), Heft 12, ed. R. Buber, K. Cramer, and R. Wiehl, 1977.

In Chapter 4, "The Body-Mind Relation," originally published in *Spinoza's Metaphysics*, ed. James B. Wilbur, 1976; and in Chapter 5, "The Order and Connexion of Ideas," originally published in *Spinoza on Knowing, Being and Freedom*, ed. J. G. van der Bend, Van Gorcum, Asson., 1974.

In Chapter 6, "The Essence of Man and the Subject of Consciousness," originally published in *Spinoza's Philosophy of Man*, ed. J. Wetlesen, Universitetsforlaget, Oslo, 1978.

In Chapter 12, "Schelling and Spinoza: Spinozism and Dialectic," originally published in *Spinoza: Issues and Directions*, ed. Edwin Curley and Pierre-Francois Moreau, E. J. Brill, Leiden, 1990.

In Chapter 13, "The Concept of Substance in Spinoza and Hegel," originally published in *Spinoza nel 350⁰ Anniversario della Nascita*, ed. Emilia Giancotti, Saggi Bibliopolis, 1985.

Abbreviations

E   *Ethics.* References to this work are indicated as has now become customary, with the Part in arabic figure immediately following the title abbreviation, propositions, etc. shown and numbered thus: P12; Axiom, A2; Definition, D4; Scholium, S; Demonstration, Dem; Corollary, C. (e.g., E1P5Dem = *Ethics,* Part I, Proposition 5, Demonstration).

Epp   *Epistolae doctorum quorundum virorum ad B.d.S. et Auctoris Responsiones* (Letters of certain learned men to B.d.S. and the Author's answers). Ep for singular references.

KV   *Korte Verhandling van God, de Mensch, en deszelfs Welstand (Short Treatise on God, Mankind, and Human Well-being).*

PPC   *Principia Philosophiae Cartesianae, More geometrico demonstratae (Principles of Cartesian Philosophy, Demonstrated Geometrically).*

TdIE   *Tractatus de Intellectus Emendatione.* Section and paragraph numbers as in the Bruder edition.

TP   *Tractatus Politicus.*

TTP   *Tractatus Theologico-Politicus.*

PART I

Epistemology
and
Metaphysics

1

Spinoza's Method and His Metaphysics

Contrary to the view defended by several commentators, Spinoza's method and epistemology are dependent upon his metaphysics and not vice versa. Some of the most revered Spinozists have complained that Spinoza's doctrine was molded by his method and have attributed what they considered its defects to that relationship. Both H. H. Joachim and John Caird have made this submission, accusing Spinoza of a rigid determinism dictated by his geometrical method, which, they say, is suited only to abstract subject matters and is altogether inappropriate to the concrete philosophical thinking for which Spinoza is most renowned.[1] G. H. R. Parkinson expresses a similar opinion in his book, *Spinoza's Theory of Knowledge*, treating the methodology as fundamental and the metaphysic as consequential.[2] This opinion, however, is based upon a misconception of Spinoza's actual procedure, which, largely due to his own statements, is superficially misleading, and only if the relation of the methodology to the metaphysic is rightly understood can either of them be properly assessed.

It is clearly an error to attribute features of Spinoza's doctrine that are set out in the *Short Treatise on God, Man, and Human Welfare* as well as in the *Ethics* to his use of the geometrical method; for the method is not used in the earlier treatise. Even apart from that circumstance, no philosopher's views on method can rightly be divorced from his (or her) epistemology, for epistemology is inseparable from ontology and from metaphysics generally. In Spinoza's system, this interdependence is unmistakable because he makes it abundantly clear that he conceives the nature of the intellect, the essential form of knowledge, and the proper method of attaining truth as dependent upon the nature of Substance and its attributes. Unless these are rightly conceived, Spinoza's method and his whole account of knowledge in its three forms are liable to be misunderstood and grossly misrepresented.

The dependence, for Spinoza, of epistemology upon ontology is apparent from his definition of the third kind of knowledge (*scientia intuitiva*) — the only kind fully worthy of the name — as proceeding from an adequate idea of the formal essence of certain attributes of God to an adequate knowledge of the essence of things (E2P40S2). An adequate idea of God's attributes is thus the precondition of adequate knowledge. Further, attribute is defined as what the intellect perceives of Substance as constituting its essence (E1D4); so the nature of Substance is prior both to the meaning of attribute and to the proper understanding of the nature of knowledge. "The intellect," it must be remembered, is not simply the human intellect, but always, for Spinoza, the infinite (divine) intellect; for, unlike Descartes, he speaks of only one "thinking thing," that is, God (cf. Epp 32, 44), in whose intellect the human mind is but one idea — that of the human body. What the intellect perceives of Substance, therefore, is God's idea of Himself: *infinita idea Dei*, which is the adequate idea of God's attributes, or what constitutes His essence, and from this all else follows.

This observation, however, requires the qualification that *infinita idea Dei* is itself one idea, in the sense that there is only one Substance; although it is an infinitely complex idea, coherently one despite innumerable internal differentiations, or modes, of which the human mind is a finite example. What human knowledge is and how it is acquired can be understood, therefore, only in the light of the metaphysic which reveals the nature of Substance, its attributes and their modes, both infinite (like *infinita idea Dei*) and finite.

Of course, the metaphysic is a product of human thought and an example of human knowing; but, as Spinoza insists, human consciousness is self-reflective; the idea of the human body necessarily involves an idea of that idea (i.e., of the human mind), and every finite mode, as a modification of Substance (one of its innumerable self-differentiations), contains immanent within it the essence of Substance under the appropriate attribute. And as there is an idea of every mode in the divine intellect, an adequate idea of the essence of God as expressed through one of His attributes is necessarily involved in every finite mode. This is true, in particular, of the human mind and of its idea of itself, so that once it has been purified of confused ideas (*imaginatio*), it can conceive the essence of God adequately through the adequate idea of the attribute of Thought, and it recognizes the intellect as that the nature of which is to frame true ideas (TdIE, IX, 73); and, as it is the idea of the body, it can also grasp the nature of God as extended, and so has an adequate idea of that attribute as well. Thus it can enjoy adequate knowledge of the essence of things by the third kind of knowledge. Accordingly, by insisting that metaphysics is prior to methodology, we are not arguing in a vicious circle, but are merely exemplifying the essentially self-reflective character of philosophical thinking, which *is* circular, but in a valid and productive way.

Moreover, in the *Tractatus de Intellectus Emendatione*, Spinoza observes early on that the search for a method does not, and must not, involve an infinite regress. We cannot and do not need to discover first a method of investigating the method, and before that to seek for a prior method ad infinitum. For the intellect possesses innately its own instruments of discovery, the objective essences of the things it requires to know. The objective essence is the truth, for it is the same in idea as the formal essence is in reality, and once we possess it, its truth is apparent on its face—for to know something is to know that you know, and the method is simply the reflective awareness (*ideae idearum*) of true ideas.

The *Tractatus*, in which Spinoza discusses method, he undoubtedly intended as a propaedeutic to what he calls "my philosophy." In it he sets out the method, or *debitus ordo*, by which truth is to be sought, and that eternal and infinite object is to be attained the love of which alone feeds the mind with joy and is devoid of all tribulation. But no sooner has he announced his intention in the proemium, and stated the practical aim of his quest, than it becomes apparent that the method is secondary to the conception of that object itself.

Descartes, following Aristotle, had maintained that the simplest truths, the starting points (*archai*) of all strict reasoning, were self-evident (*per se notae*), and in his early work Spinoza seems to agree. But it soon appears, even here in the *Tractatus*, that this is not his more considered position. For, although he says that once we have a true idea we know immediately that it is true, he tells us how we are to test and establish its truth. When the mind attends to some fiction, something fictitious and false by its own nature, he tells us, and deduces from it whatever is deducible in good order, its falsity becomes easily apparent; but if a hypothesis is true by its own nature, when the mind attends to it, understands it, and begins to deduce what follows from it in the right order, we may proceed propitiously without any interruption (TdIE). The truth or falsity of the hypothesis thus depends on the systematic coherence of the consequences validly deducible from it. This Spinoza reiterates somewhat differently a little further on. So far as what constitutes the form of truth is concerned, he says, it is certain that true knowledge is distinguished from false, not so much by an extrinsic indicator, as by an intrinsic one; for if, say, an architect were to conceive a building properly, his thought would be true and would remain so whether or not the building had ever existed (ibid). In the last resort, as he said before, the truth consists in the objective essence of that which is conceived in and through itself—in short, it is the comprehensive and systematic coherence of the whole.

All we need, then, to begin our pursuit of truth is a true idea— "and we have a true idea." Moreover, since objective essences are related to one another as are the corresponding formal essences (are in fact substantially identical with them), the idea of a perfect being is more excellent than any other idea, and is the obvious criterion of all truth; and the best method is that which directs the mind according to this norm. The most perfect being would obviously be a coherent whole such as has been mentioned above, uniting in itself all its "parts" or modes coherently and systematically in the highest degree (compare Ep 32); and we are later to learn (from the *Ethics*) that there can be only one such. Here, in the TdIE, we are told that if we are to acquire true knowledge of nature we must derive all our ideas from the idea of the source and origin of every reality, as well as of all other ideas—which is undoubtedly the perfect being the idea of which is to be our norm.

In all this the metaphysical doctrine of the *Ethics* is clearly implicit: that all things exist in and are conceived through Substance (or God), which exists and is conceived through itself; that Substance has infinite attributes in all of which the order and connection of things (or causes) is the same, and one of which is Thought, so that the order and connection of ideas is also the order and connection of things.

Once it has been established that all we need is a true idea, and that the idea of a perfect being, which indeed we do possess, is the norm and the best from which to deduce everything else, there would seem to be no need to pursue the search for a method any further. All that is now required is to define accurately the infinite idea of God and to proceed forthwith to derive from it, by developing its implications, every other truth. This, in effect, is what Spinoza professes to do in the *Ethics*; and the remainder of the *Tractatus*, concerning the nature of fictions, false ideas, doubt, and forgetfulness, seems largely premature and irrelevant. Nor does the abortive preparation for the definition of the intellect seem to be in place as the source of enlightenment about how we can attain knowledge of eternal things. If what has been laid down at the beginning is sound, this would be *hysteron proteron*, for both the nature of the intellect and its manner of acquiring knowledge should follow from the definition of eternal things rather than the other way round. This may well be the reason why Spinoza abandoned the TdIE at this point and never returned to it. What it set out to do was subsequently more satisfactorily accomplished in the *Ethics*.

Nevertheless, even if we accept Spinoza's contentions that the reflective knowledge which is the idea of the most perfect being is more excellent than reflective knowledge of any other ideas, and that, in consequence, the best method will be that which shows how the mind is directed to the norm of the given idea of a perfect being, we must surely seek to know what the proper order is in which other truths are deduced from the norm. What follows in the same passage in the TdIE provides a significant clue to the answer:

> Add to this that an idea is objectively in the same case as its ideatum is in reality. If, therefore, there were anything in Nature which had no interconnections (*nihil commercii*) with other things, then, if its objective essence were also given, which ought in every way to agree with its formal essence, it too would have no connections with other ideas; that is, we could deduce (*poterimus concludere*) nothing from it. On the other hand, those things which have connections with other things, as do all things that exist in Nature, which are intelligible and their objective essences have the same connections, that is, other ideas are deduced from them, which again have connections with others, and so instruments for proceeding further increase (*crescent*). (TdIE, VII, 41)

From this we gather that what Spinoza calls deduction is nothing more nor less than the unfolding of the connections between ideas which are implicit in the one under scrutiny and follow from its place in the system of Nature, the texture of the real. This is embraced as a whole in, and is determined by, the nature of Substance (the most perfect being), the fount and origin of all things. It follows that if this is properly understood, all else will necessarily follow from it, because (as is later to be proved in the *Ethics*) infinite things follow in infinite ways from the necessity of the divine nature. All that is needed, therefore, is to trace out the implications of the divine essence.

The nature of this deduction and its difference from what traditionally has been, and still is, understood by the word (especially by Spinoza's critics) is further established by the following considerations.

It is commonly assumed that deduction is a form of reasoning following the rules of Aristotelian syllogistic, in which universal premises, propositions linking class concepts or abstract common properties, yield universal conclusions (e.g., All men are mortal). As a valid syllogism requires a distributed middle, particular premises by themselves cannot give any valid conclusion, and resort must be had to inductive argument if we are to proceed fruitfully from particular facts. Inductive argument, as Spinoza was fully aware, presents difficulties as to validity, which he was not the only one to consider insuperable, so he rejected it as unreliable. On the other hand, Aristotelian deduction permits no derivation of new factual knowledge, whether from universal or from particular premises, and modern logic reinforces this rule by insisting that all deductive argument is purely analytic and that its validity reduces strictly to its tautological character. Spinoza's methodological procedure can thus be neither inductive nor deductive in the traditional senses of those terms. He rejects empirical premises because, he holds, they assert at best only accidental associations, and in inductive reasoning yield invalid and unreliable conclusions. Equally he rejects universal propositions as abstract, maintaining that they are for the most part the product of imaginative confusion (E2P40SS1 and 2), and are at best only *entia rationis*. As long as we are investigating realities, we are never to begin from abstractions.

> For genuine cognition of effects is nothing other than acquiring a more perfect knowledge of causes. Whence we are never permitted, as long as we pursue inquiry into things, to conclude anything from abstracta, and we must earnestly beware that we do not confuse those things which are only in the intellect with those which are real. (TdIE, XII, 93)

On the contrary, the best results are achieved by drawing conclusions from some particular affirmative essence or from a true and legitimate definition. This appears to concur with the traditional doctrine so far as it prohibits concluding from abstractions to concrete and particular facts, but traditional and contemporary logic equally prohibit deduction from a particular affirmative essence (in Spinoza's sense of that word) to any other particular matter of fact.

The customary understanding of essence, if ever the term were used today, would be a general concept expressing properties common to the members of a class. But Spinoza explicitly deprecates generalities of this kind. He means by the essence of a particular thing precisely what that thing is: that without which the thing could not be or be conceived, and which would neither be nor be conceived without the thing (E2D2). If the essence is given the thing is necessarily posited, and if it is removed the thing likewise is abolished (ibid.). Particular affirmative essences, therefore, are certainly not abstractions. Nor is a true and legitimate definition, according to Spinoza. In fact, such a definition should, in his view, adequately express the actual essence of the *definiendum,* so that from it all the properties of the thing could be deduced (cf. TdIE).

Deduction from such true and legitimate definitions and from particular affirmative essences must, therefore, be a very different kind of procedure from deduction as understood by modern logicians. Just what it might be is further to be gathered from what Spinoza tells us in the TdIE. He maintains that we must inquire first and foremost, and as reason requires, whether there is a being which is the cause of all things, so that its objective essence will be the source of all our ideas; that is, our ideas will flow from the idea of the universal cause in the same way and in the same order as all things are produced by it. It follows, he insists, that we should deduce all our ideas from those of physical and real things, proceeding according to the series of causes from one real thing to another, and never going over into abstractions or universals, whether we seek to derive them from realities or realities from them. It is clear that Spinoza here envisages a procedure which follows the causal connections and interrelations of actualities in a systematic fashion, without abstract generalization.

More light is shed on this procedure by Spinoza's further explanation that he is not referring here, when he speaks of the series of causes of real entities, to the series of singular and mutable things, but to the series of "fixed and eternal things." For the existence of finite things is not a necessary consequence of their essence, nor can their essences be derived from the order of their occurrence. On the contrary, if they are to be properly understood, both must be sought from the fixed and eternal things and the laws ("which are inscribed in them as if in their true codes") according to which all particular things are produced and ordered. Without the fixed and eternal things, we are told, the particular mutable things can neither be nor be conceived; and though they are themselves *singularia,* the fixed and eternal things, because of their ubiquitous presence and wide-ranging power, serve as universals or the genera of the definitions of particular mutable things and the proximate causes of everything (TdIE, XIV, 101).

In the TdIE Spinoza does not tell us what these eternal things are, but it must be obvious to any careful student of his writings that they are the attributes of Substance, which, as they constitute its essence, represent its infinite and ubiquitous powers. They are everywhere present and active. Moreover, it is in them that all things exist and through them that all things are conceived (as is stated in the passage referred to above). From these attributes, we learn from E1PP21–23, there follow immediately the infinite modes, which like them are eternal and necessary. These, then, must be the fixed and eternal things of the TdIE, which, while they are real and concrete (*singularia*), nevertheless serve as universals and genera of the definitions of the mutable and finite.

That they are at the same time universal and *singularia* could be possible only if they were what later philosophers have called "concrete universals"; that is, they are not abstractions, but are concrete systematic wholes, ordered according to universal principles of structure, which determine the nature and interrelations of their parts or elements, what Spinoza calls finite modes.

Spinoza's understanding of the relationship between the infinite modes and the finite is nowhere more fully and clearly set out in his writings than in his 32nd Letter (to Oldenburg), where he answers the question how we know in what way each part of Nature accords with the whole of it, and by what principle (*ratio*) it is connected with other parts. Spinoza begins by explaining how he conceives whole and part, a notion which elsewhere he decries as *auxilium imaginationis*, that is, when the whole is conceived merely as an aggregate of elements that are regarded as logically prior to and existentially independent of the interrelations which unite them into the whole. In Ep 32 he says that he regards that to be a whole of parts in which the parts accommodate themselves one to another so that they do not conflict but are mutually adapted in nature and in the laws of their behavior. He then gives his famous example of the blood, which, he says, constitutes a whole, or single fluid body, although it consists of numerous diverse components in constantly changing relations that nevertheless maintain throughout the same proportion of motion and rest. Bodies that maintain a dynamic equilibrium of this sort are individual wholes retaining their peculiar characters despite internal changes. So far as any such body (e.g., the blood) is affected by no external causes, it remains constant and so is to be regarded as a whole; so far as it participates with other bodies external to it in a similar systematic relationship to that maintained internally by its own parts, it is to be regarded as a part of a larger whole.

In the Scholium to Lemma VII of Part II of the *Ethics*, Spinoza explains how bodies form a hierarchy of such wholes, ranging from the simplest, which are distinguished from one another solely by motion and rest, rapidity or slowness, to those very complex bodies whose parts transmit one to another their motion and rest so as to maintain a constant proportion, and which attain in consequence a higher degree of self-sufficiency and self-sustenance. Such complexity and intercommunication increases by stages continuously until it includes the whole of the physical (extended) world, which thus constitutes a single infinite individual, subject to no external physical influences; hence it remains always the same despite infinite internal changes. In the 32nd Letter Spinoza writes:

> Hence it follows that every body, so far as it exists modified in a certain way, must be considered a part of the whole universe, in harmony with its whole and cohering with every other part; and since the nature of the universe, unlike the nature of the blood, is unlimited and is absolutely infinite, its parts are controlled by the nature of this infinite power in infinite ways and are compelled to suffer infinite changes.

The whole here described is what he calls *facies totius universi* (cf. Ep 64), which is one of the infinite modes of Extension (the other being Motion-and-rest). And these, we have maintained, are among the eternal things which function as universals and genera of the definitions of mutable things. Now we can see how they serve in this capacity, as infinite powers determining the nature and modifications o finite modes in such a way that the whole remains constant. In short, the totality is organized in accordance with a principle of order that determines its overall structure and the individual nature of its parts, governing the changes they must undergo in order to maintain the dynamic equilibrium. It is in this principle that the laws governing finite things are contained, as in their proper codes, so that the eternal things are concrete universals.

If, then, we can grasp the nature and principles of order implicit in the eternal things as wholes, we shall be able to deduce from them the order and connection of the particular finite entities which make up their "parts." And as the order and connection of ideas is the same as that of things in general, what is true of one attribute (e.g., Extension) will be equally true of any other (e.g., Thought), the wholes and parts in each being correspondent to those of every other.

Thus we come to understand how Spinoza conceived the best method of ascertaining the truth about the nature of things as the derivation of all our ideas by reference to the idea of what is the fount and origin of the whole of Nature, as it is also the source of all other ideas. The deduction involved is not formal deduction as conceived either by Aristotle or by Descartes (*illatio*, in his *Regulae ad directionem Ingenii*, ii and iii), still less as conceived by modern logicians, but is the systematic development in thought of the connections of things, as determined by the principle organizing the structure of the whole to which they belong. As the ultimate whole is the absolutely infinite

Substance, expressing its essence (or power) through infinite attributes, each whole and complete in its own kind, the adequate knowledge of things must be deduced from adequate ideas of God's attributes.

It is not, however, obvious that we can at once comprehend the principles of order implicit in the absolutely infinite Substance and its attributes. We may, in fact, doubt whether this is possible prior to a long and arduous investigation. Yet unless it is possible the procedure recommended by Spinoza in the TdIE can hardly begin. Undoubtedly Spinoza believed that the nature of the most perfect being could be understood sufficiently well for it to function as the starting point of all reliable knowledge, and he thought that the actual procedure of deduction was that pursued in Euclidean geometry and in mathematics generally; so he called it *geometricus ordo* and arranged his own argument in a form superficially similar to Euclid's, beginning with definitions and axioms, formulating theorems, and proving them in deductive fashion with the definitions and axioms as first premises. He had good precedents for regarding mathematics as providing the paradigm of scientific method. The tradition goes back to Plato, or even to Pythagoras, and the method had been advocated by Descartes. Spinoza was impressed by the objectivity and rigor of mathematical reasoning and the cogency with which its conclusions followed. When asked by Albert Burgh how he knew that his philosophy was the best, he replied,

> I do not presume that I have found the best philosophy, but I know that I understand the true one. But if you ask me how I know that, I shall answer, in the same way as you know that the three angles of a triangle are equal to two right angles. (Ep 76)

Nevertheless, it requires but little scrutiny to discover that, in spite of the format used, Spinoza's argument proceeds in quite a different manner from Euclid's and is not typically mathematical, although it may quite legitimately be described as philosophical.[3] The question remains, of course, what is precisely the form and character of mathematical reasoning? Euclid's is certainly not syllogistic in the Aristotelian style, and it is dubious whether it is, as some modern logicians have claimed, purely tautological, for it does seem to have some bearing upon the nature of physical space in which motions of low velocity over small distances occur, so that in certain circumstances factual information not contained in the premises seems to be derivable from them. Claims have been made by others besides Kant (e.g., by H. Poincaré) that mathematical reasoning is synthetic a priori—but we are not here concerned with the question whether this is so, or what the precise nature of mathematical thinking may be. Our object is to discern the type of procedure advocated and adopted by Spinoza.

It is clear from what Spinoza writes in the 32nd Letter and in the Scholium to Lemma VII in Part II of the *Ethics* that he was firmly convinced of the unity of the universe as a single organic whole; and if he is correct in this, the principle of order and structure determining every part and all relations between its constituents must be immanent in every detail. This, indeed, is Spinoza's own submission (E1P28S). Therefore, sufficiently searching scrutiny ought to be able to discover in any and every existent, and in all relations between things, at least some trace of that universal principle which is the key to all understanding. Instead of insisting upon the idea of the most perfect being as the proper starting point, therefore, we might think that Spinoza need only have claimed that we could begin with any true idea whatsoever. In fact, at one point in TdIE he does, in effect, make this claim, for he says that all we need to begin with is a true idea, although obviously the best would be that of the most perfect object. He says also that the greater the number of natural objects the mind understands the better it knows its own nature, and (in the TTP) that the more we know of Nature the more we know of God. All these statements fit in with his deep conviction of the unity and coherence of the universe.

The proper method, then, should be to develop from the implications of any true idea what we may call elements of structure, and thence to discern that universal principle that governs the whole. From this we should be able to read off further details of the series of natural causes and the disposition of natural events. In the *Ethics* Spinoza begins with the definition of Substance. Like Descartes, he sees clearly that the awareness of defect and imperfection in finite things (oneself included) implies the tacit assumption by the mind that judges of a standard of perfection. This standard, he sees further, must be the idea of a being that is self-complete and all-inclusive, absolute and infinite, for (to be such a standard) it cannot be susceptible of limitation such as would follow from any exclusiveness. It can therefore not be dependent on anything else, it cannot be consequent to anything prior, it cannot be the effect of any cause external to or other than itself. It must then be *causa sui*, and its existence will be necessitated by its essence. It follows that it will be the ultimate source of everything dependent and contingent. There cannot be more than one such being, because multiplicity involves mutual limitation by the numerous entities and mutual relations which will connect them all together in one comprehensive whole, which would then be the ultimate totality, or "perfect being." Of necessity, therefore, there must exist one infinite and eternal whole, which Spinoza calls God-or-Substance-or-Nature. This is what the first fifteen propositions of Part I of the *Ethics* establish.

That we do have in our minds the idea of such a being is inevitable if, as we have said, and as is undoubtedly the case, we are aware of imperfection whether in ourselves or in other things; and although, as Spinoza admits in the *Short Treatise* and in correspondence, we do not and cannot have complete and detailed knowledge of the divine nature, we do possess a sufficient concept of it for us to be able to develop its necessary implications, and this must be so as long as we entertain any ideas of any reality at all. For any such ideas can have significance for us only in the context of a system to which they and their objects belong, a system that must in principle and in the last resort be complete and all-inclusive. For Spinoza, the necessarily implied system is the divine essence, immanent of necessity in everything. This is the foundation at once of his metaphysics and of his methodology.

Further development of the implications of the nature of Substance reveals that it differentiates itself into a scale of forms—infinite attributes, infinite modes, finite things that follow from it of necessity in infinite ways (modes). Every attribute (seeing that each expresses in its own way the essence of a single identical Substance, so that the modes under each follow the same order of existence and ranking) is again differentiated into a hierarchy of finite modes ranging in complexity and self-dependence *ex summo nimirum ad infimum perfectionis gradum* (E1A), all governed and determined by the same principle of order inherent in the attribute (as the essence of Substance). Elsewhere I have argued that a graded scale of this kind is dialectical in form,[4] and although Spinoza does not set out the scale which he obviously assumes and actually describes in this form (largely because of his somewhat misguided predilection for *geometricus ordo*), it is a thought structure that has emerged in the work of great philosophers ever since Heraclitus, and has been continuously developed until it became explicit and systematic in the philosophy of Hegel, and was in our own time expounded afresh by R. G. Collingwood.[5] That this is the method actually latent and operative in Spinoza's thought the passages to which reference has been made as well as those quoted from TdIE bear witness, and the whole structure of his ontology puts beyond reasonable doubt.

I have tried to show in some detail, by direct reference to the relevant passages in Spinoza's text, that his conception of method is not the linear formal deduction of traditional logic, but is a crypto-dialectical development of the structural implications of a systematic whole. To do this, I have been prompted by the fact that contemporary commentators, by neglect of this evidence, seem to me to have misrepresented important aspects of Spinoza's doctrine. In *Salvation from Despair* I took issue with some of these; here I shall confine myself to one of the more recent, Professor Jonathan Bennett.

In his book *A Study of Spinoza's Ethics*, Bennett makes important comments on Spinoza's methodology, some of which seem plausible, but most of them are flawed by Bennett's misconception of Spinoza's procedure as linear deduction subject to the laws and criteria of validity traditionally applied. If, however, as I have claimed, it is crypto-dialectical, it cannot be linear, but will be at the same time both deductive and inductive;[6] in fact, as the whole is being progressively explicated, and as it is immanent throughout, the course of the argument is constantly and in a special way circular without invalidity, the conclusion confirming the premisses as much as the premisses support the conclusion.

The appeal is always to the systematic structure of the subject, in which relationships are reciprocally determining. This does not mean that all relations are symmetrical, but that when they are not they are still regulated by the universal principle of structure governing the totality, so that it is immanent in the terms. In "deduction," therefore, the conclusion is simply the explication of the system of which the ordering principle is immanent in the premisses. The same circularity is occasioned by the self-reflective and self-conscious nature of knowledge, without which there would be no apprehension of relation or system at all.

This give-and-take between antecedent and consequent, between hypothesis and confirmation, gives some color to the view, expressed by Professor Bennett, that Spinoza's method is hypothetico-deductive; but the exposition of that procedure by its major proponents, R. B. Braithwaite, Sir Karl Popper, and his follower J. O. Wisdom,[7] makes its attribution to Spinoza inept. According to the accepted view, the method involves first the postulation of a hypothesis more or less arbitrarily— a mere guess or conjecture—from which lower-level hypotheses and subsequently observable predictions are deduced by the orthodox linear tautological process. These predictions are then tested by experiment and observation, and if the results are favorable, the hypothesis is corroborated (but not confirmed, for no amount of empirical corroboration would be sufficient), and if the results are unfavorable, the hypothesis is refuted. Crucial experiments may thus decide between rival hypotheses, and those which remain unrefuted survive until decisive evidence against them is forthcoming.

Quite apart from internal difficulties that beset this theory of method,[8] it is quite clearly not Spinoza's. His propositions (if we are to consider them "hypotheses" in Popper's sense) are not conjectures made at random, but are the implications (dialectically) derived from his conception of Substance as an infinite whole differentiating itself into infinite attributes that express its essence. This conception again is no hypothesis, but is an absolutely certain idea self-evidently true (because its denial is self-refuting). Spinoza establishes it at the beginning of the KV thus:

> Whatever we clearly and distinctly understand to belong to the nature of a thing, that we can also assert of the thing with truth. But we clearly and distinctly understand that existence belongs to the nature of God; Therefore . . . .

This is the so-called Ontological Proof that existence cannot consistently be denied of an absolute and infinite being. Without entering here into the interminable dispute about its validity, we may say without fear of contradiction that it is the fundamental principle of holism, for the completed system is necessarily presupposed in and by every finite existent and by any and every significant and coherent judgment about the real. The denial of its existence, therefore, is either totally irrational and arbitrary, or must rest on the tacit admission of its own falsehood. For from the absolute whole everything else follows with dialectical necessity. So it is for Spinoza. This is the norm offered in the TdIE as that to which the mind must be directed. It is the fount and origin of all things and all ideas to which every proposition must be traced back. Any "deduction" involved is dialectical and not tautological linear transformation of formulae (as maintained by Braithwaite).

Further, what is "deduced" by Spinoza from this indispensable first principle is not a prediction for empirical testing. Even if Spinoza does sometimes claim that experience bears out some of his conclusions, any such evidence is adduced by the way, and is not offered as the main reason for accepting the propositions (although it does strengthen our conviction of their coherence with the rest of the system). The systematic interlock is what is all-important. Finally, Spinoza is unequivocally emphatic in his rejection of empirical evidence as scientifically appropriate. For him, empirical judgments are mostly the product of *imaginatio*, which is vague, haphazard, and unreliable. Only if it can be incorporated into a systematic structure as demanded by the intellect can it be accepted as scientific.

Entirely in keeping with this view, Spinoza says, in PPC 3, that a good hypothesis is one which, considered in itself, implies no contradiction, is as simple as possible, and is one from which everything observable in Nature can be deduced; but it does not follow that Spinoza's geometrical method is (as Professor Bennett suggests) hypothetico-deductive in the modern sense. It is as futile to seek after the data by reference to which Spinoza confirms or disconfirms his hypotheses, as it would be to ask the architect of the example in TdIE whether the building of which he has formed a true idea ever has existed or ever will. What matters is whether the implications of the idea are coherent and mutually supportive, and whether they can be traced back to the ultimate norm.

Further, it is quite illegitimate to impugn the validity of Spinoza's arguments by the criteria of modern formal logic, as Professor Bennett does. That is simply to misconceive the whole Spinozan position. Bennett, for instance, objects to the proof of Proposition 14 of *Ethics*, sp. I, although he does not mention any specific fallacy, describing the demonstration as a creaky, leaky affair which cannot be fully salvaged. What Spinoza is arguing here is simply that an absolutely infinite Substance, which necessarily has infinite attributes, each in its own kind expressing its essence, could not possibly share an attribute (and there can be none which it does not possess) with another substance; for to assign a common attribute to both would, in effect, to be to identify them—they would both have the same essence. Hence no other substance than God is conceivable. What Bennett finds creaky or leaky about this reasoning is not obvious. The cogency of the demonstration rests upon the necessary implications of the nature of an absolutely infinite Substance as defined, and the contradiction(s) which follow from assuming that more than one such could exist. The concept with which Spinoza is dealing is not an abstract generalization, nor a class concept or common property; it is a concept of the concrete system of the universe, *Deus-sive-substantia-sive-natura*, and he is trying to unfold the necessary implications of this concrete universal.

Contrary to the claims of some contemporary commentators, Spinoza is certainly not operating a calculus or anything of that sort; nor can his reasoning, despite attempts that have been made, be reduced to a formal deductive system in contemporary logic.[9] Arne Naess, who more than most employs symbolic formulae in his exposition and interpretation of Spinoza, admits that the use of symbols is merely heuristic and is not an attempt to philosophize.[10]

Some logicians [he writes] have discussed the possibility for formalizing the system of Spinoza. Such an undertaking, however, is doomed to be unsuccessful considering the complexity of his texts. What I have done . . . has little, if anything, to do with formalization of doctrine.[11]

Naess gives warning that one of the few things of which we may be sure is that the intended meaning and the import of a sentence within the system are changed in definite ways when it is symbolized.[12] We may add that the possibility of formalizing Spinoza's thought is not only impeded by its complexity and the alteration of the import of sentences when symbolized, but is due to the profound divergence of the basic metaphysical assumption underlying symbolic logic of the relation between bare particulars and abstract universals, from the conception of the concrete universal which is fundamental to Spinoza's system.

To return to Bennett, the objections which he raises to the demonstration of Proposition 14 are based partly upon a fallacy he claims to have detected in the demonstration of Proposition 5 (on which Proposition 14 depends) and partly on his rejection of the Ontological Argument as stated in Propositions 7 and 11, upon which 14 also draws. The fallacy is that of moving from "*Fx* and possibly *Fy*" to "possibly *Fx* and *Fy*"; but the argument that this invalidates is not Spinoza's and has been imported, wrongly and unnecessarily, into Spinoza's proof by Bennett, who virtually admits that he does not understand Spinoza's argument here.

The proposition to be proved (E1P5) is that there cannot be two or more substances with the same natures or attributes (attribute = essence = nature). Spinoza says that distinct things differ only in either their attributes or their *affectiones* (their "states"); but as substances are prior to their *affectiones*, these may be set aside—Professor Bennett says he cannot understand why. The reason is clearly that any differences between *affectiones* must be traceable back to differences between the natures (or essences) of the substances themselves, hence to their attributes. But if they are distinguished by differing attributes, that is, by their essences, they can have nothing in common. Since *affectiones* are taken by Bennett to be accidents (which for Spinoza they certainly are not), he interprets them to mean what the substance might have lacked, and he infers, if accidents which are actually different might have been similar (which Spinoza would have denied), then the substances would have been perfectly alike and so identical. Thus "*Fx* and possibly *Fy*" is improperly taken to imply "possibly *Fx* and *Fy*", which is fallacious. But this is not Spinoza's argument and has been gratuitously imported into it.

Both here and in his objections to the Ontological Proof, Bennett confuses essence with abstract common property, which is never what Spinoza means by it. Of course the Ontological Proof is invalid if God's essence is taken to be an abstract universal (common to all perfect beings); but for Spinoza there is only one Substance, the essence of which is the organizing principle of the universe, in effect the concrete universal. This is the indispensable ground of all finite existence, of all relations, and so of any and every proof of existence. The being of the concrete whole, the absolutely infinite Substance, cannot therefore be denied without absurdity. As Spinoza says: "*vel nihil existit, vel Ens absolute infinitum necessario etiam existit*" (E1P11D3). It is because Spinoza's God is the concrete universal that his argument is, notwithstanding superficial appearances, essentially dialectical.

Oversight of Spinoza's holism leads to widespread misinterpretation of his doctrine. Professor Bennett, for instance, reduces the attributes of Thought and Extension to types, or classes, of concepts—abstract items in logical space,[13] taking concept as an abstract universal with an extension covering a collection of similar particulars. Nothing could be more alien to Spinoza's way of thinking, for whom all abstractions were anathema and the attributes of Substance were concrete universals, as explained above. This notion of universals (and essences) as abstract bedevils Bennett's whole treatment of Spinoza's doctrine, and his neglect of the distinction between an aggregate and a whole, as Spinoza explains it in Ep 32, distorts his interpretation of the concept of Substance.

A dialectical argument is one that demonstrates the systematic character of the concept under scrutiny, whether it is the system as a whole, or an element within it. If it is no more than the latter, it will reveal its partiality, or relative abstraction, as its implications are developed in thought (as Spinoza indicates in TdIE); and as its deficiencies are explored, what is needed to supply them will be brought to light. The argument will unfold "in fuller degree as it proceeds" the implications of the ordered whole.

Strictly such reasoning should begin without presuppositions, taking as little for granted as possible. The starting point would seem to be the most general and immediate notion, underived from any prior assumption. The obvious defects of the initial concept would then be progressively supplied from the implications of whatever significance it is seen to have, leading through the gamut of dialectical forms eventually to the disclosure of the complete concrete and absolute system. But when the zenith is reached, as the organizing principle of the whole is the source of all significance and structure at every stage, it will become clear at once that the whole is what has been developing and specifying itself throughout the entire process, and was, despite the initial profession of presuppositionlessness, implicit from the very beginning and immanent at every level. The process would thus have been circular, but without fallacy. As the absolute totality and its ordering principle were implicit from the outset, the argument did, in effect, start from it—it will have supplied the nerve and direction of the argument throughout. But at first it was *only* implicit, and the advance of the argument is the process of its explication.

Spinoza, however, begins explicitly with the idea of the absolute whole, the absolutely infinite Substance; but in fact the first conception is general and relatively unspecified, so it requires development. Although the idea of Substance, entertained in isolation, is concrete in the sense that it is the idea of an actual and individual thing (*res*)—*quamvis sit singularia*—it is relatively abstract as long as its systematic implications remain latent. It is defined by Spinoza as that which exists in itself and is conceived through itself; that is, what does not need the concept of anything else (an external cause, or a wider whole) from which it must be derived. It is, in short, presuppositionless, self-contained, and self-dependent. As absolutely infinite it comprehends all Nature and is God.

Now, whatever is finite, although it will have some attributes, will (as finite) lack others, and as we move up the scale of finite entities, as set out in E2P13S and E2L7S, finite modes increase in "excellence" or "reality." Spinoza tells us that the more reality anything has the more attributes it will possess, and that what has infinite reality must possess infinite attributes (E1P9 and Ep 9). What has all possible reality, the absolutely infinite whole of Nature, will have all possible attributes. In that case, (a) it will not be conceived through anything other than itself, (b) it will obviously be Substance as defined in E1D3, and (c) it will necessarily be the one and only substance because, as infinite, it must be all-inclusive.

Because of Spinoza's preference for the geometrical manner of exposition, the dialectical character of this development is obscured and remains hidden, but it requires not much perspicacity to recognize it. Because the whole and its self-specification is the wellspring of dialectic, Spinoza's insistence on Substance as his starting point, and his specification of it into attributes and modes as he explicates its structural order, supply the framework of a dialectical system that from time to time becomes evident, breaking through the geometrical disguise, as in the passages to which attention has been drawn.

The attribute of Extension, expressing the essence of Substance (its

power) dynamically as Motion-and-rest, differentiates itself into bodies
ranging from the simplest to the most complex, in a graded scale of
overlapping structures, each of them a specific instance of the generic
essence. As the complexity increases, so does the holism and self-
dependence of the body in its endeavor to maintain itself as a distinct
individual. And the series continues until it embraces the entire physical world, *facies totius universi*. Thus we have a dialectical scale. But it
is only one aspect of the complete system that constitutes Substance,
and it is complemented by innumerable corresponding series of modes
in other attributes, such as the order and connection of ideas.

Spinoza does not arrange the attributes among themselves as a similar dialectical series, if only because, while he claims that there must
be infinite others, we know only Thought and Extension. So he is left
with the apparently insoluble problem to which Tschirnhaus drew attention (Ep 65). If the order and connection of ideas is the same as
that of things, why are we not aware of other attributes than Extension? And if the divine intellect is cognizant of all the attributes, is
not Thought more extensive than any of the others (Ep 70)? In succeeding chapters I try to suggest ways in which this difficulty might be
overcome, and have come nearest to a solution by viewing the attributes
themselves as a dialectical scale.

As long as the holistic character of Spinoza's thinking is neglected
and the consequent dialectical structure of his system overlooked, no
adequate understanding of his metaphysics is likely to be gained; and
it is from his metaphysics that his epistemology follows, along with his
conception of *methodus perfectissima* and his reasons for preferring a
deductive manner of exposition that professes to be geometrical.

Notes

1. Cf. H. H. Joachim, *A Study of the Ethics of Spinoza* (Oxford, Clarendon
   Press, 1901; repr. New York, Russell and Russell, 1964), Introduction, Book
   I, Appendix, pp. 115–119, Book II, Ch. III, pp. 189–190, Appendix, pp.
   230–232; *Spinoza's Tractatus de Intellectus Emendatione* (Oxford, Clarendon
   Press, 1940), Ch. II, §6, Ch. III, Excursus, Ch. IV, §21, and passim. Cf.
   John Caird, *Spinoza* (Edinburgh and London, Blackwood and Sons, 1910),
   Ch. IV. See also H. G. Hubbeling, *Spinoza's Methodology* (Assen, van Gorcum,
   1967), p. 10 and passim.
2. Cf. G. H. R. Parkinson, *Spinoza's Theory of Knowledge* (Oxford, Clarendon
   Press, 1954).
3. Cf. my *Salvation from Despair: A Reappraisal of Spinoza's Philosophy* (The Hague,
   Martinus Nijhoff, 1973), pp. 28ff.
4. Cf. my *Foundations of Metaphysics in Science* (Atlantic Highlands, N. J., Humanities Press, 1992) Ch. XXII, and *Hypothesis and Perception: The*

Roots of Scientific Method (London, G. Allen and Unwin, 1970), Chs. IX and X; also *Salvation from Despair*, Ch. VI.

5. Cf. R. G. Collingwood, *An Essay on Philosophical Method* (Oxford, Clarendon Press, 1933), Chs. II and III, et seq.

6. Cf. ibid., Ch. VIII.

7. Cf. R. B. Braithwaite, *Scientific Explanation* (Cambridge, Cambridge University Press, 1946); J. O. Wisdom, *The Foundations of Inference in the Natural Sciences* (London, Methuen, 1952); K. Popper, *The Logic of Scientific Discovery* (New York and London, Basic Books, 1959).

8. Cf. *Hypothesis and Perception*, Chs. II and IV, esp. pp. 79–81.

9. Cf. Braithwaite, *Scientific Explanation*, Ch. II.

10. Cf. A. Naess, *Freedom, emotion, and self-subsistence: the structure of a central Part of Spinoza's Ethics* (Oslo, Universitetsforlaget, 1972), p. 29.

11. Ibid., p. 15.

12. Ibid., p. 27.

13. Jonathan Bennett, *A Study of Spinoza's Ethics* (Indianapolis, Hackett, 1984), Ch. 2, §12,2.

2

Finite and Infinite in Spinoza's System

"That queer quantity 'infinity' is the very mischief and no rational physicist should have anything to do with it." Sir Arthur Eddington's declamation was prompted by problems in classical and contemporary physics, but it is equally apposite to philosophical theories. "That queer quantity infinity" has been a perennial stumbling block to metaphysicians, not least to interpreters of Spinoza, who makes use of it undaunted by the paradoxes which seem to proliferate with every attempt to understand its nature and relations to finite individuals.

Spinoza defines God as an absolutely infinite substance possessing infinite attributes each expressing eternal and infinite essence in its own kind (E1D6). Commentators have asked why God should have infinite attributes, and von Tschirnhaus appealed to Spinoza to prove that it was so (Ep 63). Others have puzzled over the nature of infinite essence; but perhaps the problem that has given most trouble, after that of the relation between the infinite attributes, is how the infinity of Substance and of its attributes relates to the infinity in number and variety, also asserted by Spinoza, of the finite modes of Substance.

Ex necessitate divinae naturae infinita infinitis modis (hoc est omnia quae sub intellectus infinitus cadere possunt) sequi debent. [Infinite things in infinite ways (modes) follow of necessity from the divine nature (that is, everything that can be comprehended by an infinite intellect).] (E1P16)

How, then, are we to conceive an absolutely infinite Substance with infinite attributes, each of which is infinite in its own kind (Ep 36, E1P16D), and from which there follow of necessity infinite things in infinite ways?

Spinoza was confident that he had shown conclusively why an absolutely infinite Substance must have an infinity of attributes. Because a thing has attributes in proportion to its reality or perfection, the more reality it has, the more attributes must belong to it. Its essence expresses what it is, and its attributes express its essence; therefore, the more it encompasses, the more attributes are needed to express its essence. If it is absolutely infinite it must have an infinity of attributes. All this seemed self-evident to Spinoza, and his proof of Proposition 9 in Part 1 of the *Ethics* in consequence states simply *patet ex Def. 4* (i.e., the definition of the attribute). To Simon de Vries he wrote:

> But you say that I have not demonstrated that substance (or being) can have many attributes, perchance you have not attended to the demonstrations. For I have offered two, the first, that nothing is more evident to us than that anything whatever is conceived under some attribute, and the more reality, or being, a thing has the more attributes must be assigned to it. Whence an absolutely infinite thing must be defined etc. The second, and what I judge the best, is that the more attributes I assign to any thing the more I am compelled to attribute existence to it, that is, the more I conceive it under the principle of truth (*sub ratione veri*). (Ep 9)

Although this reasoning may seem clear and cogent, it gives rise to the notorious difficulty concerning the relation of the infinite attributes to the Attribute of Thought, placing Spinoza between the horns of a dilemma. Either there must be an asymmetry between Thought and every other single attribute, or else the human mind should be capable of knowing all the attributes and not only Thought and Extension (to which he maintains it is restricted). His reply to von Tschirnhaus on this point (Ep 66) is cryptic and unsatisfactory. But this matter may be left to subsequent chapters; in this one I wish to address myself to another problem involved in Spinoza's conception of infinity and its relation to finite things. It is this and the treatment of it by certain other writers to which I want to attend here.

The main question centers on E1P16. How does the multitude of things follow from the infinite essence of Substance in infinite ways? In one sense of "follows" we may find a tolerable answer, although its legitimacy has been denied by several commentators. Spinoza says that the modes follow from God's essence in the same way as the properties of a triangle follow from its definition; but H. H. Joachim and John Caird, in agreement with Hegel, have maintained that Spinoza failed to provide any principle of differentiation in the nature of Substance that could explain how this diversity of modes, or for that matter the infinite attributes, could follow from God's absolute and infinite unity.[1] What has been quoted above answers, at least by implication, criticisms of this kind. God has been defined as the absolutely infinite Substance, and the very conception of absolute infinity involves infinite reality (or perfection). A blank and featureless unity is the diametrical opposite of an infinite reality (that is, of concrete and complete wholeness); so to try to conceive God as undifferentiated unity is to strive to entertain a flat contradiction. It does, therefore, follow from the God's essence (as Spinoza defines it) that it is infinitely diversified—that is, that it has infinite attributes. And it follows in the same way, because the attributes express God's essence, that each of them must be infinitely diversified in its own kind.

Spinoza's insistence and proofs that Substance cannot be divided and that no attribute is internally divisible do not conflict with the above conclusion. Division and diversification are not the same. Within an indivisible whole there may (nay, must) be numerous distinct differences, numerous aspects, interdependent elements, and mutually indispensable factors, so related that no division or separation is possible between them, although among themselves they may be infinitely changeable and diverse. This is the case, for example, with any living organism, which is one and indivisible (while living) although it is composed of numerous distinguishable, but inseparable, metabolic cycles, organs, and members. Spinoza gives an account of such wholes, and at least one famous example, to which reference has already been made. The point to be emphasized here is that a blank and undifferentiated unity is not a whole at all, finite or infinite, and ipso facto cannot be what Spinoza defines as God-or-Substance. For "whatever is, is in God, and nothing can either exist or be conceived without God" (E1P15). God, therefore, comprehends the totality of the existing universe, the internal diversity of which nobody (not even Parmenides) can consistently deny. The importance and signification of Spinoza's doctrine is that this infinite diversity is a veritable whole, understood in the only proper and legitimate sense of that word; that is, a unity which, though diversified, is indivisible.

Again, although it is true that at times Spinoza denies the propriety of applying the category of whole and part to Substance (e.g., Ep 35), neither is this denial, rightly understood, at variance with what has just been maintained, nor with other statements of Spinoza's in which he uses whole and part in speaking of the infinite (e.g., Ep 32). The inappropriate conception is that of a whole as an aggregate or collection of separable parts, which are taken to be real and viable independently of the whole, so that the latter is made up of the parts by putting them together externally. The appropriate conception, on the other hand, is of a whole of different elements the existence and character of which depend entirely upon the structure and pattern of the whole, which is prior to them, while they are consequent both for their being and their nature (essence) to it.

If the second conception is adopted, the diversity of Substance follows from its nature or essence, and Spinoza's assertion in E1P16 is established precisely for the reasons given in the demonstration:

> ... from a given definition of anything, the intellect deduces more properties which truly follow necessarily from that same definition (that is, the essence of the thing), to the extent that the definition of the thing expresses more reality, that is, the more reality the essence of the defined thing involves. Since, however, the divine nature has absolutely infinite attributes (by Def. 6) of which, moreover, each expresses in its own nature infinite essence, by the same necessity, therefore, infinite things in infinite ways (i.e., everything that can be comprehended by an infinite intellect) must necessarily follow.

From all this it is apparent how the infinite variety of modes follows from the divine essence in the same way as the properties of a triangle follow from its definition—that is to say, they follow logically and are conceptually involved in the nature defined. But Spinoza asserts besides that God is the cause of all things, and this causal relationship is fraught with difficulties which are not immediately dispelled by the explanation of the logical connection. In fact, for some critics they are compounded by it.

Logical implication obtains between ideas and propositions. What follows from the *essence* of Substance may well be conceived in such terms. But causal connection is between events, or facts, or existences; and, at least since Kant, there has been a general consensus among many philosophers that existence does not follow logically from mere ideas. Not only does the Ontological Proof, which also prompts doubts about Spinoza's assimilation of causal to logical connection, come under attack on this account. He constantly speaks of an effect as logically implicated in its cause, and that raises problems for many; first, because logical entailment is commonly taken to reveal only equivalence of meaning and not factual information, which causal connection requires; and second, because cause and effect are normally conceived as temporally earlier and later, while logical implication is timeless. Here, however, we plunge into the depths of metaphysical perplexity surrounding the relation of time to eternity, which is inevitably involved with that of the finite to the infinite. In a single chapter one can hardly do justice to every facet of this difficult issue, and here I shall confine my attention to the doctrine propounded by Spinoza of the causal relation between Substance and its modes.

With respect to the attribute expressing God's essence and its infinite modes, little difficulty is to be encountered, for here ground and consequence coalesce fairly intelligibly with cause and effect. The reason is that the infinite modes are themselves eternal, as are the attributes from which they immediately follow. The issue of temporal succession does not, therefore, arise. The attributes are the powers of God, and their infinite modes are the first and immediate ways in which they manifest themselves. The attribute is naturally prior to the primary infinite mode, and the primary to the secondary, but the relation is at once logical and causal.

In Thought, the Infinite intellect is immediately implied by the attribute. Substance, conceived as a thinking thing, is ipso facto an infinite intellect, and (as for Aristotle) the content of its thought is itself, the infinite idea of God, which follows immediately from the notion of an infinite intellect. There is no temporal sequence here: infinite thought and the infinite thinker are one and the same, God's essence (the attribute) is one with His intellect, and what He thinks is equally Himself. For Spinoza, as for Aristotle (and incidentally Hegel), God is *noésis noeseōs*.

Under Extension, motion and rest follow immediately from the infinite attribute, the power of spatio-temporal existence and movement, and the *facies totius universi*, the configuration of bodies and the constant interchange of motion and rest among them, directly follows from the manifestation of the power of motion and rest. Here temporality begins to emerge, for changes in motion and rest are events and must be successive; but the problem does not become acute as long as the emphasis remains on the words *facies totius*. It is the configuration of the whole that is the infinite mode, not the particular changes, which produce, and occur among, the finite modes. Motion-and-rest must be conceived as a single indivisible "state" of the entire physical world, an all-inclusive energy system which at once involves a structure, a dynamic pattern, of matter and interchange.

Some might question (as did Tschirnhaus, in Epp 49 and 80) whether an energy state follows directly, or at all, from extension pure and simple; but Spinoza's answer is firm and clear, and is much what the modern physicist might give:

> Indeed from Extension as Descartes conceived it, that is to say, as a quiescent mass, not only is it difficult (as you say) to demonstrate the existence of bodies but altogether impossible (Ep 81).

... it is impossible insofar as matter has been ill defined by Descartes as Extension, but it ought to be explained through an attribute which expresses eternal and infinite essence (Ep 83).

As God's essence is the same as his power, an attribute expressing eternal and infinite essence is nothing static and quiescent, but is *energeia*—the activity of God.[2]

The main problem is how the finite modes follow from the infinite, for here there seems to be a hiatus between the causality (or logical sequence) which produces the infinite modes from attributes and that which produces finite things. Is this, perhaps, "the great gulf fixed" between God and finite creatures of which the Bible speaks? In attempts to understand Spinoza's system it presents a familiar puzzle, but it is one which I believe is soluble, as long as we understand aright what was explained in the last chapter: Spinoza's conception of logical deduction and what he held to be the true nature of "the fixed and eternal things, [which] although they are individuals, yet because of their ubiquitous presence and far-reaching power, will be for us like universals or the genera of definitions of individual changeable things, and the proximate causes of all things" (TdIE, XIV, 101).

Spinoza maintains that God is the immanent, but not the transient, cause of all things (E1P18). As we have seen, He is the immediate cause, under each of His attributes, of the infinite modes. But the finite modes can neither exist nor be determined to action unless they are affected by a cause which is also finite, and that again by another likewise, and so on ad infinitum (E1P28). This infinite regress, it seems, never extends to the infinite modes and God's eternal essence itself, yet Spinoza insists that "God cannot properly be said to be the remote cause of individual things, unless perhaps in order to distinguish them from those which He has immediately produced, or rather follow from His absolute nature" (E1P28S), because nothing can exist or be conceived without Him. How, then, are we to understand God's immanent causation of finite things, and how does it converge with logical implication?

The problem had already been faced by the medievals and can be traced back, in one form or another, to Plato and Aristotle. It underlies the Cosmological Argument for the existence of God. Every finite and contingent existent requires a cause which is itself finite and contingent, and therefore in itself inadequate ground for any existence. The entire series of causes reaching back to infinity cannot ex hypothesi be summed. Unless it can be grounded (as a whole) in a necessarily existent first cause, therefore, it is ultimately unaccountable. But even if there is a necessarily existing being, which to exist of necessity must be both infinite and eternal (for finitude implies contingency), how it can be causally connected with any finite thing remains a mystery. In its traditional form, the Cosmological Proof fails, in consequence, not simply because, as Kant maintained, it presupposes the Ontological, but because even if the validity of the latter were granted, the proffered foundation of contingent existence remains paradoxical.

Spinoza, however, makes no appeal to the Cosmological Argument to establish God's existence, possibly because he was sensible of its dependence on the Ontological, but more likely because he was aware of this difficulty. But he does assert the dependence of the finite on the infinite and eternal, and he interposes the infinite modes to bridge the gap between God and his temporal creatures. It is this mediation that we seek to understand.

Contemporary commentators have answered these questions to their own satisfaction by interpreting Spinoza's theory as a form of naturalism and by understanding his notion of deduction in terms of medieval or contemporary formal logic. Their interpretation has considerable plausibility, but (as we have already seen in our consideration of Bennett) it fails to do justice to Spinoza's insight, which went beyond the ideas of the medievals and of his own day. In some degree it even goes beyond his own explicit exposition.

The view on which I propose to comment in this chapter has been expounded most clearly and systematically by E. M. Curley in his book *Spinoza's Metaphysics*.[3] In general, if not in detail, his position is similar to those of Stewart Hampshire and A. C. Watt,[4] but it is worked out in more detail and with greater elaboration. In brief, what Curley does is to correlate Spinoza's concepts with modern notions derived from Bertrand Russell and Ludwig Wittgenstein, and (professedly) to show that their interrelation can then be explained so as to resolve the difficulty I have indicated.

Curley asserts that what Spinoza calls ideas are really propositions, for every idea involves affirmation and is said by Spinoza to be a "concept of the mind" rather than a perception (E2D3). In this Curley is on the right lines, although, because Spinoza insists that an idea is an activity of the mind (E2D3, Explanation), I should prefer to substitute "judgment" for "proposition."[5] The *ideata* of ideas will, therefore, be facts rather than (as Spinoza habitually suggests) bodies. We need not discuss the effect of this emendation on Spinoza's contention that the human mind is the idea of the human body, and nothing else; for Curley regards the relation of proposition to fact as analogous to that of Aristotle's form to matter, which is almost (if not precisely) the relation which Spinoza (like Aristotle) contemplates as that between mind and body.[6]

According to Curley, the attribute of Thought (or should he have said the divine intellect?) then becomes "a set of propositions—call it A—which constitutes a complete and accurate description of the world of extended objects." These propositions state all facts about the world and are divided into three main classes: nomological generalizations, accidental generalizations, and singular propositions. Nomological general propositions are universal and necessary, and they assert laws of nature; an accidental generalization, on the contrary, is reducible to a collection of singular statements. An example of the latter would be "All the books in my library were published after 1850," which is equivalent to "This book was published after 1850, and this next book . . . , etc.," until all the books I possess have been enumerated.

The world, we are told, mirrors our description of it, so it consists of nomological facts corresponding to laws, and individual facts, i.e., particular events and states of affairs. Nomological propositions may be axiomatic or derivative (the theorems of a deductive system), and correspondingly the facts they describe will be basic or in varying degrees derivative. The basic facts are Spinoza's attributes, the primary derivatives are his primary infinite modes, and the secondary derivatives are his secondary infinite modes. Singular propositions correspond to finite modes—individual facts and events. In sum, the basic nomological facts comprise *Natura Naturans* and the rest *Natura Naturata.*

The set of propositions, A, constitutes the complete body of unified science. Nomological general propositions being universal and necessary, and singular facts being causally related in accordance with universal laws, all the propositions of our unified science are logically interdependent, so we are justified in assimilating causal to logical sequence. Thus within the scientific system any individual fact is explicable by deduction from a general nomological proposition in conjunction with singular propositions stating the relevant antecedent conditions. Hence we may say, in Spinoza's terms, that a finite mode follows from an infinite mode along with other finite modes which constitute the series of causes of which it is an effect, and our problem is solved.

As Curley puts it, we should understand Spinoza as maintaining that finite things follow from God both and at once so far as he is affected by finite modes and so far as he is affected by infinite modes. Neither by itself is the adequate cause of any given finite mode, but together they provide a complete explanation.[7]

Such an interpretation is intriguing and well-nigh unexceptionable.

As far as it goes it is commendable, especially if we add that Curley follows Sir Frederick Pollock in recognizing the identity of the attributes and in finite modes with what Spinoza calls "the fixed and eternal things" in TdIE. I shall take issue with his rendering of Spinoza, not so much for what it says as for what it leaves undisclosed.

The crucial issue, or at least one of them, is the status of nomological propositions. Curley tells us that they rank as axioms and theorems in a system of unified science and are laws of nature. He tells us also that they are universal and necessary. For Spinoza, unquestionably, the laws of nature, which are the "eternal decrees of God" (E2P49S and TTP, Ch. 3), are universal and necessary. But this is not the way they are conceived by contemporary thinkers under the influence of Hume and Wittgenstein. Curley rightly maintains that Spinoza rejects the logical atomism fundamental to Wittgenstein's early position (in his *Tractatus Logico-Philosophicus*), but he persists in trying to interpret Spinoza in its terms. It would hardly seem possible to do this consistently.

For contemporary thinkers, like A. J. Ayer, R. B. Braithwaite, and E. Nagel, laws of nature are empirical generalizations which can be established only by inductive reasoning and cannot be deduced a priori. In the light of Hume's analysis, inductive reasoning can never establish universal and necessary laws, but only the constant conjunction of events or characters in particular things as they occur contingently in common experience. On this basis no general propositions could, in principle, be other than accidental generalizations. Because there is and can be no logical entailment between distinct matters of fact (no necessary connection), according to this doctrine, such generalizations can refer only to contingently occurring conjunctions which, so far as we have had experience of them, happen to have been regular. The fact that something more than this is required for scientific prediction has been a persistent source of difficulty for the theory of induction throughout modern history, which different writers have tried to overcome, either by postulating synthetic a priori principles, in conflict with their own basic philosophical position, or by offering a priori proofs of the principle of induction which have invariably turned out to be fallacious.[8] Be that as it may, the current doctrine remains that scientific laws of nature are contingent upon experience and changeable with it. If Spinoza thought otherwise (as he certainly did) and we wish to make his view intelligible, it is not sufficient to say, as Curley does, that he believed it possible to deduce the laws of nature a priori, and that this belief was shared (as indeed it was) by Galileo, who is usually regarded as the founder of experimental science. We must understand how such a view can be justified and how laws of nature must be conceived if they are really to be universal and necessary.

Curley's best answer seems to be that they describe nomological facts, but what kind of facts are these? The example given is the law of inertia, but this, if it is taken as a description of fact, is precisely what a contemporary philosopher would insist is an empirical generalization. Otherwise it is an arbitrary rule defining motion uninfluenced by external forces, from which no factual information can be deduced purely a priori.

Neither of these alternatives would have been accepted by Spinoza, who regarded empirical generalizations as confused ideas, at best as aids to the imagination, existing only in the mind and without any real referent (E2P40S1), or else as a haphazard way of ascertaining "accidental properties which are never clearly understood" (TdIE, IV, 21 and V, 27), and who dismissed stipulative definitions as asserting only what we conceive and nothing *sub ratione veri* (Ep 9). Unless laws of nature are very differently understood, and nomological facts are more clearly explained, one can hardly agree with Curley that Spinoza's "substance . . . is that set of facts to which the axioms of our unified science correspond";[9] nor will Spinoza's conception of the dependence for existence of finite things upon infinite modes and attributes be faithfully represented by saying that singular facts can be deduced from laws of nature in conjunction with statements of antecedent conditions.

What, then, must be the character of the laws of nature if they are really to be universal and necessary, and how will they be related to particular facts? These questions must be clearly answered if Spinoza's system is to be coherently understood and successfully vindicated. To fulfil these aims we must examine closely what he meant by infinite and how he conceived the relation between whole and part. For, as Curley agrees, it is "the fixed and eternal things" of which Spinoza speaks in TdIE, wherein the laws of nature "are inscribed," that constitute the nomological facts of the system; and these (Curley also agrees) are the attributes of Substance and their infinite modes, all of which, following as they do immediately from the infinite and eternal nature of God, are themselves infinite and eternal.

In his famous "letter on the infinite" (Ep 12) the kernel of Spinoza's argument is that the infinite and eternal substance cannot be compounded of separable parts,[10] and that it is only when we try to imagine the infinite and fail to conceive it (adequately) that it appears to be divisible. We conceive quantity, he says, in two ways, namely, abstractly or superficially as we have it in imagination with the help of the senses, or as substance, which can be conceived only by the intellect (*quod non nisi a solo intellectu fit*). If we attend to the idea of quantity as it is in the imagination (which is easy) we find it divisible and composed of finite parts; but if we consider it as it really is in itself, as conceived by the intellect (which is very difficult), we find it to be infinite, indivisible, and one (*unica*). The important point is that mere addition of finites does not produce the infinite, which is not an aggregate nor compounded of separable parts, each independently real. The indefinitely continued addition of finites produces only a spurious infinite, the true infinite being a single and coherent whole.

The argument is clearly set out in KV, I, 2, where Spinoza writes:

> Whole and part are no true or distinct (*daadelijke*) beings, but only beings of reason, and consequently there are in Nature neither whole nor part. Secondly, for a thing to be put together from different parts it must be such that the parts, taken separately, one without the other, can be grasped and understood.

And that, Spinoza proceeds to show, is not possible in the case of Substance and its attributes (in particular, Extension).[11] He repeats and elaborates the argument in E1P15S, castigating those who deny the infinity of corporeal substance because it is composed of finite parts,

> doing nothing different, by Hercules, than one who pretends that a circle has the properties of a square, and hence concludes that a circle does not have a centre from which all lines drawn to the circumference are equal. For corporeal substance, which cannot be conceived except as infinite, unique (*unica*) and indivisible, they conceive, in order to prove it finite, to be conflated (*conflari*) out of finite parts, and to be multiplex and divisible.

In the *Short Treatise* (cited above) we are told that extended substance is a self-dependent reality (*sefstandighijd*), and is accordingly indivisible; but what are distinguishable are its modes, and these we divide into parts. Likewise in the *Ethics* it is said that matter is indivisible "unless we conceive it as affected in different ways, in which case we distinguish its parts modally only, but not in reality" (E1P15S). Just previously, in this Scholium, the passage quoted earlier from Ep 12, in which the apparent divisibility of quantity is attributed to the imagination, is repeated almost verbatim. In the letter Spinoza says that

> because we are able to limit (*determinare*) duration and quantity as we wish, when we conceive the former abstracted from substance, and when we separate the latter from *a mode, which flows from eternal things* [my italics], time and measure arise,

defining duration and quantity in such a way as to enable us to imagine them more easily.

From all this we are left somewhat in doubt whether the succession of events and the distinction one from another of finite modes are mere appearances produced by imaginative thinking, or have some status in reality. There are cogent reasons for maintaining that the latter is the case, not only from the evidence of the quoted passages, but more decisively because imagination is itself a consequence of the finiteness of the human body as a mode of Extension, and so cannot be the original source of modal distinction. Moreover, it is by the necessity of the divine nature that from it infinite things follow in infinite ways (*modis*).

So far we have examined only the negative side of the argument. The infinite is not composite, not an aggregation (and this is the essential point) of separately independent and separately intelligible parts, which, in consequence, would be prior in conception to the whole. The positive side of the case, that the whole is prior to, and determines the conception, the nature, and the behavior, of the parts, is developed in the 32nd Letter and (more briefly) in E2L7S, from which we learn what Spinoza held to be the true and legitimate conception of whole and part and of their mutual relation. To these allusion has already been made in the previous chapter, but it may be worth quoting the actual explanation to Oldenburg of how each part of Nature agrees with the whole and by what principle (*ratione*) it coheres with the rest:

> By the coherence of parts . . . I understand nothing other than that the laws or nature of one part so accommodate themselves to the laws or nature of the others that they conflict as little as possible. Concerning whole and parts, I consider things as parts of some whole or other to the extent that their nature accommodates itself one to another (*invicem*) so that as far as possible they agree among themselves. (Ep 32)

The lemmae inserted after E2S13, with the axioms and definition from which they follow, explain how complex bodies answer to the above description. They are complex, not merely in being combinations of simple bodies (mutually distinguished only by motion and rest), but also because, despite diverse changes among their parts, they are so adjusted one to another as to transmit a constant ratio of motion and rest to one another, and to preserve the individuality of the whole.

In the letter the example of the blood is given, the aptitude of which is the more remarkable in that the science of physiology in Spinoza's day was still in its infancy. A modern description of the complex mutual accommodation of chemical components in the blood, of how oxygen, carbon dioxide, sugar, and insulin levels are regulated and kept in constant equilibrium, would even more spectacularly support Spinoza's theory.[12]

But Spinoza's insight goes beyond the conception of finite organisms. He realizes that organic individuality can embrace even larger wholes; and today we know that ecosystems and the entire Earth answer to his principle of wholeness. Complex bodies, he maintains, can be constituted by parts themselves already complex, and these may be combined hierarchically in yet more complex structures until

> if thus still further we proceed to infinity, we easily conceive [he optimistically tells us] that the whole of Nature is one individual, whose parts, that is, all bodies, vary in infinite ways, without any change of the individual as a whole. (E2L7S)

In the letter, it will be recalled, Spinoza tells us that the infinite power of the whole (i.e., the attribute, the power of Substance or God) compels the parts (or modes) to suffer infinite changes, and they are modified in infinite ways. In short, the whole regulates the parts so as to keep the total structural pattern constant. This entire structure is *facies totius universi*, the infinite mode of Extension following from Motion-and-rest. Thus it is apparent how bodies, the differentiations of Motion-and-rest, which is the primary infinite mode of Extension, are determined and regulated by the configuration of the whole universe.

In the light of twentieth-century physics, Spinoza's theory makes good sense. Modern physicists assimilate elementary particles (simple bodies) to energy (Motion-and-rest) according to the equation $E = mc^2$; and these combine in hierarchical series, quarks forming protons and neutrons, these together with electrons constituting atoms, and these again combining to form molecules, which continue to complexify to produce the macromolecules that are strung together in polymers and become the basic materials of living organisms. At each stage the peculiar entity is a whole maintaining itself by sustaining a dynamic equilibrium among its constantly interactive constituents. Each is thus, on its own level, an individual body such as Spinoza envisages. At the same time, the energy from which the series begins is characterized as a field, represented in relativity theory as a curvature in space-time; each particle represents a particular energy field, and each type of field has its equivalent exchange particle. The whole physical universe is conceived as a single indivisible system in which every entity and process affects every other and all are coordinated and regulated by laws implicit in the structure of space-time. David Bohm characterizes this conception of the world as a "holomovement" (a dynamic totality) in which an implicate order is enfolded and is immanent at every point. He writes:

> ... in the implicate order the totality of existence is enfolded within each region of space (and time). So whatever part, element, or aspect we may abstract in thought, this still enfolds the whole and is therefore intrinsically related to the totality from which it has been abstracted. Thus, wholeness permeates all that is being discussed, from the very start.[13]

When Spinoza speaks of "how each part of Nature accords with the whole of it," he intends much the same as what Bohm has described in this passage.

Heisenberg some years ago pronounced that the ultimate aim of physical theory was to discover a fundamental equation from which all the primary forces and elementary particles could be derived,[14] a goal which contemporary S-matrix, Grand Unified, and super-string theories bid fair to achieve. Such an equation would represent the universal organizing principle of the entire physical world, much what is suggested by Spinoza's *facies totius universi,* from which, as his doctrine implies, all finite modes of Extension should, in principle, be derivable. As the order and connection of ideas is the same as that of things, what is true of Extension will be equally true of Thought, and all finite ideas should thus be deducible from the *infinita idea Dei.*

We can now see what should be meant by "nomological facts." They are those dynamic systems the organizing principles of which determine the activity and disposition of the finite modes that differentiate and express their intrinsic natures. The configuration of the whole, in every case, remains constant despite, or because of, the perpetual changes and relevant variations among the parts. These configurations correspond to the fixed and eternal things in which the laws of finite mutable things are inscribed. It has also become clear why these laws are universal and necessary: universal because of the comprehensiveness of the wholes whose nature they express, "because of their ubiquitous presence and far-reaching power"; and necessary because conformity to them alone makes the internal diversification and the component elements what they are, and "compels" them to vary as they do.

Such universal laws are in no sense empirical generalizations from frequently experienced conjunctions. They are not generalizations at all; for apart from comprehension of the principle of structure of the whole it would be impossible to perceive the particulars from which the generalizations could be made. As Spinoza says:

For it would be impossible for human weakness to follow through the series of individual changeable things, both on account of their multitude surpassing all count and because of the infinite circumstances in one and the same thing of which any one may be the cause that the thing exists or does not; since indeed their existence has no connection with their essence, or (as we have just said) is not an eternal truth. (TdIE, XIV, 100).

This is why he proscribes "generalities and abstractions" and insists on deduction from "real entities," that is, from the fixed and eternal things. Fully adequate knowledge, he concludes, will be an adequate idea of the essence of things derived from an adequate idea of the formal essences of certain attributes of God (E2P40SS1 and 2). In short, Spinoza's nomological facts are concrete universals, a concept wholly foreign to the thought of the early Wittgenstein, anathema to Bertrand Russell and his following, and utterly incompatible with logical atomism, in terms of which Curley professes to be interpreting Spinoza.

A concrete universal is a self-differentiating system, of which the principle of organization determines the nature, mutual relations, and behavior of the parts (or internal specifications), as an algebraical equation determines the contours and mutual relation of points in a geometrical figure. From the formula (*ratio*) expressing the universal principle of order the specific instantiations follow, and so can be deduced. The consequent logical relations are concrete or real relations inherent in the actuality of the whole, so that they determine and are manifested in the causal relations which govern the succession of changes within the dynamic structure. For Spinoza, therefore, "deduction" is no mere transformation of formulae according to arbitrary rules. It is the self-development, at once in thought and in actuality, of a dynamic principle. It is the self-specification, both inferentially and as organic causation, of the concrete universal.

The divine essence is an infinite whole of this nature—a genuine infinite, a self-complete totality, in which the regress of finite causes is but a subordinate (its temporal) aspect constituted by the perpetually varying manifestation of the dynamic principle of equilibrium that maintains its constancy. It specifies itself systematically as an organically coherent universe, the configuration of which is invariant, but the specific detail of which is the endlessly diversified succession and profusion of finite things and events. The finite modes are, therefore, the manifestations of God's eternal activity. The infinite regress of causes is nothing other than the inexhaustible dynamic flow of *Natura naturans*, which under Extension fills out *facies totius universi* and under Thought is the content of *infinita idea Dei*. Each of these is an eternal invariant

Gestalt regulating the nature of every transient detail and "compelling" the infinite changes suffered by the innumerable diversifications of *Natura naturata*.

Notes

1. Cf. Joachim, *Study of the Ethics of Spinoza*, Book I, Appendix; Caird, *Spinoza*, Ch. VIII; G. W. F. Hegel, *Werke in zwanzig Bänden, Band 20: Vorlesungen über die Geschichte der Philosophie*, (Frankfurt-am-Main, Theorie Ausgabe, Suhrkamp Verlag, 1971–1978), Dritte Teil, Abs. II, A2, pp. 157–197 (trans. E. S. Haldane and F. H. Simson, *Hegel's Lectures on the History of Philosophy*, Vol. III, pp. 252–290).
2. In contemporary relativity physics, space-time (Spinoza's Extension) and energy coincide. The first is the metrical field, and fields of force are represented in it as curvature. All movement is along geodesics.
3. Cambridge, Mass., Harvard University Press, 1969.
4. Cf. Stuart Hampshire, *Spinoza* (Harmondsworth, Penguin Books, 1946); A. C. Watt, "The Causality of God in Spinoza's Philosophy," *Canadian Journal of Philosophy* Vol. II, No. 2 (1972).
5. Further, judgments do not exhaust the denotation of Spinoza's modes of Thought, which include emotions (*affectus*) as well as ideas; but, as he asserts in E2A3, affects do not occur without ideas, although ideas may occur without any other mode of thought. There are other reasons for objecting to the identification of *idea* with "proposition" so far as that connotes a verbal or symbolic formula, but these need not be pursued here as they are not germane to our central theme.
6. Cf. my *Salvation from Despair*, p. 83.
7. Cf. Curley, *Spinoza's Metaphysics*, p. 66.
8. Cf. my *Hypothesis and Perception*, Ch. II.
9. Curley, *Spinoza's Metaphysics*, p. 75f.
10. "*Quare ii prorsus garriunt, ne dicam insaniunt, qui Substantiam Extensam ex partibus, sive corporibus ab invicem realiter distinctis, conflatam esse putant.*"
11. He has special reasons (into which we need not enter) for confining attention here (and in E1P15S) to Extension.
12. Cf. J. S. Haldane's description in *The Philosophical Basis of Biology* (London, 1931).
13. Cf. David Bohm, *Wholeness and the Implicate Order* (London, Routledge and Kegan Paul, 1980; rpt. Boston, Ark Paperbacks, 1983), p. 172.
14. Cf. Werner Heisenberg, *Philosophic Problems of Nuclear Science* (London, Faber and Faber, 1952), p. 105; *Physics and Philosophy* (New York, Harper, 1958, 1962), p. 72.

3

Infinity of Attributes
and *Idea Ideae*

In a very scholarly paper, Professor George Kline has drawn attention to the fact that Spinoza (like other major philosophers) uses certain key terms in different senses, some more or less technical in relation to the philosophical system being expounded, and some unsystematic, more conventional and common.[1] Among such terms *absolutus* and *infinitus* (with their adverbial counterparts, *absolute* and *infinite*) are of special importance and interest. Professor Kline distinguishes three senses of *infinitus*, two systematic and one unsystematic. The first systematic sense, he says, means "perfect without limitation"; the second means "all without exception." The nonsystematic sense is numerical, meaning "countless" or "indefinitely many," "an indefinite number," akin to the sense of "infinite" that Hegel calls "*die schlechte Unendlichkeit.*" As Kline reminds us, Joachim had suggested that the term as applied by Spinoza to substance and attribute is intended to mean "complete" and "all-inclusive" rather than endlessly numerous.[2]

There can be little doubt that Joachim is right and that Spinoza conceived the infinity of Substance and of each of the attributes as complete in itself and whole (in the *Short Treatise*, the word used is *volmaakt*), and that he reserved the meaning of the term as endless, or indefinitely many, for finite entities and for the idea of infinity entertained by the imagination. In the 12th Letter (to Meyer) Spinoza writes that the difference is between "what must be infinite because of its own nature, or in virtue of its definition, and that which has no limits, not indeed in virtue of its essence, but in virtue of its cause" (A. Wolf's translation). He also says that the first is what we cannot imagine but can only understand, whereas the second is what we can also imagine.

38

But these distinctions still leave us in a quandary as to their application to the attributes. When Spinoza is speaking of any attribute as infinite in its own nature, he is almost certainly considering it as complete in itself and, in its own kind, all-inclusive. But when he refers to the infinity of attributes possessed by the absolutely infinite Substance, does he mean that they are indefinitely many, or does he mean that there is a definite number which exhausts them (all there are)?

Joachim contends that there is no indefiniteness in the absolutely infinite Substance, and that the infinity of the attributes does not imply that there is. In this again I am sure he is right. Yet the argument by which Spinoza satisfies himself that Substance must have infinite attributes strongly suggests that he is here using the term in the numerical sense. His argument, it will be remembered, is that any thing must be conceived under some attribute, and the more reality it possesses the more attributes it will have, thus if anything is absolutely infinite it must have infinite attributes. This may be understood in either of two ways: that an absolutely infinite thing must have attributes each of which is infinite in its own kind, or that an absolutely infinite being must have an infinite number of attributes. There are passages in Spinoza's writings that suggest that he understood the phrase in both of these ways (possibly both at once, or sometimes in one sense and sometimes in the other).

In Spinoza's philosophy no problem of interpretation has been more persistent or has occasioned more dispute and discussion than that of the infinity of the attributes, yet none of the proffered solutions have been satisfactory, and the disputed questions remain finally unanswered. Familiar as the problem is, it may be best, for the sake of clarity, to begin by stating it afresh as it was originally, and perhaps most clearly, seen by Spinoza's correspondent Walther von Tschirnhaus.

From the proposition that the more reality a thing has the more attributes belong to it (E1P9 and Ep 9) the presumption must be that one is speaking numerically, but Spinoza's conclusion from the definition of God as an absolutely infinite Substance is that He must have infinite attributes each one of which expresses eternal and infinite essence (KV, I, 2n1, Ep 9, E1D6 and P10S, P11). Here the suggestion is strong that Spinoza conceives the infinity of the attributes in both the above senses. If, however, we accept Professor Kline's submission that infinite can (and does here) mean "all without exception" then both senses are appropriate. As almost certainly Spinoza did not entertain the idea that God had an endless succession of attributes, this is probably the best way to understand the conclusion, although I should prefer "every possible" or "every conceivable" to "all without exception."

Even so, von Tschirnhaus' questions are not answered. The only attributes known to the human mind are Thought and Extension (KV, I, 2, E2PP1 and 2, Ep 64), and why this is so Spinoza explains in the 64th Letter, in answer to von Tschirnhaus, whose question was relayed to him by Schuller (Ep 63). It is because the human mind is the idea of an actually existing body, and nothing else (E2P13), and can thus come to know only what is involved in, or can be inferred from, this idea, namely, what is bodily or extended and what is ideal or thought. No other attribute of God is involved in the body or in its idea. It does not follow from this that there are infinite worlds, one for each attribute, in each of which the finite beings know only their own attribute and that of thought (there being an idea of each in the divine intellect), as von Tschirnhaus had supposed (Ep 63); for, as proved in the scholium to E2P7, there is only one Substance, and the corresponding modes in all attributes constitute only the diverse ways in which the essence of one and the same thing is expressed.

The explanation gives rise to the further question, however, why, since the human mind is the idea of the body, and the body is the same thing expressed in every other attribute as a corresponding mode, we are cognizant only of the extended body and not of the corresponding modes in all other attributes (Ep 65). There is general agreement that Spinoza's reply in Ep 66 is unsatisfactory. He writes:

> . . . although each thing is expressed in infinite [all possible?] ways in the infinite intellect of God, yet the infinite ideas by which it is expressed cannot constitute one and the same mind of an individual thing (*rei singularis*), but an infinity of minds: seeing that each of these infinite ideas has no connection with the others . . .

(The infinite ideas by which it is expressed cannot mean here "infinite in its own kind" or "expressing infinite essence" but can mean only "innumerable" or "all without exception," and the same must apply to the infinity of minds.)

The answer is unsatisfactory because it leaves unexplained the difficulty raised subsequently by Schuller and von Tschirnhaus (Ep 70), "that in this way the attribute of thought is made much more extensive than the other attributes," which should not be possible inasmuch as each attribute equally expresses the essence of Substance and the order and connection of modes is the same in all. Spinoza never responded to this last objection, deferring his reply to the objections raised in the letter as a whole because of an obvious error of interpretation by von Tschirnhaus of E2P5, which is, however, irrelevant to the matter in hand.

Even if the infinite ideas in which the infinite variety of modes, each expressing a single thing in a different attribute, cannot constitute one and the same mind of a singular thing, they are all ideas in the infinite intellect of God and are all modes of Thought. The attribute of Thought, therefore, and the infinite intellect, its primary infinite mode, must range over all the other attributes and must be infinitely more complex than any one of them or than any infinite mode under an attribute other than Thought.[3] In that case, the order and connection of ideas is not the same as the order and connection of things (unless in a different sense from that in which the order and connection of modes in all the other attributes is one and the same). For whereas the order of causes in any attribute other than Thought is, so to say, one-dimensional, the order of ideas in God's intellect is, as it were, multidimensional to any conceivable extent.

Moreover, if the ideas of modes in different attributes constitute separate minds, each appropriate to its own attribute, we have returned to the view formerly assumed by von Tschirnhaus that there must be innumerable separate and different "worlds," a view rejected by Spinoza and incompatible with the Scholium of E2P7.

A further difficulty is that the corresponding modes in different attributes constitute one and the same thing (*res*) (E2P7S). So body and mind are one and not two entities, identical in substance. It should follow that the corresponding modes in other attributes are identical with our bodies in substance; yet the ideas of those modes are apparently not identical and can have no connection one with another, but are so different that they cannot constitute one and the same individual mind. Nevertheless, all ideas are ideas, and all belong to Thought, and if each is the same *thing* as, is identical in substance with, its *ideatum,* one would expect the idea of that thing to be one and the same no matter how many attributes there might be under which its *ideatum* could be expressed. Yet as an attribute is defined as what the intellect perceives as constituting the essence of Substance, there must be as many different ideas of each thing as there are different attributes.

Spinoza nowhere resolves these apparent incompatibilities, although his demonstrations of both theses seem incontrovertible: (a) that an absolutely infinite Substance must have infinite attributes (all possible, all without exception—in any case, more than one or a few), and (b) that the human mind can become aware of two only.

In the history of Spinozistic studies various resolutions of the problem have been suggested. It has been maintained that Spinoza should have assigned only one attribute to God (Stumpf), or that there could be no more than two—Extension and Thought—and that in either case God's absolute infinity would not have been prejudiced (Leibniz, Jacobi, Schelling, Erdmann, Friedrichs, etc.).[4] These suggestions are refuted by Spinoza's own propositions and are (perhaps admittedly) not Spinozistic, the presumption being, perhaps, that no solution of the problem is possible consistently within Spinoza's theory. M. Gueroult,[5] however, rightly rejecting all of these, has offered a solution which claims to remain within the bounds of legitimate interpretation of Spinoza and to answer von Tschirnhaus' question as Spinoza would have done had he addressed himself directly and satisfactorily to Epp 65 and 70.

When Spinoza says that God's power of thought is equal to his power of action, M. Gueroult asserts, he means only that however great God's power of action is conceived to be, his thought is equal to it, not absolutely, but only in its own kind. For clearly, God having infinite attributes has infinitely more power in all taken together than in any one taken alone (e.g., Thought). Nevertheless, von Tschirnhaus' problem seems to remain with us, because clearly God's thought comprises ideas of all the modes in all the attributes, and must therefore exceed infinitely the modes in any one (other than the attribute of Thought itself). Gueroult rejects the proffered solution of Lewis Robinson, that a mode of thought has infinitely less reality than a corresponding mode in any other attribute, as the image has less reality than the original (hence the ideas of innumerable modes in other attributes would not exceed in power any one mode in any attribute.[6] He also rejects the suggestion that one cannot attribute more reality to the attribute of Thought on account of the number of its modes, on which its infinity does not depend, and must not equate what is produced in one attribute alone with what is produced in infinitely many. This suggestion, he says, runs counter to E1P16.

The solution offered by Gueroult depends upon the distinction between formal and objective essences. Power of action, he says, is power to produce formal essences, and there is no discrepancy in degree of reality between God's power of thinking, by which he produced ideas as formal essences, and his power as expressed through any other attribute. But an idea, the formal essence of which is identical in substance with its *ideatum*, refracts into infinite objective essences reflecting, or corresponding to, its correlative modes in other attributes. This refraction makes no difference to its formal essence, which "abstraction having been made from every represented object" remains identically one and the same thing (or cause) in the attribute of Thought. Reference to support this contention is made to E2P21S,[7] where Spinoza speaks of the mind as *idea ideae*, and repeats what he had written in the Scholium to P7 to show that it is the same thing as the mind itself, just as the mind is the same thing as the body. Hence, Gueroult maintains, we must understand the *infiniti modi* and *infinita* of E1P16 differently from those of E2P4, the first being the modes of Substance, but the second only modes of modes (that is, modes or modulations of ideas) each of which is a representation of a mode in one of the other attributes, and all of which constitute only one mode of thought with one and the same formal essence.

Now this solution is no more acceptable than those which have been rejected, for it is incompatible with Epp 64 and 66 and appears to misinterpret the sense of *forma ideae* in E2P21S. In fact, this Scholium, which is quoted in support of the interpretation, if rightly understood, is incompatible with it.

Spinoza's statements in the *Ethics* about the identity in substance of *idea* and *ideatum* must be taken in conjunction with what he says in TdIE about objective and formal essences. In the *Tractatus* he says that a true idea is nothing other than the objective essence of its *ideatum*, but he there says that the formal essence of the idea is not the same as that of its object—an idea of a circle has no center or circumference as a circle has—and that in *idea ideae* the formal essence of the idea itself is made the object of the reflexive idea. In E2P21S he says that the idea of an idea is the *form* of that idea apart from its relation to its object. By this Spinoza cannot mean that *idea ideae* is the formal essence of the idea, for he has in TdIE specifically told us that its formal essence is made the object of the reflexive idea, whereas here it is the reflexive idea which is called the form. In E2P7S we are told that *idea* and *ideatum* are one and the same thing (*res*), because corresponding modes in different attributes are all identical in substance. But the formal essence of a mode cannot simply be its substantial being, i.e., the *res* of which it is a modal expression; for if it were, its modal characters under the various attributes would be quasi-objective. Accordingly, it should follow that one identical *res* has infinite formal essences, differing one from another as do the attributes under which they fall. The idea of each formal essence is the objective essence of the thing, and the formal essence of the idea must then be either the same for all objective essences, or each objective essence must be a different idea with a distinct formal essence of its own. If there is only one idea which is *formaliter* the same for all the differing objective contents, the idea of the human body must be the same idea *formaliter* as that of all the modes corresponding to the body in all other attributes, and it should comprehend all these diverse modes *objective*. To use Gueroult's image, it should be refracted into infinite modulations constituting the objective essences of the same thing as modes in all the infinite attributes of Substance. But the idea of the human body is the human mind, which we are explicitly told does not become aware of any attribute other than Thought and Extension. It is the *formal essence* of the idea which becomes the object of the idea of the mind (*idea ideae*), and if this is the same for all the objective essences of all the modes corresponding to the body in all the attributes, the human mind, as well as God's, should be aware of all the attributes and not only two. But this is not the case, and Spinoza's argument in Ep 64 that it cannot be seems cogent.

Accordingly, there must be different ideas with different formal essences corresponding to the differing objective essences of the modes in other attributes than Extension, and God's intellect must include not only one idea of each individual thing modulated into infinite ideal modes objectively representing the formal essences of all the modal varieties under the differing attributes, but, as Spinoza says in Ep 66, infinite ideas, the formal essence of each of which is the objective essence of the mode of its *ideatum* under a particular attribute. If there were formally only one idea, nothing would prevent its being the same mind of an individual thing under all attributes, the possibility of which Spinoza denies. But if there are formally infinite ideas, because they are of modes in different attributes and so are not mutually connected, they cannot, as Spinoza says in the letter, constitute one and the same mind of an individual thing (bearing in mind that modes of any attribute must be explained through that attribute alone and not through any other; E2P7S). At the same time, Spinoza has insisted that all the infinite minds (ideas) of all the modes under the different attributes of any individual thing are identical in substance.

This is clearly Spinoza's explicit doctrine, however difficult it may be to comprehend, and Gueroult's interpretation cannot be accepted because it is incompatible with what Spinoza maintains in the 64th and 66th Letters. It would, in short, imply the possibility of human knowledge of all the attributes. Nor would it help to believe (if one felt so inclined) that Spinoza had changed his mind between writing the TdIE and the second Part of the *Ethics*, and that what he means in E2P7S is that the formal essence is one and the same for both *idea* and *ideatum*, while the objective essence differs with each attribute. For that would make the difference between the attributes merely ideal, an interpretation conflicting with E2P6C, as Gueroult points out.[8] It would, moreover, be incoherent, for it would involve the formal identity of extension and thought (it would imply, for instance, that the idea of a circle was circular).

Gueroult's reference to E2P21S is obscure. He says that the formal reality (*réalité formelle*) of the idea, "*abstraction faite de tout objét représenté,*" remains identical and unchanged by the refraction into an infinity of reflections (*reflets*) which are the objective essences of all (an infinity of) modes corresponding to it in other attributes.[9] In the Scholium, however, Spinoza says that *idea ideae* is "*forma ideae, quatenus haec, ut modus cogitandi, absque relatione ad objectum consideratur,*" and (as we saw from TdIE) the formal essence of the idea is the object of *idea ideae*. *Idea ideae* itself, then, must be the objective essence of the idea, though not of the body (its object) from which abstraction is to be made. The *forma ideae* here is, therefore, not the formal essence but rather the objective essence, the form of the formal essence. Gueroult, on the other hand, speaks of the formal reality of the idea as that which remains when abstraction is made from its object. It would, then, be a natural inference, in view of his reference to the Scholium, to regard the modulations or refractions of the idea into an infinity of modes of the mode of thought as *formae ideae* coinciding with the infinite series of *ideae idearum* of which Spinoza speaks. In that case, the *ideae idearum* would become the ideas representing *objective* the corresponding modes in the attributes other than Extension.

This Gueroult does not allege, and had it been his intention he must have known that he would have been reverting to an interpretation very similar to that offered in the last century by Windelband and Bratuschek, worked out with great ingenuity by the latter, but no less in conflict with Spinoza's statements. Gueroult must also have known that the failure of this interpretation had long since been exposed by Gabriel Huan. We must, therefore, conclude that, although it is suggested by the reference on page 83 of his book, it is not what Gueroult meant to convey. Nevertheless, it may be of some interest to consider the implications of this older hypothesis once more and to expose the reasons for its failure anew.

The interpretation takes two main forms, one corresponding to that which, if he had meant it, we might attribute to Gueroult, and the other put forward by Ernst Bratuschek in his *Habilitatsvortrag* before the Berliner Hochschule in July 1871.[10] According to the first, the infinite ideas is God's intellect which represent corresponding modes in each of the attributes would be the *ideae idearum* occurring in series from the ideas of particular bodies in Extension. The corresponding modes themselves would be the *ideata* of these ideas. But this version is obviously untenable, first because the object of *idea ideae* is explicitly said by Spinoza to be the idea of the body (E2P21D), and the *idea ideae* is itself *ideatum* to a further *idea ideae ideae* (for "whosoever knows something knows that he knows it and knows that he knows that he knows"), and there is no question here of *ideata* in any attribute other than Extension or Thought.

Bratuschek, however, alleges that *idea ideae* cannot belong to the attribute of Thought, because, as all the bodies comprising the *facies totius universi* exhaust the infinity of Extension, so must the ideas of these bodies exhaust the attribute of Thought—for the order and connection of modes is the same in both. *Idea ideae* must therefore fall outside the attribute of Thought and must itself be a mode, corresponding to the body and its mind, in a third attribute. The same will be true for *idea ideae ideae*, and so on ad infinitum. It is this infinite series, then, wherein the infinite attributes of Substance consist.

If *idea* and *idea ideae* both belonged to the attribute of Thought, Bratuschek argues, they could be distinguished neither *modaliter* nor *realiter*, and two infinite series of identical modes cannot exist under one attribute. Spinoza maintains that they are related as body and mind are related, but body and mind are the same thing under *two* attributes, not one.

Bratuschek contends that *idea ideae* appears to the human mind as belonging to the Attribute of Thought because the human intellect can perceive only two attributes, and in being self-conscious is unaware of *idea ideae*. This he supports by reference to Spinoza's assertion in TdIE that *idea ideae* is not necessary for certainty, because the *essentia objectiva* is itself the truth and is all that is required. But the intellect of God is identical with God Himself; thus they encompass the whole of God's nature in all its infinite attributes. In the divine intellect, therefore, the distinction of *ideae idearum* from *ideae* as a separate attribute from that of Thought is explicit, and so with *ideae* raised to a third power, and so on ad infinitum. Accordingly, Spinoza can rightly say in the Scholium to E2P21 that the idea of the mind and the mind itself are in God by the same necessity and follow from the same power of thinking.

There is, however, no suggestion in the Scholium that the reason why "the idea of the mind and the mind itself are one and the same thing which is conceived under one and the same attribute, namely, Thought" is that the human mind is restricted to two attributes; and it is clear that "one and the same power of thought" is intended by Spinoza to refer to the Attribute of Thought. It is indeed the same power by which God perceives all his other attributes, but no reference to that fact is made in this context.

In fact, what follows from Spinoza's statement is that *idea* and *idea ideae* are the same mode of thought. There is some justification for saying, with Gueroult, that every idea refracts into an infinite spectrum, but its spectral lines are the reflections of itself, not of modes in other attributes. Otherwise, there would be no point in Spinoza's repeated insistence that to know is to know that you know, and to know that you know that you know. In short, the infinite series of *ideae idearum* has nothing whatever to do with the infinity of the attributes. It is simply Spinoza's recognition of the infinite capacity of thought for self-reflection and self-illumination. If we were to accept Bratuschek's argument, that *idea ideae* must belong to a new attribute, we could not escape the conclusion that all the infinite attributes are immediately accessible to the human mind, for to know that one knows something would immediately be to know it under some other attribute, different from either Extension or Thought, and this is obviously false. Yet whatever we know involves unlimited self-awareness of our knowing. Spinoza's point is that it is impossible to know something, in the proper sense of "know," and to be unaware that you know it. This self-illumination, self-reflectiveness, and self-transcendence is the peculiar character of thought, and much of consequence follows from it; but it does not involve the automatic ability to conceive modes in other attributes than Thought and Extension, nor to generate them, as Bratuschek's interpretation would imply.

So the problem of the infinity of the attributes (all without exception, all there are, however many there may be, the totality of God's powers), and the relation between Thought and attributes other than Extension, remains unsolved by any of the devices, ingenious though they may be, hitherto suggested.[11]

Quite probably no solution of this problem is possible according to the strict letter of Spinoza's doctrine; and modifications of it which do not radically depart from it fail to produce a coherent theory. It has been submitted that Spinoza need not have opted for infinite attributes, but should have been content with two, relying simply on the infinite self-reflectiveness of thought to fill out the absolute infinity of Substance. At times I have myself been inclined towards this way of avoiding the impasse. But it will not really serve, because Spinoza's reasons for limiting the human mind to the knowledge of two attributes, and for declaring that God must have an infinity of attributes, are too strong for us legitimately to abandon them. And the capacity of the human mind to reflect upon itself ad infinitum is not impaired by its limitation to two attributes; so that it should, despite the finitude of the body, be at least potentially capable of comprehending God's absolute infinity in detail, which it obviously is not.

Yet there are elements in Spinoza's thinking that, as one continues to reflect upon them, continuously provide more light.

Bratuschek makes the point that in the *Short Treatise* Spinoza writes "up to the present only two of these infinites are known to us,"[12] as if the restriction of human cognition to two attributes was merely provisional, and that he repeats in Ep 56 that he knows only some of God's attributes, as if he had hoped, with increasing knowledge, to become cognizant of others.[13] Possibly, then, we may be allowed the liberty of expanding Spinoza's doctrine in the light of more modern scientific discoveries. In the seventeenth century the only developed sciences were mathematics and physics, and in the latter little more than geometrical optics and mechanics had as yet been systematized. One might well have asserted, therefore, that "up to the present" only two attributes were known, namely, the extended physical world and that awareness of it the existence of which we cannot deny (as Descartes had stressed), if only because to be aware is to be aware that one is aware. But the succeeding century saw the rise of chemistry and the next the development of biology, followed by empirical psychology.

Today we can conceive the world in a more complex and more illuminating fashion. Science discloses to us a physical world disposed in a space-time continuum which is inseparable from the energy and matter that differentiate it and determine its contours. It is a single indivisible whole, "finite but unbounded." A conception such as this of a self-contained yet unlimited universe is entirely consonant with Spinoza's definition of an attribute, infinite in its own kind, and with his notion of infinity as he explains it to Meyer in the twelfth epistle. It is indeed an "infinite which cannot be divided into parts," because the whole and its configuration determine (like Spinoza's *facies totius universi*) all physical entities and processes in the minutest detail.[14] The extended physical universe can be completely described and explained in terms of "motion and rest," or in modern scientific language, in terms of space-time curvature and quanta of action.

But that does not exhaust its nature; for it can also be regarded without any diversity of substance, as an organic whole, the principle of which is life. Organism is physico-chemical throughout, yet is "teleonomic" (that is, all its processes tend towards the self-maintenance of an organic system); and this teleonomic character is not explicable by purely physical laws.[15] An organismic principle is involved. Further, organism and environment are not separable, but are organically united; and the flow of matter and energy from one to the other is continuous. The world is not just a collection of organisms fortuitously associated, any more than the physical universe is a mere collection of bodies. It is an integrated biocoenosis, a system of ecosystems to which no limit can be set short of the entire biosphere. Once again, it is, in

Spinoza's sense, an infinite whole, indivisible into independent parts.[16]

Further, every organism is, according to its degree, animated or beminded. It is sentient and registers, not simply chemically or physically, but sensuously, the innumerable influences of the surrounding world. The entire infinite system can be deployed as the content of a psychological whole which is correlative to, but not describable in terms of, the biological and physico-chemical entities upon which it supervenes, and with which it is substantially one and the same.[17]

Finally, the whole is again expressible in purely intellectual terms, as what Sir Karl Popper has called "the third world"—the world of pure theory, setting out systematically and in conceptual terms the entire system in all its gradations and phases.

Might we not regard each of these levels as a distinct attribute of Substance? Each is a complete, self-contained, infinite whole (where "infinite" means self-dependent and self-sustaining, not endless or interminable). Each comprehends the entire universe. They are all substantially one and the same world, in which every thing (*res*) is expressed in all the specific attributive forms. And each level of reality expresses the nature of the whole in its own kind. "Up to the present" we know only these few, but nothing in principle prevents our becoming aware of others. Nevertheless, we may well—or rather, cannot but—agree with Spinoza that "God does not lack material for the creation of all things from the highest to the lowest grade of perfection" and that the complete essence of God must be expressible as a whole in infinite degrees. For the gradation is continuous and must include infinite specific levels, infinite things in infinite modes under infinite attributes.

But if we were to think of the attributes of Substance in this way, we should not be confronted with von Tschirnhaus' problem. There is only one world, as Spinoza requires, and not infinite separate worlds. The Attribute of Thought, while it expresses the whole essence of Substance in all its degrees and in all other attributes, does not repeat itself in innumerable series of minds, each corresponding to a separate attribute. The human mind is, as Spinoza intended, the awareness of its body, and as such is identical with it as felt (or, as Merleau-Ponty might have said, "lived"). The body is one and the same thing in all attributes; it is an extended physical thing, an organism, a felt whole (a sentient field), and is self-aware at the same time as it is aware of the world, the interaction of which with it is registered in it, as a whole at all levels. All minds taken together make up the intellect of God, which is the infinite mode of Thought and comprehends the whole of God's nature (*idea infinita Dei*). But there is no reduplication of minds, and Thought does not become "much more extensive than the other attributes" (Ep 70).

The human mind, on this view, still is aware of only some of God's attributes (Ep 56), but the potentiality of knowing more is not ruled out in principle, and it remains true that, being the awareness of a physical, organic body, it can know only such attributes as are involved in that fact. God constitutes the human mind so far as He is considered as a thinking thing, and the human body of which the mind is conscious (which is its object or *ideatum*) insofar as He is considered as an extended, and as an organic, whole. Nothing here alleged, therefore, conflicts in principle with what Spinoza has written in the 64th Letter; and it is in harmony with his references to the limitations of our knowledge of God in the *Short Treatise* and in the 55th Letter. The only conflict is with Ep 66, which from the start has been found unsatisfactory, by von Tschirnhaus and by all commentators ever since.

That this is a fully satisfactory resolution of the problem of the infinity of the attributes may not be conceded by all Spinozists. It is the best I can think of; and as far as it goes, it does not seem to be incompatible with Spinoza's ideas, nor to involve any serious distortion of his system.

Notes

1. G. L. Kline, "On the Infinity of Spinoza's Attributes," in S. Hessing, ed., *Speculum Spinozanum, 1677–1977* (London, Routledge and Kegan Paul, 1977), pp. 333–352.
2. Cf. Joachim, *Study of the Ethics of Spinoza*, pp. 27–35.
3. Alternatively we might say that there must be an infinity of infinite intellects, one for each attribute other than Thought, so that while every other attribute has but one primary infinite mode, Thought has an infinity of infinite modes.
4. Cf. G. Huan, *Le Dieu de Spinoza* (Arras, 1913), p. 216.
5. M. Gueroult, *Spinoza* (Paris, Hildesheim, 1968–1974), Vol. II, Ch. IV, §§XX and XXI.
6. It is not clear whether Gueroult or Robinson attributes this comparison to Spinoza. The reference is to *Cogitata Metaphysica*, I, Ch. I, where it does not occur. Gueroult, however, affirms that what Spinoza says there about *entia rationis* does not entail a denial of reality to ideas as *essentiae objective* (cf. TdIE).
7. Gueroult, *Spinoza*, p. 83.
8. Ibid., p. 79.
9. Ibid., p. 83.
10. *Worin bestehen die unzähligen Attribute der Substanz bei Spinoza?* (Berlin, 1871). Cf. also Wilhelm Windelband, *Die Geschichte der Neuern Philosophie* (Leipzig, 1878) Vol. I, p. 213.

11. Cf. also Constantin Brunner's interpretation in *Science, Spirit, Superstition,* trans. Abraham Suhl, ed. Walter Bernard (London, G. Allen and Unwin, 1968), Pt. II, Ch. iv; and Ch. 14 below.

12. *Short Treatise of God, Man, and Human Welfare,* Pt. I, Ch. VII, note 1.

13. Joachim draws attention to the same point: cf. *A Study of the Ethics of Spinoza,* p. 39, n. 5.

14. Cf. Sir Arthur Eddington, *The Expanding Universe* (Cambridge, Cambridge University Press, 1933), *New Pathways in Science* (Cambridge, Cambridge University Press, 1953); D. W. Sciama, *The Unity of the Universe* (New York, Doubleday, 1961); Fritjof Capra, *The Tao of Physics* (London, Wildwood House, 1976; rpt. London, Fontana, 1983); David Bohm, *Wholeness and the Implicate Order*; and my *Cosmos and Anthropos* (Atlantic Highlands, N.J., Humanities Press, 1991), Ch. 3.

15. Cf. Jaques Monod, *Le hasard et la necessité* (Paris, 1970), and my discussion in *Proceedings of the XVth. International Congress of Philosophy,* 1973.

16. Cf. L. von Bertalanffy, *Problems of Life* (London, Watts, 1952); Lewis Thomas, *The Lives of a Cell* (New York, Viking Press, 1974); James Lovelock, *Gaia: A New Look at Life on Earth* (Oxford, Oxford University Press, 1979); and my *Cosmos and Anthropos,* Ch. 7.

17. Cf. *Cosmos and Anthropos,* pp. 106f., 139, 149f.

4

Spinoza's Doctrine of Body-Mind Relation

The key passages in the *Ethics* for the correct understanding of Spinoza's theory of the relation of the mind to the body are:

1. Definitions: By body I understand a mode which expresses in a certain determinate manner the essence of God insofar as he is considered as an extended thing. By idea I understand a conception of the mind which the mind forms because it is a thinking thing. (Explanation: I say conception, rather than perception, because the term perception seems to imply that the mind is affected by the object. But conception seems to express action of the mind.) (E2D1, 2)

2. Whatever can be perceived by the infinite intellect as constituting the essence of substance all pertains to only one substance, and consequently ... thinking substance and extended substance is one and the same substance which is comprehended now under this attribute and now under that. So also, a mode of extension and the idea of that mode is one and the same thing (*res*), but expressed in two ways; ... Thus, whether we conceive nature under the attribute of Extension, or under the attribute of Thought, or under any other whatsoever, we shall find one and the same order, or one and the same connection of causes, that is, the same things following one another. (E2P7S)

3. The first thing that constitutes the actual being of the human mind is nothing other than an idea of some single thing actually existing. (E2P11)

4. Whatever happens to the object of the idea constituting the human mind must be perceived by the human mind, or there is necessarily an idea in the mind of that thing: that is, if the object of the idea constituting the human mind were a body, nothing could

52

happen in that body which would not be perceived by the mind. (E2P12)

5. The object of the idea constituting the human mind is a body or a certain mode of Extension actually existing and nothing else. (E2P13; compare KV, II, Preface, Note, and Appendix)

6. From these [propositions] not only do we understand that the human mind is united to the human body, but also what ought to be understood by the union of the mind and the body. But nobody can understand that [union] adequately or distinctly unless he first knows adequately the nature of our body. For what we have shown hitherto is generally applicable, and does not pertain to men more than to other individual things, which are all besouled (*animata*) although in different degrees. For of everything whatsoever there is necessarily an idea in God, of which God is the cause, in the same way as the idea of the human body; and to that extent, whatever we have said of the idea of the human body, must necessarily be said of the idea of anything whatsoever. Nevertheless, we also cannot deny that ideas, like objects themselves, differ from one another, and one is more excellent than another and contains more reality, as the object of the one is more excellent and contains more reality than the object of the other; and for this reason in order to determine how the human mind differs from the rest, and how it excels others, it is necessary for us to know the nature of its object, that is, as we have said, the nature of the human body. . . . This I shall say in general: to the extent that any body is better fitted than others for doing or suffering many things at the same time, to that extent is its mind more capable than other things of perceiving many things at the same time; and the more the actions of one body depend on itself alone, and the less other bodies are involved (*concurrunt*) with it in acting, the better is its mind able (*aptior*) to understand distinctly. (E2P13S)

Body and mind are one thing (*res*), one entity, not two. They are substantially one and the same; but the essence of the one substance is expressed differently under different attributes, and what is, under the Attribute of Extension, a body, under the Attribute of Thought, is an idea or mind. This identification of mind with idea is as apt to be a source of misunderstanding, as is the distinction between thought and extension. So our first task must be to explain and to clarify what Spinoza means by these terms and how he conceives their interrelation.

The idea of an object (which is the *ideatum* of the idea, or what is "ideated" in it) is the mind of that object. The idea is not a mere replica of its object, as if in a different medium; it is not a dumb picture on a tablet, nor something merely passively received into the mind; but it is an active self-illuminating awareness of that which it brings to consciousness (or ideates)—its *ideatum*.[1] The idea of a body is thus the consciousness which that body has of itself, or the body as felt—not, of course, merely tactually perceived, but as experienced or, in the language of contemporary phenomenologists, "lived." The idea of the body is thus its self-awareness, or mind. We must, however, take care not to read too much into the term "self-awareness," at least in the first instance, or in its primary phase. It is not immediately and ab initio an awareness of a developed self or personality, but simply the way the body, and everything in it or what happens to it, is felt. The body under the attribute of Extension is a finite physical thing (about which we shall presently have more to say); its idea or mind is the same thing (*res*) under the attribute of Thought, that is, qua felt or self-sentient.[2] Further, just as the body is an active metabolic and physiological system, maintaining itself in dynamic equilibrium, so the idea, its mind, is an activity of thinking, hence no dumb picture.

We commonly speak of the "idea" of a body as some sort of mental image or concept in a mind, and the body which is the object of the "idea" is taken to be external to and other than the body which has the mind. I have the idea in my mind (I may say) of a table, and the table, though a body, is no part of my body. But Spinoza declares that the idea which constitutes the human mind is the idea of a particular body (or mode of Extension) actually existing, *and nothing else*. This is because I can have "ideas" (whether mental images or concepts) of other bodies than my own only if and so far as other bodies in some way affect my body physically—be it by reflecting light into my eyes, or pressing upon my skin, or transmitting sound waves to my ears, or the like. The effects of these on my body I feel or sense, and they, together with numerous other processes and events in my body, constitute my self-sentience—the idea of my body.

When I see a table, what I sense is an effect registered through my eyes in my brain, although in seeing the table I am not directly aware of either. Nevertheless, my vision of the table is a sensing of something happening to and in my body and thus is a factor or component in my bodily awareness. It is this bodily awareness as one whole that Spinoza calls the idea of the body. It informs me, Spinoza says,[3] (although I may fail in my confusion of thought to recognize this) more about the nature and condition of my body than about the table; and as far as I think inadequately and confusedly, I fail to make the proper distinctions between the objects of my ideas and I attribute to the table what are really properties of my body.

That this is a sound doctrine is simply illustrated by the ways in which our perception of other bodies is affected by changes in our own bodies. Their colors are modified if we have jaundice; we see double if one eye is pressed; outlines become blurred if our eye muscles malfunction and fail to focus or accommodate properly; chemical changes in the bloodstream caused by drugs produce all sorts of hallucinations.[4] There is no need to multiply examples which are all too common and familiar. Normally we learn to distinguish what pertains to our own bodies from what we take to be the qualities and characters of others, but frequently (perhaps constantly) we confuse the two, as when a bubble floating in the vitreous humor of the eye is taken for an insect crawling over the page we are reading. Thus the self-sentience of the body, what for Spinoza is the idea of the body, includes everything of which I am sensuously aware; and it is from this, and on this as foundation, that all my "ideas" of whatever kind are elaborated. As the medievals maintained, *nihil in intellectu est quod non fuit in sensu.* In this way, my mind is constituted by the idea (Spinoza's term) of my body.[5]

Spinoza tells us, however, that all bodies are in different degrees *animata,* for there is of necessity an idea in God of everything whatsoever. In the infinite intellect ideas are no more dumb pictures than they are in our minds, and the mind of God is not a sort of infinite picture gallery, or a celestial *camera obscura* in which the world is depicted. It is the idea (or mind) of the entire universe and is articulated in modes of Thought, as the extended world is diversified into bodies, so that each and every body has its appropriate idea—again not a replica of itself in some other medium, but its very self as felt. In the mind of God (or even of man) this is conceivable; but how are we to understand the self-sentience of a stone or a molecule? The answer we are given by Spinoza is that ideas differ in excellence, or degree of reality, as do their *ideata,* and the mind of so relatively simple a body as a stone (which today we should call inorganic) would be so rudimentary as to be far below the level of anything worthy of the name consciousness.

The idea in my mind of a stone is a feature in the elaboration of the felt content of my mind—the idea of my body. I say "felt" content advisedly, because Spinoza regularly uses the Latin word *sentire* to indicate the kind of awareness that we have of ourselves. In E5P23S, for instance, he says that we feel (*sentimus*) ourselves to be eternal. By using this word he does not mean that we suspect or "have a hunch," but literally that we sense or ideate. Thus I "feel" (*sentio*) the stone of which I have an idea, or alternatively I "perceive" it (*percipio*). My ability to do so, however, is consequent upon the highly complex organized structure and the dynamic equilibrium of motion and rest that characterize my body. Its action is, like that of organisms generally, much more dependent on itself alone than upon the concurrence of other bodies. It is largely self-constituting, self-maintaining, and self-renewing. As Spinoza says, it is "more excellent" than other bodies (such as stones or molecules).[6] The correlative idea or mind will, therefore, be similarly more developed, so that the effects upon my body (e.g., through sense organs like eyes) of external things (like the stone) are felt in *idea*, and I say that I have an idea *of the stone* so far as I am able to bring to consciousness the idea of my body and to articulate it. On the other hand, although Spinoza does not make the point explicitly, it would be natural to suppose that conscious self-sentience would not really be possible below a certain level of organic development, although the germ and potentiality of consciousness might nevertheless be present. So the stone itself, although it has an idea (there is an idea of it in God), is not aware of itself.

Even human ideation at the sensuous and merely imaginative level is very confused. For although our minds are ideas of our bodies, they do not initially involve adequate, clear, or scientifically complete knowledge of our bodies, or, consequently, of our minds either (the reason for this will become apparent later).[7] How much less, then, will inorganic bodies be "capable of perceiving many things." Only organisms have, or approximate to, mental capacities like our own, and the suggestion of pan-psychism in Spinoza's statement that everything is in some degree "animate" is not eccentrically speculative. It does not involve a belief in animism any more than does the modern physical principle of exclusion in quantum theory, which endows elementary particles with a sort of intrinsic capacity to avoid others with the same quantum numbers.

Spinoza's intention here may best be grasped if one realizes that there is for him strictly only one thinking thing (*res cogitans*), as also there is only one extended thing (*res extensa*), and that it is the same thing in both cases—namely, God. The thinking thing is the infinite intellect, and all ideas strictly belong to it. But just as bodies are "parts" (a term to be used only with qualification, as has already been noted) of the extended thing, so all ideas (or minds) are "parts" in a somewhat different (nonspatial) sense of the thinking thing. Because these "parts" are finite, incomplete, truncated, and fragmentary, as compared with the whole, they are in varying degrees inadequate: the more so the more elementary and exclusive the *ideatum*. Thus a simple body has a mind or idea which, if taken in and by itself, is so inadequate that it hardly amounts even to rudimentary sentience.

The human body is not a simple body, and the idea of the body that constitutes the human mind is, accordingly, not a simple idea; being one and the same in substance, each is as complex as the other. This Spinoza tells us in so many words (E2P15 and D). The idea that constitutes the human mind includes the very obscure feelings of bodily processes and conditions that never, or only on rare and special occasions, rise to clear consciousness. It also includes feelings and percepts of the direct effects of causes external to the body, which impinge upon it from other bodies. It is therefore legitimate when appropriate to refer to these differentiations themselves as single ideas, distinguishable within the mind, as we commonly do, and as Spinoza henceforth habitually does.

The fact that the order and connection of causes is the same under Extension as under Thought does not imply "parallelism," if by that is meant a double series of episodes in one-to-one correspondence. There is strictly no double series but only a single train of events, which can be viewed in either of two different ways. Events in the bodily process are physical, occurring in space and time, and they are felt as "ideas" or sensations, which may be refined and elaborated to any degree. But the refinement, which corresponds to thought, to knowledge of the second and third kinds (*ratio* and *scientia intuitiva*, as opposed to *imaginatio*), is not something without any physical or physiological aspect. The more apt a body is to do and suffer many things at the same time and the more self-dependent and self-sufficient it is in its own organic functioning, the more capable is its mind of adequate thinking.

To understand the implications of this contention better, we must take some note of the rather scant account Spinoza gives us in the *Ethics* of the nature of bodies. Extension is nothing merely inert and static. It is a form of dynamic activity, or power, of God.[8] Its primary self-expression is Motion-and-rest, what today we should be more inclined to call energy. Bodies distinguished from other bodies only by the quantity of motion and rest that constitutes them are the simplest. One is reminded of modern elementary particles, although Spinoza knew nothing of them, distinguished from one another by the kind of radiant energy they represent: photons, gluons, gravitons, electrons, and the like. Contiguous bodies, Spinoza goes on to say, which transmit to one another motion and rest in constant proportions, constitute a single individual body, which may retain its identity and dynamic equilibrium despite internal changes. Such complex bodies, again, may unite with others, and these more intricately organized complexes with yet others, in a hierarchy, developing up to organisms such as human beings, and beyond—for Spinoza asserts, as we have earlier observed, that "if thus we proceed to infinity, we can easily conceive that all nature is one individual whose parts, that is, all bodies, vary in infinite ways without any change in the individual as a whole" (E2L7S).

We need not go as far as that, however, to see that bodies like our own may be highly complex, and that all kinds of changes may go on within them without their losing individuality or identity. Moreover, changes in one part (or process) may proceed in one direction while others go in other, even contrary, directions, yet the overall proportion of motion and rest transmitted throughout may remain the same. If this occurs we shall expect the idea of the body to reflect similar changes and, in spite of them, to retain its constancy and self-identity. Thus a mind capable of perceiving many things and of understanding clearly and adequately may, nevertheless, be hampered by untoward sensations and obstacles to its intellectual achievement. It may be able, all the same, to overcome some or all of these obstacles by the very capacities that Spinoza describes, both physical and mental. The confused awareness of its body may be clarified sufficiently for it (through medical science, for instance) to remedy some of its own physical ills, and the strengthening of its bodily powers (through organic self-restitution and regeneration) will be reflected in increased mental capabilities. The constant effort, which Spinoza maintains is inherent in all things, to persevere in their own being, and which is, in consequence, an effort to increase their power of action, would provide the incentive for such self-improvement. That this *conatus in suo esse perseverandi* is always an effort to increase one's power of action is clear, because Spinoza identifies it with the essence of the thing that exerts it; and action, properly so-called, is that of which one's own nature (or essence) is the adequate cause.[9] Accordingly, the effort to persist in one's own being is ipso facto the endeavor to act solely from one's own essence or nature.

As an idea is no dumb picture, but is an active awareness, it involves an idea of itself, *idea ideae.* This reflexive idea is one with the first-order idea, as that is one with its *ideatum* (the body). The *idea ideae* is the idea of the mind, but its *ideatum* is just as much the body as the mind, for there is only one Substance. In the last chapter we argued that the object of *idea ideae* was the formal essence of the idea, but that is the objective essence of the body, and the objective essence is one and the same in substance as the formal essence (i.e., as the body itself). The idea of the mind, therefore, is simply a heightened power of self-awareness. One cannot be conscious without being aware of one's own consciousness (as Descartes emphasized), and the consciousness is the self-awareness of the body.

Thus knowledge of the mind and knowledge of the body are concomitants in the same way as body and mind are concomitants; as Spinoza states it, "This idea of the mind is united with the mind in the same way as the mind itself is united with the body" (E2P21). The idea of the body, in the first instance, is obscure and confused, and so likewise is that of the mind; but both may, while remaining concomitants, become clearer and more distinct by being related to the common characteristics implicit in their dependence upon and inherence in the infinite modes of God's attributes—in short, by being related to God's essence, or seen in the light of the whole to which they are integral.

It is not my purpose in this chapter to discuss in any detail Spinoza's theory of knowledge, but that is so intimately bound up with his doctrine of body-mind relation that some account of it can hardly be avoided. Already we have been forced to allude to certain features of it, and a little clarification of those allusions will not come amiss.

The idea of the body is, in its immediacy, the sensory level of awareness. It is, as we have said, confused, and in some respects it may be so obscure as to amount to little more than a vague tonality in consciousness without specific content. In other respects, however, it does present a differentiated field of sensation within which objects can be and are distinguished. It thus provides the "objective" content of the first kind (or phase) of knowledge, *imaginatio*.[10]

Imaginal ideas are never adequate, and Spinoza maintains that *imaginatio* is the one and only source of error. This is not because its ideas are other than, or even in conflict with, the truth, so much as because they are fragmentary and mutilated, because they are only partial and leave out significant aspects or factors belonging to the objects they present. In themselves and within the limits of their own positive content they contain nothing that is false. Their deceptiveness arises merely from what they omit, and their falsity is the result of mere negation or privation of supplementary content, by the inclusion of which their whole aspect would be transformed.[11] Even fictitious ideas are simply remembered fragments floating, as it were, in isolation and out of context. They are not positively or intrinsically false.[12]

Such inadequate ideas, if properly supplemented and set in proper context, approach the truth, which is no more nor less than these same ideas as they are in the infinite intellect of God. There they are fully adequate, completely filled out, and fitted into the web of their actual relations to all others. The nearer ideas approach to this completeness (as is equally the case with their *ideata*) the more reality, and the more perfection, they possess.

Because any and every idea is self-reflexive and involves an idea of itself, the mind, even at the first level of knowing, is capable of reflection upon its ideas, and so is capable of comparing and relating them. In this way it can come to identify and form ideas of those things which are common to its objects and are equally in the part and in the whole. Such ideas, Spinoza tells us (E2P38), are necessarily adequate, for they must be the same in God as they are in us. They cannot be affected by the fragmentariness of our ideas, because what is common to both whole and part must be the same in both. Ideas of such common characteristics (Spinoza calls them *notiones communes*) constitute the second phase of knowledge, *ratio*, and as they are adequate they must necessarily be true.

Precisely what Spinoza means by these common notions is not immediately obvious, and is easily misunderstood. What he most definitely does not mean is the sort of common property, or class concept, which we abstract from similar objects and in terms of which we form general ideas. Such ideas, he holds, are confused and are the product of attempts to combine a multitude of similar images too numerous to hold together in our minds.[13] At best they are mere aids to the imagination (*auxilia imaginationis*) to which nothing in reality corresponds, and they are anything but adequate ideas.

On the other hand, what is common to parts of all things as well as wholes are those features characteristic of the attribute under which they fall. For instance, ideas of the characteristics inherent in the nature of Extension as such provide us with the propositions of geometry, which are about characteristics common to all extended things, both parts and wholes, and are necessarily true.

That this is what Spinoza intends is strongly suggested by what he writes in TdIE about the "eternal things," which, while they are themselves real and individual, are "like generalities or kinds of definitions of singular mutable things and the proximate causes of all things." The eternal things, we have maintained, are the attributes and their infinite modes the characteristics of which are all-pervasive throughout Nature, inasmuch as each attribute expresses, in its own kind, the essence of Substance as a whole. The infinite modes, we have seen, are (or involve) principles of order determining the nature and relations of their component finite modes, so they provide the definitions of all things and in them "as in their true codes" are inscribed the universal laws governing the changes that take place within their invariant configurations.

When our knowledge has advanced thus far, it is a relatively short step further to relate the idea of every particular thing to the complete system as a necessary consequence of the infinite and eternal essence of God. As perceived by the (infinite) intellect, that eternal essence is expressed in the attributes of Substance.[14] Adequate knowledge of the essence of individual things is then attained by seeing them in the light of an adequate idea of the formal essence of one of God's attributes. This is the third and most perfect phase of human knowledge, *scientia intuitiva*,[15] and what is known in this way is known as it is by God, as it is in the eternal and infinite intellect.

How, we may ask, are *ratio* and *scientia intuitiva* related to the human body, that finite mode of Extension from which we began, the idea of which (and nothing else) constitutes the human mind? Can this be so elaborated as to comprehend ideas as they are in God? The answer to these questions is to be sought in the self-reflectiveness of ideas by means of which, as we have been told in TdIE, the human intellect can be purified of errors and confusions. These are matters to be discussed in the following chapter.

While the human mind is said to be the idea of the human body and nothing else, Spinoza also maintains consistently and repeatedly that the essence of the human mind is the intellect. It realizes its true nature in adequate thinking. It is of the nature of the intellect, he contends, to frame true ideas (TdIE, IX, 73). The essential nature of the mind, then, is displayed in *ratio* and *scientia intuitiva*, and at these stages of intellectual development the idea of the body is an adequate idea. It is the idea of the body as it is eternally in God.

Does this abrogate what has been said of the mind as the self-sentience of the body, which is, after all, only *imaginatio*, and is the source of error? Some commentators seem to suggest that its products are mere appearance, the reality of which (whether of body or of mind) is their eternal essence in God. That, of course, is true, but it does not require us to treat the temporal existence of the body, nor its self-feeling, as unrealities. They are not *mere* appearance in a pejorative sense, for even *imaginatio* in its positive content is real as a mode of Thought, as is its *ideatum* in Extension. The adequate idea is a systematic elaboration of the confused idea in the light of its total context in reality, not a simple addition to it, or a sheer substitution for it. It comprehends the physical (and biological) system to which the finite body is integral, in relation to other bodies as determined by the configurationof the whole (*facies totius universi*). These relations are in large measure causal and are registered in the finite body, so that they are already present in its initial self-sentience. The clarification that articulates the system and discloses the true nature of the body and its eternal essence does not cancel out its finite and temporal character, it only supplements it, even if this supplementation reveals it in a new light.

The intellect as the essence of the human mind, therefore, is no less the idea of the body, but is that idea developed, clarified, made adequate and complete. The important question is not so much how it can remain the idea of the body (a merely finite mode) while it comprehends the whole of Nature, but how confused self-sentience can become clear and distinct. This question will be pursued further anon. Our next task, however, is to consider certain interpretations of Spinoza's theory and to correct misunderstandings which all too readily tend to arise.

That the theory is not one of parallelism or psycho-physical dualism has already been shown, yet this is how it is most frequently represented, presumably because Spinoza explicitly denies interaction between body and mind. The theory is one of identity, but it is not the same as the neural-identity theory which has been advocated by contemporary philosophers, such as Herbert Feigl, U. T. Place, and J. J. C. Smart. The modern writers in effect deny the existence of ideas. They maintain that mental states are evidenced only in behavior and in physiological processes, so that an introspective account of experience is only an alternative description, in alternative language, of behavioral and physiological facts, which are equally well describable in physical language.

Spinoza, however, does not reduce mental states to physical, for each belongs to a different attribute. The description of either must therefore be different from that of the other, but the distinction is not merely linguistic, not merely a matter of how the single process is described. Certainly the description of a mode under one attribute is no description at all of the same mode under a different attribute; yet, although substantially they are the same thing, it exists (not merely is describable) in two different forms, each with its own formal essence. One cannot reduce the green appearance of a leaf to light waves plus neural discharges in the brain, nor is it a description of these physical and physiological occurrences. To say that I see a green leaf is to describe my idea, not my physiological condition, even though the two modes are necessarily concomitant. The idea and the physiological state differ in essence although they are the same in substance, and therefore a different account must be given of each if they are to be accurately described—of one in physiological, of the other in psychological, terms. Neither is reducible to the other, nor is either the cause of the other; they are both the same substantial being.[16]

A painting may be described as different colored oil paints smeared over a canvas, and also as the portrait of a woman. They are both the same thing, but neither description is a substitute for the other. This is a close analogy to Spinoza's position. As a portrait the picture has to be recognized, to be perceived by an intelligent subject; it is a portrait only for the perceiving mind. But substantially it is one and the same thing as the paint on the canvas, which is a physical state of affairs independent of its being perceived by an intelligent percipient, and one of which an exhaustive physical description can be given, which is in no sense a description of the portrait and would in no way impart the fact that the painting was a portrait rather than a landscape or a still life. In the same way a physical or a physiological description of what goes on in the body is in no way a description of how it is experienced by the mind, nor is the latter a description (even in a different language) of the former.[17]

When Spinoza says that mind is the idea of the body he means, as has been argued, not the conception of the body, nor its mental image, not a complex model of its physiological functioning constructed by abstract scientific thinking, but the feeling or self-sentience of the body—sensory awareness purely as such. Awareness of this kind is notoriously obscure, and even though everything that occurs in the body is registered in it somehow or other, it is at this lowest level never recognized precisely for what it is. Even when raised to higher levels, as it may be by self-reflection, not everything in it can be clearly and distinctly perceived. Its adequate articulation, moreover, is not primarily an elaboration of physiological theory or a physiological description. It begins with the distinction of the felt body itself from external bodies, the properties of which are initially confused with it, and which, even when distinguished in imagination, are often credited with qualities properly belonging to the body of the sentient subject. Careful and systematic discrimination, however, can clarify the relations between the body felt as mine and other bodies, and can determine the causal connection between them, including the effects they have on my body and the way in which I feel them. Thus a science of physiology, among others, becomes possible. But it is a bad mistake to conclude that, because, according to Spinoza, the human mind is the idea of the human body and nothing else, the clarification and articulation of that idea is confined to physiology of the body. That would not even be possible unless the distinction of the human body from others had first been accurately made and an adequate knowledge of external bodies had been acquired. Thus the articulation of the idea of the body, qua feeling, as Spinoza understands it, is really the development of adequate knowledge of the physical world as a whole, and not simply of physiological processes. Sir Frederick Pollock, accordingly, for all his perspicacity and appreciation of Spinoza's thought, somewhat mis-leadingly represents the idea of the human body, as perceived by God in its complete adequacy, as no more than physiological knowledge. God, he says, is the "accomplished physiologist."[18] No doubt, He is, but His idea of the human body, despite the fullness of its physiological detail, is far more than that; for that idea is the human mind in its true and essential nature, and human knowledge is far from being confined to physiology.

Failure to appreciate the Spinozistic doctrine that the idea of the body is bodily self-feeling can lead to the grossest and most fantastic errors. Carroll R. Bowman,[19] who seems to construe "idea of the body" as mean-ing either image of the body or conception of the body, takes Spinoza's statement that a body apt to do and suffer many things will have a mind capable of perceiving many things to imply that gymnastics should be propaedeutic to cosmology.[20] He sees that this is absurd, but not that it is an egregious misinterpretation of Spinoza. Hard muscles and acrobatic skills no doubt have their counterpart in self-sentience, but it does not amount to a knowledge of "the order of causes in nature as a whole" (as Bowman implies, misprising a correct and perspicacious remark quoted from W. van Leyden).[21] The kind of "excellence" in the body which Spinoza finds relevant to adequate knowledge in the mind is not merely a developed musculature. If it were, horses might be wiser than men. He refers to the degree of organic development involving sensory and nervous systems which are intricately and subtly adaptable and responsive to diverse stimuli. Intelligence is not concomitant with the body of a slime mold; it requires an incalculably more complex and highly organized living system, in which different organs perform different functions and contribute variously to the adequate performance of higher activities. Gymnastics may not, indeed, be wholly irrelevant to a sound mind. Plato believed it to be essential. But nobody would consider physical strength a sufficient condition of sanity.

Moreover, Spinoza's theory of bodies permits even of the compatibility of disease with clear thinking, depending on the extent to which the disease affects the proportion of motion and rest transmitted from one part of the body to another. It is well known that any bodily defect may, and probably all do, have concomitant reflections in experience. Even physiological processes which are wholly "unconscious," like digestion and glandular secretion, have obscure counterparts in our moods and mental attitudes. But not every physical functioning affects our capacity for logical thinking, nor is it disrupted by every physical defect.

Our ability to frame adequate ideas is, for Spinoza, intimately bound up with the eternity (or "immortality") of the mind, which does not involve or necessitate the indefinite duration of the body (although the essence of the body as a temporal and finite mode is eternally in God).[22] Dr. Bowman's remark "Perhaps the consumptive lungs will collapse before the *Ethics* is finished"[23] is irrelevant and pointless in this connection. The state of Spinoza's lungs might well have decreased that organic "excellence" of his body which enabled him to write the *Ethics,* but his body was so highly complex an organism—its degree of excellence was so great—that even phthisis did not reduce the quality of his thinking significantly. The sensations occasioned by the disease would not be rational ideas, but would be obscure and confused ideas at the level of *imaginatio.* Adequate ideas of the relevant *ideata* may well have led Spinoza to regard these affects as of minor importance relative to the blessedness attending upon knowledge and love of God. "If the idea of a dying body feels and knows that it is dying, the idea of the idea of a dying body feels and knows that it is eternal"—so says Bowman.[24] If he were not so confused about the doctrine of *idea ideae,* he might have gotten this right. In fact, the idea of a dying body is its mind, and every body is mortal, with or without phthisis, and the idea of a dying body is the complete knowledge of its relations with everything else in the world, which may well reveal its mortality as a matter of minor significance in the disposition of the completed whole. The realization of this relative unimportance of death might well be an implicate of the awareness of the eternity of that adequate knowledge which reveals it, so that "a free man thinks of nothing less than of death, and his wisdom is a meditation not upon death but upon life" (E4P67).

Insistence on the difference between the attributes is essential to Spinoza's theory of the eternity of the human mind in its adequate thinking and in its knowledge and love of God. If we do not recognize and respect this difference we cannot reconcile that doctrine with his theory of body-mind relation. If thought represented only an alternative description of a reality that was in itself purely physical, mind would be as mortal as the body. But it is obvious that even this way of stating the matter altogether misrepresents Spinoza, for the physical is the extended, and extension has no application at all to ideas. The identity in substance of idea and extended body underlies their essential difference.

This difference rests primarily in the self-illumination of idea. It is precisely because idea is self-reflective, is conscious, in being idea is aware of itself as idea and so involves *idea ideae,* that it transcends the spatio-temporal limits of the body—because it is no mere dumb picture on a tablet but a self-conscious activity of thinking. Body is an extended thing (or is part of an extended thing). It is therefore necessarily confined within the limits of its finite extension, both spatial and temporal. Strictly this is but half the truth, for when we come to conceive it adequately we cannot sustain the sharp separation of each singular body from every other. But for our present purpose we may say, without grave distortion of the truth, that bodies as mutually distinct extended things must be limited in space and time. Ideas are not extended things and are mutually distinguished qualitatively or conceptually and not by spatio-temporal boundaries. The same is true of their causal relations. Physical events are related as cause and effect so far as they are spatially and (or) temporally disparate, but cause and effect among ideas are mutually implicated so that the cause is taken up into the effect and combines with it. The movement of the catapult precedes the flight of the missile and ends before the free movement and trajectory of the missile begin; but the idea of the lyre, which calls to mind the lyre player, is combined with its effect. Without the lyre there is no idea of a lyre player at all.

More important, ideas, so far as they are the awareness of finite extended things, involve the awareness of the limits which define their objects, and such awareness ipso facto surpasses those limits; for if it did not it could not be an awareness of them. Thus the self-awareness, or idea, of the body, by its very ideal nature, transcends the limits of that body both spatially and temporally. This is how it is possible for the idea of the body, which begins as mere self-sentience and *imaginatio*, to develop into adequate knowledge of the world, of Nature, Substance, or God; and how it is legitimate for Spinoza to say, as he does in E5P23, "The human mind cannot be absolutely destroyed with the body [it cannot be absolutely confined within the spatio-temporal limits of the body], but something of it abides which is eternal."

Being eternal, the mind does not *endure* after the death of the body, for "in eternity there is no *when, before,* nor *after*" (E1P33S2). The eternity of the human mind so far as it understands adequately is not an "after-life" or a continuance in time beyond the temporal death of the body. It is a quality of being and knowing. There is no question of a disembodied spirit persisting after the extinction of the body, and Spinoza's identification in substance of the body and the mind remains intact.

What dies with the body is the psychical stream of consciousness (memory and imagination) what develops out of it as adequate knowledge is not in time, and is not strictly any part of the psychical stream, if only because it can envisage and be aware of that stream as a temporal series. But, not being part of the stream, neither is it any other part of the temporal series of events outside that occupied by the body. The whole question of temporality in the attribute of Thought, however, is problematical, for time is a form (or dimension) of Extension. For Spinoza time is the measure of duration and is a product of imaginal thinking. Duration he defines as quantity of existence, and he distinguishes from it another sense of existence in which the eternal essences of things exist in God. Such eternal being is obviously not in time. But ideas can be both adequate ideas of such essences or inadequate imaginal ideas. The latter are concomitant with the passing states of the extended organism, which are temporal, but the ideas themselves seem to be temporal (i.e., to belong to the "stream of consciousness") only so far as they are inadequate, that is, false. And so far as they are not inadequate they are eternal.

Any attempt to reach a satisfactory solution of this problem would take us beyond the limits of the subject of this chapter. The most fruitful clue to it in Spinoza is his account of the infinite modes, and especially of the *facies totius universi*, a totality which remains eternally the same in structure despite a continual flux of changes among the finite transitory modes which constitute it in detail.[25] The corresponding infinite mode of Thought is the *idea infinita Dei*, which is also eternal while, presumably, it includes all the finite and transient ideas (or feelings—*affectus*) of finite states in finite modes of Extension. At this point, however, we can carry the discussion no further.

Notes

1. Cf. E2P43S: *"Nec sane aliquis de hac re dubitare potest, nisi putet ideam quid mutum instar picturae in tabula, et non modum cogitandi esse."* Also D3 quoted above.
2. Cf. R. G. Collingwood's account of the body-mind relation in *The New Leviathan* (Oxford, Clarendon Press, 1942), Pt. I, I–V.
3. Cf. E2P17S.
4. Cf. Sir Russell Brain, *Mind, Perception, and Science* (Oxford, Blackwell, 1951), p. 14: "In other words, the spatial setting of the red patch is derived from my body; and the proof of this is that when this bodily machinery goes wrong I no longer see the red patch 'there'. I see two red patches, or the red patch goes round and round, or though I see it, I simply do not know where it is and cannot find my way to it."
5. Cf. H. F. Hallett, "On a Reputed Equivoque in the Philosophy of Spinoza," *Review of Metaphysics* III (1949), pp. 189–212.
6. For Spinoza, "reality," like "perfection" or "excellence," means systematic comprehensiveness, or completion.
7. Cf. E2PP24,27,28,29.

8. Cf. Epp 81 and 83.
9. Cf. E3DD1 and 2.
10. I use "objective" here in its seventeenth-century meaning referring to what is ideally present to the mind, not in its modern sense of external and public.
11. E2P35.
12. TdIE, VIII.
13. Cf. E2P40S1.
14. Cf. E1D4.
15. Cf. E2P40S2.
16. In Ep 9 Spinoza explains the relation of different attributes in Substance by means of linguistic examples. He says: " . . . by the name Israel I mean the third Patriarch, I also mean the same Patriarch by the name Jacob . . ." and follows with two equally valid definitions of the word "plane". But these examples are mere analogies, and are not meant to imply that the difference between the attributes is merely nominal, or linguistic.
17. The modern neural-identity theory involves insuperable difficulties with respect to secondary qualities to which Spinoza's position is not subject. These difficulties cannot be discussed here, but see my paper "The Neural Identity Theory and the Person" in *International Philosophical Quarterly* VI (1966), pp. 515–537.
18. Cf. *Spinoza, His Life and Philosophy* (London, 1899; repr. New York, American Scholar Publications, 1966), pp. 124ff.
19. Cf. "Spinoza's Idea of the Body," *Idealistic Studies* I (1971). Bowman is an enthusiast for Spinoza's philosophy, for whom personally I have a high regard. But this paper is so full of confusion and misunderstanding that detailed correction would involve rewriting almost every sentence. He not only confuses the image of the body with the idea of the body, he also confuses the imagination of other bodies with adequate knowledge of them; he confuses the mind with the idea of the mind; and he seems to misunderstand Spinoza's theory of the relation of *idea* to *ideatum*, as well as his theory of error and of *idea ficta*.
20. Ibid., p. 264.
21. Ibid., quoting van Leyden, *Seventeenth-century Metaphysics* (New York, Duckworth, 1968), p. 198.
22. Cf. my discussion in "Spinoza's Theory of Human Immortality," *The Monist* 55 (1971).
23. Bowman, "Spinoza's Idea of the Body," p. 267.
24. Ibid. Since this was written, Carroll Bowman, a respected and lamented friend, has suffered the same fate.
25. E2L7S, quoted above, and Ep 32.

5

The Order and Connection
of Ideas

In E2P7 Spinoza asserts that the order and connection of ideas is the same as the order and connection of things. The reason and explanation for this he states as follows: Everything that the infinite intellect perceives as constituting the essence of Substance pertains to one substance only, and consequently extended and thinking substance are one and the same. Likewise, a mode of extension and the idea of that mode are one and the same thing expressed in two different ways. It follows that whether we conceive Nature under the attribute of Extension, or under the attribute of Thought, or under any other attribute whatsoever, we shall discover one and the same order, or one and the same connection of causes, that is, the same things following one another in succession (E2P7S).

We are naturally led to ask what the order and connection is which is the same both of ideas and of things, and to wonder whether this refers to all ideas, false as well as true, or if it is only true ideas of which Spinoza here speaks. To gain some insight into this matter, it is clearly necessary to consider first what Spinoza says about true and false ideas, and how we distinguish between them, and that will lead us once more to consider what he has said about method.

We have been told in TdIE that the best method of discovery is that which reflects upon, directs the mind toward, the norm or standard of a given true idea; and that, as the relation between two ideas is the same as that between the formal essences of their objects (i.e., their *ideata*, or the things of which the ideas are the objective essences), it will follow that reflection upon the idea of a perfect being will be more excellent than reflection upon any other, so that relating all ideas to that idea will afford the best method. We ought, he says, before all else, to have in our minds a true idea, as an innate instrument of knowing, by which the intellect may understand the difference between such an idea and all the rest. The best method, then, is that which relates all ideas in the right order to that of the most perfect being.

Turning again to the *Ethics*, we read (in E1P16) that infinite things in infinite ways (*modis*) follow of necessity from the divine nature; and Spinoza never tires of repeating (both in his treatises and in his correspondence) that things follow from the nature of God in the same way as the equality of the internal angles of a triangle to two right angles follows from the nature of a triangle. From this we should gather that the order and connection of things is that necessary order in which they follow from the nature of God, and that of ideas being the same, it will be the necessary order in which they follow rationally from the idea of God, and that would be the *debitus ordo*, which is the right method of knowing, and which Spinoza considers himself to be pursuing in the *Ethics*.

One might be inclined to think that with respect to false ideas the question is inept; for Spinoza quite definitely maintains that false ideas are confused. They will surely, then, be such ideas as confuse and disrupt the *debitus ordo*, and we should not expect the quotation from which we began to apply to them. They are, however, none the less ideas, and they have their specific causes, and Spinoza tells us that we should find the same connection of causes in every attribute. We cannot, therefore, make an exception for ideas of the imagination. The difficulty is not so easily surmountable as the supposed objection would suggest. Moreover, Spinoza explicitly states (E2P18S) that the order of the imagination (in this context, memory), the order and concatenation of affections of the human body, is to be distinguished from the order of the intellect, by which the mind perceives things through their first causes. Which of these, then, is the same as the order and connection of things?

It seemed at first that the order and connection which is one and the same for both things and ideas was this order of the intellect—the order and connection of causes—and if he now maintains that there is an order or concatenation of ideas different from this, is Spinoza not being inconsistent? Alternatively, if the affections of the human body are, as they must surely be, among the things to be understood through their first causes, and if they are caused by things that are connected in the necessary order found in the attribute of Extension, why is the connection of bodily affections different from the so-called order of the intellect?

Perhaps we shall best be able to resolve this difficulty if we begin by attending more closely to the question first raised: What is the *debitus ordo*, the order and connection which is the same in all attributes? We may then be able more easily to discover how, if at all, the concatenation of bodily affections and imaginative ideas fits into it. That somehow it must be accommodated we may be certain, for all things flow of necessity from the divine nature, all things, we have been told, that fall under the infinite intellect (E1P16).

The first things that necessarily flow from the divine nature are the infinite attributes, because, as we have seen, God is the absolutely infinite Substance with infinite reality, and must therefore have infinite attributes, each infinite and eternal in its own kind, and each expressing God's essence. Further, what follows necessarily from an eternal and infinite attribute must itself be eternal and infinite (E1P22); so from the attributes there follow directly certain infinite modes. Under the attribute of Thought they are the infinite intellect and that which it conceives, the infinite idea of God. Under Extension they are Motion-and-rest and what it produces, the configuration of the entire (physical) universe (*facies totius universi*). In Part I of the *Ethics* Spinoza does not explain further how the finite modes of thought are related to the infinite, although he does say of finite modes in general that they have determinate existence, caused in each case by a finite cause itself having determinate existence, and that again likewise, and so ad infinitum, so that God is the indirect cause of finite things, through the infinite modes, of which He is the direct cause.

What we learn from Ep 32, and from E2P13S along with E2L7S, enables us to understand how the finite modes of Extension, the incessant series of changes in motion and rest that produces the hierarchy of bodies, are "compelled" and regulated by the configuration of the whole physical world, which is itself an infinite mode. Thus we can see how the finite modes of Extension follow from its infinite modes, and can infer that the same applies to the finite modes of Thought, as the order and connection of ideas is the same as that of things.

Just as the power, or essence, of God expresses itself under the attribute of Extension as Motion-and-rest (energy, in modern terms), so it expresses itself in Thought as His infinite intellect. And, as Motion-and-rest disposes itself in an infinitely diversified configuration as the physical world, preserving an invariant proportion (*ratio*), so the intellect of God forms the idea of Himself (*infinita idea Dei*), which, we may infer, is a single infinite idea internally differentiated into finite ideas in accordance with eternal (logical) laws or principles (*rationes*). We have now traced the sequence of things in the right order, without, so far, encountering any difficulty as to its concurrence with the order of ideas. When we try to go further, however, and discover how ideas occur in the human mind, matters become less straightforward.

Insofar as the infinite idea of God is (or comprises) the idea of Extension, its finite differentiations will be ideas of finite bodies, and these will be in varying degrees complex, as has been explained (E2L7S). But the idea of a body is its mind; for, Spinoza says, all things are in varying degrees besouled (*animata*), their minds differing in complexity and capacity as do their bodies. The more reality they possess, the more apt will the bodies be for doing and suffering many things together, and the more capable will their minds be of perceiving many things. To the extent that they can act from their own nature alone without the concurrence of other causes—as we may say, the more self-sustaining they are as organisms—the more capable are their minds of understanding clearly and distinctly. The objective essence of any body being correlative with its formal essence, the degree of capability that its mind (or idea) will have for clear understanding will be proportional to the amount of reality that the body possesses.

It is at this point that we encounter the complications that give rise to the difficulty from which we began. As every body is beminded, so the human mind is neither more nor less than the idea of its body. It is the awareness of everything that happens to and in the body. We feel (*sentimus*) all the changes and processes that occur in our bodies, but not all of them, or always, do we understand clearly. As we affirmed in the last chapter, the idea of the human body is a very complex idea, as the human body is a very complex body. The idea that constitutes the mind includes internal differences which are of three grades, each representing a different type or level of knowledge that varies from the other two in clarity and distinctness; and within each grade there are further manifold distinctions.

We must now try to understand how the diversifications of this idea (no dumb pictures on a tablet, but active, conscious, assertions) all belong to that order which is the same as the order of real causes, how they can, as they must, all be in, or part of, the mind of God, while at the same time some of them are confused and false and belong to the order of the imagination, which, we have been assured, is not the same as the order of the intellect, to which others belong.

Ideas of the imagination are the ways in which we feel or become aware of the effects in our bodies caused by external bodies. These effects are all determined. They all belong to the series of real causes governed ultimately by the structure of the physical universe. As so understood they constitute the order and connection of real things.

We should, therefore, expect the ideas of these causes to occur in a determined order so that they can be understood as the effects of their (psychological) causes, concomitant with those in the physical series. And so they do; but when they do, they are adequate and belong to one of the two higher grades of knowledge.

But ideas of the imagination are not themselves such understanding. When scientifically understood as the effects of the causes that produce them (their proximate causes), they are grasped in adequate ideas on the level of *ratio* or *scientia intuitiva*; but they themselves are not adequate ideas. In them, the characteristics of effects in the body appear as the properties of the external objects which are believed to cause them, and they are not perceived in their actual relationships to other ideas, nor properly understood as concomitant with modes of Extension. Consequently, they are confused, partial, and truncated; each is only a mutilated piece of the totality to which it really belongs. It is as such bits and pieces that they are imaginal ideas.

In God's mind these ideas certainly occur, but not torn from their proper setting; there they are perceived in their complete context, and so are not imagined but are adequately conceived. Our minds, however, are so limited that in them they appear disconnected and dissevered from their actual causes, and we tend to associate them haphazardly, in fortuitous concatenations. These are the concatenations of *imaginatio* which are not the order of the intellect, nor do they follow the real order and connection of things.

By means of the analogy of the blood to which Spinoza appeals in the 32nd Letter, he compares the manner and principle of generation of finite modes to the way in which states and processes occur in a living organism. The substances and quantitative relations composing the organism (or the blood) are regulated and determined by the system of metabolic cycles and physiological activities that keep the whole body in organic equilibrium and maintain its individual identity. But, Spinoza suggests, a minute creature ("a worm") inhabiting the blood would not be able to perceive or appreciate how this occurred, and would experience the diverse substances and changes as apparently mutually independent. In like manner, we observe only apparently contingent and disconnected events in a world which in reality is one individual, the universal nature (or structural principle) of which determines all the changes that occur within it and the order in which they happen.

The causes of our sensuous perceptions, our memories and our imaginings, follow definite laws or principles of order, which do regulate the actual order of which they are part. But the imaginal ideas do not constitute an understanding of themselves or of their objects according to their proximal causes. Hence, the order of the imagination is neither the real order of things nor that of ideas. For our sensuous experience along with the images of our fantasy are not real ideas at all—at least, they contain only a fragment of the reality. They are fractions, shards (as it were) of the truly adequate ideas of their objects (the actual effects in the body, in relation to their actual causes). Consequently, they are confused and are the source of error.

Just as the worm in the blood cannot perceive the way in which the diverse contents are determined in quantity and interaction by the governing principle of order maintaining the organic system, so the human mind does not initially grasp the ordering principles that determine the effects on its body of external causes. While each and every effect is determinately caused, the way in which it is perceived suppresses or confuses the connections by which it is interlocked with other events, or simply fails to apprehend them. What it does apprehend, however, is still part of the order and connection of things, with which the order and connection of *adequate* ideas coincides, while the order of the imagination is fragmentary and confused. It is this fragmentariness that is the source of error and falsity.

Does this falsity, however, introduce into the order of ideas something foreign to the order of things? According to Spinoza it does not, because it consists in nothing positive. The ideas in themselves are not false, only truncated; what is false is the assertion of them as substantive and whole, and as presenting something real, when in fact they omit so much, and are at times concocted simply as aids to the imagination, enabling us to remember more easily what is complex and diverse. But their omissions are mere privation, nothing really in them, only a lack of something needed to complement them. The complement, when supplied, does indeed alter their aspect or intention—their meaning—but it makes no difference to their actual content, which is just as necessary to their adequation. For instance, the sun may appear to the eye like a relatively small luminous object some hundreds of feet away; and even when we learn that it is not so, but is a vast incandescent mass many times larger than the Earth and millions of miles distant, the appearance does not change. It does, however, come to have a new meaning. We are no longer deceived by it, but come to realize that it is the consequence of the small angle projected by the sun's surface in our eyes from an immense distance. When we understand how the sun comes to appear to us as it does, our idea of it is true, as well as our idea of its sensible appearance. These ideas, then, belong to the order of the intellect, but they include the content of the imaginative (or sensory) idea, now set in its right context.

Thus we see that the order and connection of ideas is the same as that of things. That of imaginative ideas is the same as that of the causes which affect our bodies, but taken out of context they are false. Taken in their proper order and relations they are understood, as they are in the intellect of God. True understanding is the grasp of ideas in their proper relations, according to the principle or law (*ratio*) established by the divine intellect.

Objection has been raised that the assertion of a part as if it were the whole is itself a positive error, and the idea of a fragment misplaced in the wrong context or affirmed out of context is itself a misplaced idea. Spinoza cannot, therefore, accommodate such ideas in his theory. Again, the possible answer that the content of these ideas is the same when they are rightly placed and seen in their proper setting is rejected on the ground that the content is changed when in a different context, as the elements of a *Gestalt* vary with a change in the total pattern. There is some substance in this demurral, and no explicit answer to the criticism appears in Spinoza's text, but there is one implicit in his doctrine, which I shall try presently to develop. We may, however, note immediately that the error of *imaginatio* is more one of attitude than of subject matter, and this attitude (to which Spinoza refers as "affect") is incidental to the level of apprehension. It is proportional to the degree of reality or "perfection" of the idea, and, as we shall see, the order of things for Spinoza does involve a scale of degrees of perfection, "from the highest to the lowest."

The position so far may be summed up as follows: ideas of *imaginatio* are concomitant with the occurrent effects on the body of external causes; ideas on the level of *ratio* are deduced according to the principles of order (*rationes*) immanent in the infinite modes expressing the nature of Substance under the appropriate attribute so that they follow the *debitus ordo* in which all modes follow from the essence of God; ideas on the level of *scientia intuitiva* envisage the essence of things in the total context and adequate conception of the attribute, and are thus obviously concomitant with the entire structure of things and causes in *facies totius universi.*

Turning now to the objection that, even so, false ideas have not been satisfactorily accommodated within Spinoza's system, and that they cannot, as he claims, belong to the order of ideas that is the same as the order of causes in other attributes, we must begin by observing that error is always and only the result of limitation and defect. This does not entail the converse, that error is always and necessarily

consequent upon limitation, because the limitation adequately understood within the system to which the limited element belongs is necessary and, as rightly integrated, real and true. But a limited idea affirmed as self-sufficient and self-complete is an error, and it is this that
we have to explain as belonging, along with adequate ideas, to the
order and connection that is common to all attributes.

Defect, for Spinoza, is a relative lack of perfection or reality; and
the necessary self-differentiation of Substance issues, as we have already
seen, in a series of degrees of perfection, which he has told us is the
same both for bodies and for their ideas or minds. We have also been
told that the more perfection or reality the body contains, the more
able it is to register (*patiendum*) and do many things at the same time,
the more capable is its mind of perceiving many things together, and
the more self-sufficient and self-maintaining the body is, the more its
actions are dependent solely upon itself, the more apt is its mind to
understand clearly (E2P13S). Consequently, the structure of the universe is that of a scale of things (bodies under Extension, ideas under
Thought, and so on for other attributes) differing continuously in degree of perfection. The order in which things follow from the essence
of God thus turns out to be a scale of forms decreasing "from the
highest to the lowest" in degree of perfection, and so related that the
lower are implicated in the next above, to form a continuous series of
overlapping items. This, I have contended, is a dialectical scale.

That Spinoza constantly thinks in terms of such a scale is evident
from several passages in his writings. He declares that God does not
lack material for the creation of all things from the highest to the
lowest grade of perfection—everything that can be conceived by an
infinite intellect. He describes the *facies totius universi* as a single infinite whole comprising bodies graded from the simplest through those
of increasing complexity up to its all-embracing totality. To this series
of gradations the ideas, or minds, of the bodies correspond:

> . . . *Ideas inter se, ut ipsa objecta, differre unamque alia praestantiorem
> esse, plus realitas continere, prout objectum unius objecto alterius praestantius
> est, plusque realitatis continet* (E2P13S).[1]

The common principle of order specifies itself in a scale of forms,
each progressively more adequate to the universal principle of wholeness.

In like manner, in his discussion of human welfare, Spinoza speaks
of what is "good" on different levels of perfection. First he is disparaging
of men's habit of regarding as good whatever they find useful to them-

selves. On this level the terms "good" and "evil" are purely relative and correspond to nothing in reality. Then he asserts quite seriously that the good for man *is* what is useful; but in the first instance men take to be good whatever is found pleasant and what they happen to desire, both their conceptions of the objects and their emotions being the confused products of imagination. It is only when we become aware that our true advantage is served only by what really increases our power of action, and that that is our capacity for determining ourselves by our own nature alone, that we know with certainty wherein our advantage lies so as to recognize and pursue the true good. This true good turns out to be the perfection of the intellect, bringing with it action from reason alone, which overcomes the vagaries and tempestuousness of the passions. So the conception of real freedom is reached with the enjoyment of blessedness, the intellectual love of God, and eternal life in unity with the divine intellect. This is the perfection of man that we may set before ourselves as the supreme goal of action—"the love of an eternal and infinite thing that feeds the mind with joy and is free from all pain." Once again, the generic concept, this time of goodness, is specified as a scale of forms; the degree of perfection is proportional to the degree or amount of "reality" contained in the appropriate stage of moral and intellectual development, or, what amounts to the same thing, the degree of adequacy of thinking and of the ideas involved.

Remarks dropped almost as if casually in his letters point to the same notion in Spinoza's mind of a scale of varying degrees of perfection. In his reply to van Blyenberg (Ep 23) he says that a mouse equally with an angel, and sorrow as well as joy, depend on God, but a mouse cannot therefore be a species of angel, nor sorrow a kind of joy. In the context the implication is that, while all things equally depend on God, they differ in their degree of perfection or reality. At the same time, it is implied that difference in kind follows upon difference in a certain large measure of degree. Writing to Oldenburg on the question of freedom and responsibility, Spinoza says: "A horse is excusable for being a horse and not a man; yet none the less it is a horse of necessity and not a man" (Ep 78). Again the implication is that the difference between wrongdoing and virtue is one not of culpability so much as of differing degrees of reality—as a horse is on a different level from man.

In a series of dialectically related forms, the lower phases relative to the higher become errors, unless and until they are seen in the light of the whole and in accordance with their position in the scale. As stages in the generation of perfection, or as degrees of reality (in

Spinoza's sense of those words) they are real and true, but as imperfect and truncated, without their complement, they are false. They all belong to the same order, and their actual and (for Spinoza) necessary connections are the same in all attributes; yet, without disrupting that order, the ideas of those in the lower ranges are merely confused and erroneous in isolation from the system in which, to be adequate, they have to be placed.

Now it is possible to see how ideas can be in the intellect of God, where they are properly understood in their right order and connection, and so are not inadequate, yet can be inadequate in the human mind so long as the human intellect remains finite and undeveloped, and so fails to grasp them in their total context. Their inadequacy in the human mind is incidental to the level of that mind in the scale of ideas, which does not disrupt nor involve any exception to the order and connection which is the same as that of things.

Note

1. "... that ideas differ among themselves as do their objects, that one is more excellent than another and contains more reality, just as the object of one [idea] is more excellent than that of another and contains more reality."

6

The Essence of Man and the Conscious Subject

THE PROBLEM

In E4P4 Spinoza demonstrates that man is a finite mode of Substance, a part of Nature, and, do what he can, he can never be more; but he seeks to persuade us, equally, by the arguments of the second and fifth Parts of the *Ethics* that the human mind can achieve the third kind of knowledge, in which it proceeds from an adequate idea of the formal essence of certain attributes of God to the adequate knowledge of the essence of things, and that such knowledge leads to the intellectual love of God, which is the infinite love by which God loves himself (E5P36), and in which blessedness and salvation consist (E536S).

Can Spinoza hold both of these positions consistently, or is he committing the epistemologist's fallacy of claiming a kind or degree of knowledge that should be impossible on his own metaphysical theory? If man is but a finite mode, if, as we read at the end of Part IV,

> human power is very limited, and is infinitely surpassed by the power of external causes (E4A32),

so that nobody can be free of *imaginatio* and passion nor

> suffer only change such as can be understood through his own nature as adequate cause (E4P4),

how can he ever attain to an adequate idea of the formal essence of God's attributes?

That such a claim amounts to a dogmatic fallacy was, in effect, the charge brought against Spinoza by Fichte when he accused him of overstepping the bounds of the "I am" and of denying "pure conscious-ness" to the self to whom he attributes empirical consciousness, as-signing pure consciousness only to God.[1] Spinoza's postulation of an infinite Substance of which the human mind is but one modification is made, Fichte asserts, in response to a practical demand to bring about the highest possible unity in human cognition—an unattain-able ideal that cannot be theoretically established.[2] It cannot be theoretically accomplished precisely because the ego is unable to break and exceed its own self-imposed bounds.

In Spinozistic language we may try to state the problem thus: if the human mind is only a finite mode inevitably subject to the overpowering influences of external causes, it must in all its consciousness be in-fected with *imaginatio,* and any aspiration to adequate knowledge of the Substance of which it is a mode can at most be a regulative de-mand due to its *conatus* as it presses constantly towards self-determina-tion, but a demand impossible of realization within the bounds of finite consciousness. But if this were so, how could any human conscious-ness know that it was so? How could it discover that it was only a part of an infinite nature infinitely exceeding human limitations, the idea of which it postulated only because of the practical demand of its own *conatus* towards self-completion?

To grasp the Spinozistic response to and solution of this problem we must examine the account Spinoza gives of the essence of man and attempt to locate in it the subject of consciousness, to determine what Spinoza understood its nature to be and how it was related on the one hand to external causes and on the other to substance as infinite and eternal.

It may be of some help to begin by observing how Descartes con-ceived the subject of awareness and its ontological status.[3] For him it was *res cogitans,* and every *res cogitans* was a thinking substance, of which its *cogito* was the assurance of its own existence. There can be no doubt that Spinoza accepts this last point with respect to the finite subject even though he denies that it is a substance. In TdIE Spinoza casti-gates the sceptics who doubt everything and claim to know nothing "*nam neque seipsos sentiunt,*" thus "they fear to assert that they exist" and so ought to remain silent (*obmutescere*). Being aware of oneself, therefore, is at the same time being aware that one exists; but Sub-stance Spinoza defines as what exists in itself and is conceived through itself, and the existence of which the finite self is aware, as Descartes also recognizes, is defective and dependent.[4] In Spinoza's view, there-fore, it cannot be a substance.

Nevertheless, must we not insist that it is *res cogitans?* The very awareness of defect must be attributable to the subject that knows itself to be finite, and that knowledge necessarily implies that the knower has in his or her own consciousness an idea of perfection (of the infinite) reference to which is required in order to recognize fault and dependency.[5] Both Spinoza and Descartes declare that we have an idea of a perfect being.[6] The unity of the subject of consciousness seems thus to be necessary as a prior condition even of the knowledge of God. Seemingly, therefore, it should follow that the idea of God is postulated by the ego, which, whatever may be claimed for any of its objects, must be self-existent as prior to the conception or positing of anything else.

But no such conclusion is tolerable to Spinoza; nor does it appear to be self-consistent. For the self, while in its consciousness it knows its own existence, is concurrently aware of its own deficiencies. It cannot, therefore, be *causa sui*. Both Descartes and Spinoza are quite clear on this point. And if not *causa sui* then not self-existent or absolute. In that case, it cannot be or be conceived in and through itself alone and so, for Spinoza (although not for Descartes), it cannot be a substance:

> The being of substance does not pertain to the essence of man, or substance does not constitute the form of man. (E2P10)

The problem to be faced, then, is how the finite and deficient can apprehend the infinite and perfect; nor does it suffice to say with Kant and Fichte that this is impossible except as a practical postulate, because the postulation itself involves the concept, the apprehension (or mere conception) of which by a finite subject requires explanation. For Kant and Fichte the demand for self-completeness in knowledge derives from the unity of the "I think"—of the finite subject of consciousness—and it is the status of this unity in Spinoza's system that we have to investigate.

Spinoza's answer to the question is, in effect, to reverse the roles suggested above for the finite and the infinite. Despite his remark in TdIE, what he maintains is not so much that the finite subject conceives an idea of God, as that it is God who conceives, and it is only insofar as God's thought expresses itself in and through a finite mode that the human mind is said to have an idea of anything whatsoever. Thus he writes to Oldenburg:

> As regards the human mind, I think it too is a part of Nature, since I maintain that there exists also in Nature an infinite power of thought, which, so far as it is infinite, contains in itself the whole of Nature objectively, and whose thoughts proceed in the same manner as Nature, which is indeed its ideatum.
>
> Then I maintain that the human mind is this same power, not so far as

it is infinite and perceives the whole of Nature, but insofar as it is finite and perceives only the human body, and for this reason I maintain that the human mind is part of a certain infinite intellect. (Ep 32)

In the *Ethics* the doctrine is stated, perhaps more clearly for our present purpose, as follows:

Hence it follows that the human mind is part of the infinite intellect of God; and so, when we say that the human mind perceives this or that, we say nothing other than that God, not insofar as he is infinite, but so far as he is expressed *(explicatur)* through the nature of the human mind, or in other words so far as he constitutes the essence of the human mind, has this or that idea (E2P11C).

Thus, when we say that a human being has an idea of the infinite, or of God, we say nothing other than that God has this idea insofar as he is expressed through (or specified in) the human mind. Strictly speaking, God is the sole and ultimate *res cogitans*, in whom and through whom whatever is conscious thinks.

That God, the absolutely infinite Substance, should have an idea of himself presents no such problem as the one which we have set ourselves. It follows immediately from God's nature as a thinking thing, Spinoza has told us (E1P21, E2P3), that he should of necessity have an idea of his own essence and of all that follows from it. But this idea of God must be the idea in the infinite intellect so far as it is infinite. If human creatures have an idea of God it must be the idea of the infinite so far as it constitutes the human mind; that is, not insofar as it is infinite and perceives the whole of Nature, but insofar as it is finite and perceives only the human body. It is this possibility, if it is one, that we have to try to understand. How can God have an idea of himself insofar as his nature is expressed through a finite mode and his intellect perceives only the human body?

We are told in the corollary to E2P11 that

when we say that God has this or that idea, not only so far as he constitutes the hu-man mind, but so far as, at the same time with the human mind, he also has the idea of another thing, then we say that the human mind perceives the thing in part or inadequately.

Now it is surely obvious that when God has an idea of himself he has ideas of other things—infinitely many other things—than that of the human body, which constitutes the human mind. Must we then conclude that the human idea of God is inadequate? That would conflict directly with E2P47, which proves that the human mind has adequate knowledge of the eternal and infinite essence of God.

The apparent conflict is, however, resolved by Spinoza's demonstration that the idea of any body whatsoever, or of any individual thing actually existing, necessarily involves the eternal and infinite essence of God (E2P45). For nothing can be or be conceived without God, and whatever exists necessarily involves the conception of the attribute under which it is a mode, that is, of the eternal and infinite essence of God. The human body, therefore, necessarily involves such a conception. Thus the idea of God's infinite and eternal essence is necessarily involved in the idea of the human body (i.e., in the human mind); and the idea of God's essence thus implicated is adequate and perfect (E2P46). Accordingly, God's idea of the human body, as well as of any other singular thing, involves an adequate idea of himself, even so far as he constitutes the essence of the human mind.

Stated in this way, however, the matter is so involuted as scarcely to be intelligible, and at least it calls for clarification. Nor does it appear at first sight to be acceptable; for while we must concede that nothing can be adequately conceived without God, and that the adequate idea of any singular thing involves that of the attribute to which it belongs, it hardly seems to follow that inadequate and imaginative ideas fulfil these conditions. Of course, God's ideas must be adequate, including that which he has of the human body; but the idea of the body that constitutes the human mind seems to be the idea considered in isolation and apart from ideas of other things; otherwise it would be the idea as it is in God insofar as he is infinite. Moreover, even if we waive this objection, we are still left with the difficulty of understanding how the human subject of consciousness, thinking in its own right, can be no more than an idea in the mind of another subject, albeit God's. Is this suggestion any less outrageous than Tweedledee's triumphant declaration to Alice (in *Through the Looking Glass*) that she is "only a sort of thing" in the Red King's dream?

THE ESSENCE OF MAN

Essence is defined by Spinoza (E2D2) as that which, when given, the thing of which it is the essence is necessarily posited, and when removed the thing is necessarily removed also. It is that without which the thing can neither be nor be conceived and which cannot be conceived nor be without the thing.[7] Hence, for all finite things, their essence is not God, although they can neither be nor be conceived without him, because God is and is conceived through himself alone.

But God is the immanent cause of all things, both of their existence and of their essence (E2P10C and S), a truth which we shall find to be fundamental to the solution of our problem, and one to which we shall return. The important thing to notice is that God, or Substance, the absolutely infinite whole, is prior both to the being and to the conception of everything else—it is ontologically as well as logically prior—and not vice versa. The fundamental constituents of the real are not the finite particulars; they are the derivative specifications, or differentiations, of the totality, the organizing principle of which is prior. This relation between God and his modes must be borne in mind throughout our discussion if we are not to succumb to the errors of those *qui ordinem philosophandi non tenebant*.

M. Martial Gueroult distinguishes ten different "definitions" of the essence of man and of the mind in Spinoza's writings.[8] We need not quote them in detail, for the first follows from what has already been said above, and the second is clearly Spinoza's main definition of the essence of the human mind, namely, that it is the idea of the body. The third and the fourth are explications of the first in the light of Spinoza's general account of attributes and modes; the fifth and sixth are, as it were, corollaries of those already stated; and the last four are simply explications of the main definition. Only the first three of these so-called definitions, as distinguished by M. Gueroult, bear directly upon our problem, but the relevance of the others will become apparent as we proceed. Attention has already been drawn to the first: that the essence of man is constituted by certain modifications of God's attributes. We must attend next to the main definition.

Strictly speaking, however, and Gueroult notwithstanding, Spinoza gives no formal definition of the essence of man. He enunciates propositions about the human mind and its unity with the body, and he deduces consequences from them which make clear, as he says,

> not only that the human mind is united to the body, but also what should be understood by the union of the mind and the body. (E2P13S)

In the first place the mind is the idea of a particular thing actually existing (E2P11); and in the second place the *ideatum* of that idea is the body, a certain mode of Extension, and nothing else (E2P13). This mode of Extension is finite but highly complex, capable of doing and suffering many things at the same time, and of a high degree of self-dependent action without the concurrence of other bodies (E2P13S). The human mind, then, the idea of this body, is capable of perceiving many things and of a high degree of distinct understanding (ibid.).

But we shall be prone to err unless we clearly grasp Spinoza's conception of *idea*, and unless we appreciate the force of his contention that the *ideatum* of the mind is the body and *nothing else*. Such error results from the too frequent disregard of Spinoza's repeated warnings that an idea is not a dumb picture on a tablet (E2P43S, E2P49S) and his explicit insistence that it is an activity, a conception, of the mind (E2D3). The idea of the body, accordingly, is not a mental picture, or a replica, or an image of the body (as so many commentators assume)[9] but is the body as it is felt, as it feels and is aware of itself.[10] Evidence that this is Spinoza's intention is copious in the frequent use that he makes of the word *sentire*. Note, for instance, the passage quoted earlier from TdIE in which he satirically chides the sceptics: *neque seipsos sentiunt.*

The essence of man, then, is that he is a body come aware of itself in and through sensation. The body, and nothing else, is the *ideatum* of this self-feeling; but the body is highly complex, and its relation to all other bodies in the physical world (*facies totius universi*) gives a special character and complexity to the *idea* of which it is the object. The individuality of a body, we have learned, consists in the maintenance of a fixed proportion of motion and rest transmitted among its parts (E2D before L4). Such individuality may thus persist in spite of innumerable changes and interchanges among the parts, and one complex body may consist of numerous less complex bodies, each of which, according to its own degree of complexity or "perfection," preserves its own individuality. This gradation of "excellence" proceeds from the simplest of bodies, by continuous complexification, right up to the entire physical universe regarded as one individual, the activity of all and the relations between them being regulated by the universal principle ordering the whole.

In the 32nd Letter Spinoza explained to Oldenburg how the relation of whole and parts was to be understood. The parts are mutually adapted in their activity and disposition to one another as required by the principle of order constituting the whole; and this relationship pervades the entire physical world, as outlined above. It follows, therefore, that every body will reflect, or register, in its appropriate degree and according to the measure of its complexity and self-sufficiency, every other, as well as the complete structure of the entire universe. In the case of the human body, it is its high degree of complexity and integrity that enables it to do and suffer many things together; and to the corresponding extent its mind (its self-awareness, its *idea*) will be the perception of many things. As in this way the whole is prior to the part and the principle of its structure is immanent in every part, God-or-Substance is immanent in each and all of its modes; consequently, the idea of the body involves the idea of the whole universe and of the essence of God as expressed in his attributes.

The self-awareness of the body is, in the first instance, sentience (*imaginatio*), and as such it is a confused awareness of the body, and through it a confused awareness of the whole physical universe, for the reason already given. In this confused awareness, the nature of the human body is not accurately distinguished from that of other bodies, while at the same time bodies are distinguished from one another and from that which feels in ways that are deceptive. They are all (as we have seen) mutually adapted and mutually involved, all governed by the configuration of the *facies totius universi*, which makes every one of them what it is, determines their mutual relations and the way in which they will behave and change. But in sentient awareness, or *imaginatio*, although all this is implicit, it is not clearly understood. In sense perception things present themselves as separate (although they are really mutually interdependent), as succeeding one another in time, and as mutually external and separable in space. *Imaginatio* is consciousness of the world only as "the common order of nature," the effects on the human body of successive and concurrent causes, effects on one body only—the one that is sentiently aware. Such awareness is therefore inadequate. It is an idea, which constitutes the human mind in the intellect of God only so far as it pertains to the human body and not insofar as that body is conceived in its proper relation to the rest of the universe.

Even as sentient, however, the idea of the human body is idea; that is, it is an activity of thought, which has the special character of all ideation distinguishing it in a peculiar way from all body. It is conscious of itself, is self-reflective and so self-transcendent, because being *idea* it is (ipso facto) *idea ideae.* Thus it can grasp in idea the relation between ideas and the structural principles of configurations, which are registered in, but not apprehended by, bodies as such. This reflectiveness (as we were told in TdIE) enables the human mind to clarify itself of confusion and to make its knowledge adequate. It is a capacity more fully developed in proportion as the body is more "excellent," more organically complex and integrated both in itself and with its environment. The more this is the case, the more fully is the mind, the idea of the body, apt in its reflection to comprehend its relation of its own body to other bodies and the idea of the attribute immanent in every mode, including its body and itself.

To the nature and possibility of adequate knowledge we shall return shortly. First let us observe that the idea of the body which is the human mind is not (for Spinoza) an intentional object of a transcendental subject, but is the self-awareness of a mode of Extension, and this awareness is a mode of Thought. The subject of human consciousness is, in a sense, the human body (as it is for Merleau-Ponty), yet not in a strictly Spinozistic sense. More accurately we should say that it is a mode of Substance which, under the attribute of Extension, is the human body, and under the attribute of Thought, is the human mind. But the unity, or individuality, of the subject is not separate from the unity of the attribute and the infinite mode of which the human mind is a differentiation. To this feature we must next attend.

THE INDIVISIBILITY OF SUBSTANCE

Spinoza insists that Substance is indivisible, whether conceived as Extension or as Thought, and that we tend to regard it as divisible, especially extended substance, only because we imagine it and do not conceive it adequately. Substance is not divided into modes as separable parts, for its modes, although distinguishable, are not separable.[11] This is true of infinity and of the eternal things that follow immediately from the divine nature, and we have seen how it is so in the case of *facies totius universi*, which is a single individual whole although infinitely diversified—always the same and unalterable although differentiated into perpetually changing modes, whose character and changes are all adjusted to its overall configuration and so each to every other.

As the order and connection of ideas is the same as the order and connection of things, what is true of Extension is equally true of Thought. Ideas, then, as modes of Thought are not mutually separable, but are only differentiations within the infinite idea of God conceived by the infinite intellect, the finite modes of the attribute of Thought, or of God as a thinking being.

Accordingly, neither body nor mind is a separate, self-dependent entity, and in either case individuality is a matter of degree. Ultimately there is but one individual, God, of whom all others are graded differentiations. That they are degrees in a hierarchy we know from Spinoza's description of the hierarchical series of bodies and the corresponding degrees of excellence in their minds. So we have a continuous series of progressively more organically unified bodies, the more complex consisting of organizations of less complex, and a corresponding series of progressively more adequate minds, in all possible gradations of perfection from the highest to the lowest (E1A). And this gamut of modes is, as a whole, the self-differentiation of the infinite totality which is one indivisible Substance, or God. Hence the whole constitutes one body and one mind of which all the modes are various expressions, each in its appropriate degree of perfection; and the nature of the whole is such that it is immanent as whole in every mode. That is to say, the principle of order and structure which constitutes its wholeness governs the "parts" or modifications down to the last detail.

Under the attribute of Thought, then, there is a single mind or intellect, a single power of thinking, infinitely differentiated into finite minds (or ideas) in a continuous gradation of clearness and distinctness from the most fully adequate down to the most obscure. In fact, we have in effect, under this attribute, something very like the conception of the universe later developed by Leibniz, that is, a world consisting of individuals each organically whole in itself but every one at a different level or degree of clearness of perception, culminating in the *actus purus* of God. Like Leibniz, also, Spinoza might have asserted of the world that it is made up of organisms whose parts are organisms down to the least complex, and all of which, although in different degrees, are beminded (E2P13S). All taken together in their mutual adaptation constitute for Spinoza (under the attribute of Thought) the divine intellect. Leibniz's assertion that the monads are separate and windowless actually makes no difference to this overall unity because their monadic disparity is nullified by the pre-established harmony. But Leibniz's theory helps us to understand how finite minds can maintain their individuality while, and indeed because, they reflect a single infinite mind, to which they all belong as specific expressions, or specifications, and in which their inadequacies are supplemented.

Leibniz explained the gradation of the monads by saying that those with the more obscure perceptions reflected the world, while those with the clearer perceptions reflected God. This corresponds to Spinoza's distinction between inadequate, imaginative, ideas that register the effects on the finite body of other bodies, producing the notion of the common order of nature, and adequate ideas conceiving the essences of things *sub specie aeternitatis*, as they are conceived in the intellect of God.

THE SUBJECT OF CONSCIOUSNESS

The subject of consciousness is, therefore, the mind of God specified in and as innumerable subjects which in their various degrees of excellence together differentiate the concrete infinity of the divine Substance. The power of the infinite intellect is expressed in and through each of its finite modifications. In each the whole is immanent; therefore, each thinks as a whole and has an idea of the whole, and that idea is adequate to the extent that it is clarified in self-reflection. We must understand Proposition 46 of the second Part of the *Ethics*, which states that an adequate and perfect knowledge of God is involved in every idea, to mean that such knowledge is implicit in inadequate ideas and explicit in adequate ideas. The inadequate ideas, we have seen, are not false in their positive content, but are truncated and mutilated; thus the positive content implies the principle of the whole just as much when abstracted from its proper context as when augmented and made complete in adequate knowledge. It follows that while all ideas implicitly involve the idea of God, only minds capable of distinct understanding, which are ideas of highly complex organic bodies, like the human body, can attain to an adequate knowledge of God's eternal and infinite essence.

The power of thought, therefore, so far as it perceives only the human body (EP 32) and constitutes the human mind, although it implicitly involves the whole universe and the idea of God, perceives them only inadequately and confusedly, the former as the common order of nature and God as a supreme ruler and judge. This is because God at the same time perceives other things besides, and has other ideas in intimate relation with that of the human body, which he therefore perceives adequately. The human mind, however, does not perceive adequately so far as it is only the felt body apprehended in apparent isolation or in casual contingent relations to other bodies in the order of the imagination (E2P18S).

The power of thought is God's power, and the idea of the body, however inadequate and confused, is no mere image or representation. It is an active conceiving which, like the body itself, is impelled by a *conatus in suo esse perseverandi*, that is, an endeavor to maintain itself against and in independence of external causes. The true aim of the *conatus* is so to act (and think) that the adequate cause of the action is the essence or nature of the agent alone. It is therefore the essence of the thing itself, striving to persist in its own nature, and at the same time it is the power of God working in and through it.[12]

In Thought it is this agency that is the conscious subject, and it operates through self-reflection to progress from *imaginatio* to *ratio* and *scientia intuitiva*. Reflection enables the mind to recognize that in the *idea* and in its *ideatum* which is the same both in the whole and in the part, namely, the attribute to which each belongs and the principle of which each is a specific expression. Thus the mind advances from the first to the second kind of knowledge and to the adequate comprehension of the essence of Substance involved in all things, an adequate idea of the formal essence of certain attributes of God, from which it can proceed to the adequate knowledge of the essence of things. In this knowledge the thinking activity is explicitly one with God's, and this knowing is the proper activity of the intellect, the true essence of the human mind (E5P36S).

The subject of consciousness, therefore, so far as it is considered to be human, that is, as constituted by God's perception of the human body, is initially the subject of *imaginatio*, the subject of consciousness as a stream of sensuous perception. But the subject of adequate thinking, qua human, is the adequate idea of the body *sub specie aeternitatis* (E5P23S), which is the idea of the human body as perceived by God (E5P22). This is the subject of the third kind of knowledge, nothing other than the power of the infinite intellect expressing itself in and through the human mind (E5PP29,30).

Other Minds and the Unity of Consciousness

Spinoza has insisted on the unity and indivisibility of Substance in every one of its attributes. We have seen how this is realized in Extension in the coherence and integration of bodies in *facies totius universi.* In Thought it implies a common consciousness embracing the ideas of all bodies, each of which, it has been argued, is the mind or self-feeling of its own body or *ideatum.* Spinoza nowhere elaborates this aspect of his doctrine in detail, except that he develops its consequences at the higher levels of perfection. But that there may be some form of common subconscious uniting all sentient beings with one another and with lower nature is an idea that has been seriously proposed by modern psychologists, such as Jung, and is being explored in the more sober and scientific forms of psychical research.[13] Hegel, in the early part of his *Geistesphilosophie*, espouses the same idea with most illuminating insights, giving us a theory of consciousness as rising to the level of awareness of individual subjects out of a prepersonal, preconscious totality of feeling which is not individuated. The same doctrine reappears in F. H. Bradley's essay on Immediate Experience,[14] where he speaks of a "non-objective whole of feeling" prior to the level of conscious mind with its awareness of the distinction between self and not-self. Husserl and his followers, especially Merleau-Ponty, have adopted a similar theory.[15]

On the other hand, the identity and community of individual minds in adequate knowledge and action is demonstrated by Spinoza in Part IV of the *Ethics*, where it is shown that so far as men live in accordance with reason they agree in nature (E4P35), that the highest good is common to all (E4P36), that what a reasonable person desires for him (or her) self is equally desired for others (E4P37).

But the necessity, quite apart from the possibility (which some have doubted), that subjects of consciousness can be self-identical and individual only in distinction from, as well as in communion with, other subjects of consciousness was left to be demonstrated by Hegel. That awareness of self is correlative to awareness of another, and indeed in conflict with the self-assertion of the other, he worked out in detail in the *Phänomenologie,* establishing a truth that is now widely admitted by psychologists. Contradistinction and conflict, however, are not sufficient; for the conscious self realizes its individuality fully only in the recognition of equality and identity with its other and of its other with itself; so that ultimately the mind, which is a unitary and self-dependent whole of consciousness, is a community of minds with shared content. This manifests itself, for instance, in what we describe as "contemporary knowledge," and also, on the practical side, as the common enjoyment of art, the common performance of ensembles in music and of teams in sport, and the common interest in human welfare. Ultimately, however, the community of minds, expressed severally in each individual, recognizes itself as the self-manifestation of one infinite and encompassing transcendent spirit, short of which no merely human aspiration or endeavor reaches its goal.[16]

The Unity of the Subject—Immanence and Transcendence

The subject of human consciousness (the so-called natural subject) turns out, in Spinoza's system, to be the immanence in the human mind (and its body) of the infinite intellect (*res cogitans*). The subjective unity of consciousness, which Kant and Fichte rightly found indispensable to any and every experience of objects, is by both of them confessedly correlative to the coherent wholeness of the object. It is only in the apprehension of the synthetic unity of experience that we become aware of the identity of the ego.[17] Spinoza recognizes and allows for this truth in his assertion of the immanence in all finite modes of the divine essence. God is the immanent cause of all things, without which they can neither be nor be conceived. We can as truly say of ideas (or minds) that without the immanent causality of God they can neither be nor can they conceive. For the intelligibility of all objects is consequent upon their being conceived as modes of Substance, conceived through an adequate knowledge of certain attributes of God. The immanence of God in the idea of the body is the source of the idea of God in the human mind. This consciousness of the body becomes aware of itself as a mind in being self-reflective—the idea of the human mind (i.e., the mind's consciousness of itself) is the idea of the idea of the human body (E2PP20,21). As such, it is aware of the idea of God immanent in it, and this is at the same time its awareness of its own identity or essence, as well as that of its *ideatum*, as modes of Substance under the attributes of Thought and Extension.

At the level of *imaginatio* the awareness of self is as inadequate and confused as the awareness of the body. Regarded as sentient experience they are identical. It is only at the level of *ratio* that we become clearly aware of either, and at that level we do so through, and in the light of, our relation to the eternal things which are God's attributes and their infinite modes. This relationship is delineated within the totality that is at once the divine intellect and the true essence of the human mind, the intellect whose nature it is to frame true ideas (TdIE), "because the essence of our mind consists solely in knowledge, the origin and foundation of which is God" (E5P36S; cf. also E1P15 and S; E2P47). Only so can there be any self-awareness of an identical subject, and only thus is the essence of the human mind conceivable.

This identity of subjective individuality is, therefore, at the same time the awareness of the divine essence and what follows from it;[18] and Spinoza is not the victim of any fallacy and has made no dogmatic leap beyond the bounds of the conscious ego that cannot be transcended. The *conatus*, or practical urge that demands realization of unity and wholeness in experience, is itself the power of God, immanent in and expressing itself through the finite mode. It is realized only in the knowledge and love of God, who is its original source, a knowledge and love that is identical in God and in every human mind that attains to adequate knowledge and action in the full sense. In this knowledge and love alone is the complete and genuine unity of consciousness actualized—a consciousness which may well be that which the mystic claims, although, for Spinoza, it is nothing ineffable, obscure, or ultimately mysterious,[19] rather the diametrical opposite.

The object of this knowledge and love *(amor intellectualis Dei)* is the transcendent infinite, and the awareness of a reality transcending the finite is precisely how the immanence of the infinite in the finite manifests itself. Apart from that no finite mind could be aware of itself as finite, or aware of itself (or of anything else) at all.

Notes

1. Cf. *Grundlage der gesamten 'Wissenschaftslehre, Erste Teil,* I, §100.
2. Ibid.
3. Fichte attributes priority to Descartes in formulating the principle "I = I" as fundamental.

4. Cf. *Meditations*, III.
5. Cf. Descartes, ibid.
6. Cf. TdIE: " . . . habemus enim ideam veram."
7. In my opinion M. Martial Gueroult (*Spinoza*, Vol. II, pp. 429ff., 459ff., 547ff.) is wrong in his assertion that the term "essence" is used by Spinoza in two senses, one referring to the general nature of the thing, and one referring to its nature as an individual. It is always and only to be understood in the second of these senses, even in spite of frequent appearances in Spinoza's text. Cf. TdIE, E240S1 and P48S.
8. Geroult, *Spinoza*, Vol. II, App. 3.
9. Cf. A. E. Taylor, "Some Incoherencies in Spinozism," *Mind*, Vol. XLVI (1937); H. Barker, "Notes on the Second Part of Spinoza's *Ethics*," *Mind*, Vol. XLVII (1938); Carroll R. Bowman, "Spinoza's Idea of the Body," *Idealistic Studies* I, 1971; et al.
10. See above, Ch. 4.
11. Cf. Ep 12 (to Meyer) and E1P15S.
12. Cf. M. Gueroult's definitions 8 and 9.
13. Cf. C. O. Evans, "A Parapsychological Interpretation of Freud," *Psychoenergetic Systems*, Vol. II, No. 6 (1976).
14. Cf. *Essays on Truth and Reality* (Oxford, Clarendon Press, 1914, 1962), Ch. IV, p. 189; cf. also *Appearance and Reality* (Oxford, Clarendon Press, 1897, 1962), Ch. XIX and passim.
15. Cf. Edmund Husserl, *Experience and Judgement*, trans. James S. Churchill and Karl Ameriks (Evanston, Northwestern University Press, 1973), Pt. I; Maurice Merleau-Ponty, *The Primacy of Perception* (Evanston, Northwestern University Press, 1964), *The Phenomenology of Perception*, trans. Colin Smith (London, Routledge and Kegan Paul; Atlantic Highlands, N.J., Humanities Press, 1962), *The Visible and the Invisible*, trans. A. Lingis (Evanston, Northwestern University Press, 1964), 5 (Appendix).
16. Cf. my *Atheism and Theism* (Atlantic Highlands, N.J., Humanities Press, 1993).
17. Cf. Kant, *Critique of Pure Reason*, B133–135.
18. Cf. Gueroult's definition 6.
19. Cf. TTP, Ch. VII. Spinoza derides the claim to supernatural knowledge, and the experience which many claim as mystical is at a far lower level than what Spinoza calls *scientia intuitiva*. It is, in fact, *imaginatio*, and the best account that may be given of it in Spinozistic terms is that it is a form of prophecy, that is, revelation through the medium of the imagination (cf. TTP, Chs. I and II).

PART II

Politics
and
Religion

7

Spinoza's Treatment of Natural Law

HISTORICAL RETROSPECT

The doctrine of Natural Law has a long history which may be traced back not simply to Plato and Aristotle but even to the Presocratics. It took definitive form in the hands of the Stoics, who transmitted it on to the Roman lawyers, and from them it passed to the philosophers of the Middle Ages from Augustine to Aquinas. At the Renaissance it had become common property among ethical, legal, and political thinkers, being redeployed by Vasquez and Suarez, who handed it on to Althusius and to the writers of the seventeenth century. But throughout this long history, and especially as conceived by the Stoics and in Roman Law, the notion harbors an ambiguity which is in part a merit and in part a source of confusion and difficulty.

The Law of Nature, from its very name, is the conception of a universal law governing all things, inanimate, animate, and human, but in the case of the last it becomes twofold, because while human beings, like other animals, are by nature subject to appetites and impulses, their conduct is also governed by rules which seek to restrain these natural propensities and to regulate their exercise. In society, such rules are in part customary and in part imposed by rulers upon their subjects; and as without society human life is scarcely (if at all) possible, society is seen as natural. Social living inevitably involves rules and restraints upon conduct, so that these rules also are regarded as laws of nature, especially such as appear to be universal to all nations. They operate, however, at least in some measure, against natural appetites and inclinations; so if they are held to be natural laws, Nature

96

seems in them to oppose itself, for natural laws determining the natural behavior of human beings contend with the social norms which are also claimed to be natural. Moreover, if laws imposed by rulers on their subjects are oppressive they are deplored as contrary to nature; yet that there should be rulers authorized to impose laws is a natural and necessary feature of human society.

The source of the ambiguity lies partly in the fact that laws of nature, in the sense of regularities prevailing in the behavior of things, are entirely universal and cannot be violated, for to say of any regularity that it is a law of nature is to say that whatever is subject to it always acts in accordance with the law. If it were not so, we should not call it a law of nature at all. Social and moral laws, on the other hand, can be and often are broken, so if these too are said to be natural it can hardly be in the same sense. Nevertheless, in the tradition of the Natural Law doctrine it is especially the moral law which was identified with the law of nature, no doubt due to the Stoic teaching that to live according to Nature was the right and the best way of life, and to the fact that the *jus naturale* of the Roman lawyers, being universal to all nations, was generally regarded as the norm of justice and equity. But it is just here that the two notions of Nature come into conflict, for what is right and just is far from being what the psychological nature of human beings always prompts them to do, so that if the law of equity and justice is natural at all it must be so in some other sense. The contrast is between what happens in the general course of events and what we believe we ought to do, between fact and value; and nowadays to profess to infer the latter from the former is castigated as "the natural fallacy."

The difficulty was less obvious to the Ancients and Medievals than it became in the sixteenth and seventeenth centuries A.D., because the Greeks thought of the world (or Nature) as a living being with a soul of its own, and of the rules of human morality as those which enabled the parts of the human soul to function in harmony. The laws of the *polis* similarly aimed at social harmony, so it was plausible enough to conceive them as coinciding with, or at least conforming to, a more general law that maintained harmony in the world at large and in the world soul. It was equally understandable that in both cases this law should be the law of reason: the law of the active intellect, as it appears in the philosophy of Aristotle, where it is primarily the activity of God, in which the human soul also intermittently and haltingly participates, and which all things, according to their peculiar nature and level of being, strive to imitate. This clearly would be the source of the universal law of nature and would encompass, as derivative from it, the law of human nature. The remaining anomaly of the conflict between human passions and rational action was explained away in terms of the relation between matter and form, between body and soul, as different levels of perfection within the total system.

The conception of the natural world as a living being persisted into the Middle Ages, but was overlaid by the Christian doctrine that God had created the world and mankind. Both were obviously subject to God's eternal law, from which human reason was an extension.[1] The law of nature was now plainly identifiable with the law of God and of reason, and the tension between the natural inclinations of man and his reason was eased by arguing that all natural tendencies, having been ordained by God, were good, and that reason was also a natural capacity enabling the passions and appetites better to attain their natural ends by its regulation of them in the pursuit of the supreme good of the human soul.[2]

The sixteenth and seventeenth centuries, however, brought a drastic change in this position, for the Copernican revolution in astronomy introduced a completely new world picture, which, as developed by Kepler and Galileo, presented the universe as a mechanism—still the artifact of God, no doubt, but no longer a living organism—a machine devoid of soul or mind; so that matter and mind came to be separated by an unbridgeable gulf and were (under the influence of Descartes) held to be wholly different substances.

The Law of Nature now became "the laws of nature" discoverable by men only empirically; still, of course, ordained by God, universal in their scope and insusceptible to violation. Accordingly, laws of morality and of society, which could be violated, had to be distinguished from empirical natural laws quite sharply. Still, the term "natural law" continued to be applied to the law of reason and was closely associated with, in fact inseparable from, morality and legislation. The result in the thought of moralists and political philosophers was a cleft between the natural state and the civil state of mankind, which the dictates of reason served to bridge. Consequently, there is, in this period, a latent tension between the senses of "nature" and of its laws, as applied to the external world as investigated by the scientist, and as applied to morality and legislation. On the one hand, they were conceived as empirical laws determining the behavior of natural bodies and the occurrence of natural events, including the conduct of human beings as natural animals, and, on the other hand, they were held to be the laws of reason guiding mankind out of the inconveniences and dangers of the "state of nature" into that of civil society regulated by civil law.

The postulation of a state of nature in which mankind was alleged to have lived before the establishment of the civil state is especially characteristic of the political thought of the seventeenth and eighteenth centuries, from Althusius to Rousseau; and the necessity to devise a means and an instrument of transition from one to the other resulted in the conception of an Original Contract. This Contract was the product of reason: allegedly of the reasoning of the people who entered into it, but actually of the theorists seeking to penetrate the presuppositions of social order.

The difficulty thus presenting itself of deriving moral and legal norms from natural laws, in the modern sense of that phrase, is in principle the same as that against which Hume later inveighed when he objected to attempts to deduce the "ought" from the "is." And the device of a contract hardly serves to remove it, for without a prior obligation to keep promises, no contract would be binding; and if "ought" may not be derived from "is," the obligation to keep promises cannot be a natural law in the required sense. Such an obligation, however may well be a dictate of reason. The problem, then, is to decide upon the status of reason in the scheme of Nature.

This problem did not arise in the Medieval period, as we have observed. Thomas Aquinas regarded what we should nowadays call the laws of nature as the eternal law of God, or divine Providence. This is the eternal reason to which all things are subject. But human reason, in particular, participates in divine reason, especially because human beings are themselves provident, both for themselves and for others.

> Whence both eternal reason is imparted to the rational creature itself, so that it has a natural inclination to the right action and goal (*debitum actum et finem*); and such participation in eternal law in the rational creature is called *natural law* . . .[3]

Francisco Suarez follows Aquinas in regarding reason as natural. He calls it "rational nature" and maintains that it is the rule and measure of what is right and wrong.[4] He regarded it also as an active capacity of judging what accords with this standard, and especially in the latter sense called it the law of nature.[5]

The seventeenth-century dichotomy between matter and mind, however, and the divorce of thought from extension by Descartes as separate substances, made this identification at least of human reason with the scientific laws of the physical world less feasible. Consequently, the natural state to which human beings naturally belong is sharply separated from the civil condition, and we find the postulation of a state of nature in which mankind originally found itself, and the device of a contract to account for its present social and political condition, arising more or less concurrently with the new scientific outlook. Yet, as we have seen, a contract will not solve the problem unless human reason can in some way be reintroduced into the world of Nature. If the world is a machine running blindly in accordance with the laws of mechanics and dynamics, and humanity, except so far as physiological functioning can be assimilated to the physico-chemical scheme, operates with consciousness, foresight, and intelligence, how, and in what sense, can the laws of reason and insight be viewed as "natural"? How are they to be related to the laws of mechanics (except as characteristic of the genius of the scientist who discovers those laws)? And how is the natural state of mankind dominated by appetites and passions that conform to mechanical laws to harbor a rational capacity and to submit to its regulation? What is required is an explanation of the mind-body relationship, as well as an account of reason and of law, consistent with a natural explanation of human passion and appetite, which are held to conform to the laws of physics.

SPINOZA AND AQUINAS

The only philosopher of the day who succeeded in providing a coherent theory of nature, of human passion and desire, of reason, and of legal and moral norms, was Spinoza. Grotius simply assumes the existence and efficacy of a law of nature which will suit his purpose of demanding rational conduct among men and nations. Pufendorf tries, with questionable (and perhaps question-begging) success, to derive sociality from a natural state of mankind in a transition that is purely hypothetical. Hobbes (to whom we shall return) is more circumspect, setting out to deduce the social condition from natural human propensities; but he faithfully adopts the world-view of his time and regards human beings as physical bodies that obey the laws of mechanics, even in the enjoyment of consciousness. Sensation, he says, is but the impact upon our physical sense organs of the motion of external bodies, and "motion begets nothing but motion" even if its (unexplained) "appearance to us is Fancy."[6] Reason, in consequence, becomes no more than calculation—a mechanical adding and subtracting of the consequences of names,[7] and how this can produce sociability and morals never satisfactorily emerges; for when Hobbes turns to reason as what "finds out"[8] the laws of nature, it operates very differently from a calculating machine.

Spinoza, on the other hand, identifies God and Nature as the one and only Substance, absolutely infinite and self-sufficient, so he has no difficulty in regarding natural law as the eternal law of God. Further, God's attributes express, each in its own infinite kind, the essence or power of God, and the modes (both infinite and finite) in which they manifest themselves, are all identical in substance. One of these attributes is Thought, the first infinite mode of which is the divine intellect in which all finite modes are adequate ideas; and the order and connection of ideas is the same as the order and connection of things— the same order and connection in all attributes. The eternal law of God, therefore, which is the Law of Nature, is equally the law of reason, and that is nothing other than the *debitus ordo* of adequate ideas.

In this identification of God's eternal law, the law of nature in the world at large, and the law of reason, Spinoza is in quite close agreement with Thomas Aquinas, at least in effect, although St. Thomas uses different language and does not work out the connection between God's essence, the extended world in space and time, and the rational intellect with quite the same rigor and systematic coherence as Spinoza.

According to Spinoza, the essence of Substance is an infinite, dynamic creative power, expressed in infinite attributes, each of which is one of the powers of God. It is not a static structure, but a perpetually active creative drive; and as it exerts itself in every one of the attributes through its infinitely varied series of modes, each mode has, as its essence, a *conatus in suo esse perseverare*, which is at the same time the power of God (or Substance) working through and immanent in it. Here we have an echo of the doctrine of Aquinas, who writes in *Summa Theologica* (*Prima Secundae*, Q. XCIV, A2),

... every substance seeks the preservation of its own being, according to its nature.

The *conatus* is the driving force which, in human beings, gives rise to appetite and desire, so that the law of human nature is of a piece with the general law of nature, as we should expect.

Human nature, however, is a complex notion and involves (as, it would seem, must every other finite nature in Spinoza's system) at least two attributes. For every mode (in every attribute) there is an idea in the divine intellect under the attribute of Thought; and the idea of that mode of Extension which is the human body is the human mind. Human nature may, or rather must, be considered under two aspects, that of thought and of extension; but the idea is identical in substance with its *ideatum*, and together they constitute one thing *(res)*. So whatever is true of the body will be reflected by a corresponding truth about its idea or mind, and vice versa. Further, the human body is a finite mode of Extension and so is acted upon by other finite bodies which cause contingent effects in it (contingent, not in the sense that they occur lawlessly or arbitrarily, but in the sense that they occur in the order of time, in the common order of nature). These are recorded in idea (in the mind) as affects, and so far as the causes are external these are passions. The *conatus* produces reactions to such influences in the endeavor to preserve the self, which take the form of appetites and desires accompanied by the appropriate emotions. But the *conatus* is the endeavor of the thing *(res)*—in this case the human being—to maintain itself in its own essence, and so far as it acts through its own essence alone, its actions *are* its own and are free. The *conatus*, therefore, is, in its proper and most adequate expression, the endeavor to increase the power of action of the human self. Ideas corresponding to action (as opposed to passion) are always adequate ideas, and the power of action is the power of reason. Accordingly, human nature is twofold in yet another way: it is both subject to passion and is capable of action; it is both appetitive and rational.

The way in which this comes about has been explained by Spinoza (as we have already seen) in E2P13S and L7, and in Ep 32. Every body, as a mode in the attribute of Extension, is the *ideatum* of an idea in the attribute of Thought, which is its mind. The "mind" of a simple body (distinguished from others only by Motion-and-rest) is so rudimentary as to be negligible, unless incorporated with others into that of a more complex (organic) body. But the more complex and the more versatile the body, the more excellent and capable is its mind. Bodies as organically complex as the human body, therefore, while they remain finite and subject to the impact of external causes, are also capable of "doing and suffering many things together" so that their minds are capable of developed consciousness; and the more self-dependent both body and mind become, the more capable is the individual of adequate thinking. This explains the twofold nature of human beings, who are, on the one hand, susceptible to imaginative (sensuous) consciousness, to passion, appetite, desire, and emotional stress; and, on the other hand, are able to think and to act rationally. This twofold human nature is presupposed by Spinoza in his political theory.

We should, however, observe before proceeding that the progress from inadequate to adequate thinking is as much the result of the *conatus* as any appetite or idea. The *conatus in suo esse perseverandi* determines us in all circumstances to pursue our own advantage. But what we take to be our advantage depends, for Spinoza, on whether we think inadequately or adequately. For the most part human beings think and behave on the level of *imaginatio*, that is, sensuously and perceptually, so that their appetites and desires excite in them violent and often conflicting emotions. When they do so, as is common, they imagine their advantage to lie in objects and pursuits that are mostly harmful and destructive. But they can, and sometimes do, reflect upon their experience and the consequences of their behavior. From such reflection they can learn more wisdom, even at the level of imagination and passion. Even more significantly, all thought is self-reflective; every *idea* involves its *idea ideae*, and so enables the mind to recognize those properties that are common to all things, both to the whole and to the parts. In so doing it advances from *imaginatio* to *ratio* to think adequately. Thus, with the proper schooling and discipline, in the light of critical reflection, men can develop their power of action, in which their own nature, or essence, is the adequate cause of what they do. The endeavor to maintain oneself in one's own essence, therefore, as we have contended above, is at the same time the endeavor to increase one's power of action. This really is to one's advantage, and in thinking adequately human beings are able to know for certain that it is so. The true good for man is to act rationally, to become self-determined and free. When people do this they act, as we customarily say, morally, but in all cases, whether of passion or action, they behave in accordance with nature.

Spinoza's doctrine, here again, runs parallel in several respects with that of Thomas Aquinas, who writes in the context already quoted:

> Since, however, good has the nature of an end, and evil the nature of the contrary, hence it is that all those things to which man has a natural inclination are naturally apprehended by reason as being good, and consequently as objects of pursuit, and their contraries as evil, and objects of avoidance. Therefore the order of the precepts of natural law is according to the order of natural inclinations, for there is in man, first of all, an inclination to good according to the nature which he has in common with all substances, in as much as every substance seeks the preservation of its own being, according to its nature; and by reason of this inclination, whatever is a means of preserving human life, and of warding off its obstacles, belongs to the natural law. Secondly, there is in man an inclination to things that pertain to him more specifically, according to that nature which he has in common with other animals. . . . Thirdly, there is in man an inclination to good according to the nature of his reason, which nature is proper to him. Thus man has a natural inclination to know the truth about God and to live in society. . .[9]

Here too we find a *conatus* to self-preservation, which issues in the "natural inclinations" (appetites and passions) as well as a rational capacity tending to knowledge of God and (as we shall find likewise in Spinoza) to social order.

Everything so far accounted for is, for both these thinkers, the direct consequence of the operation of the eternal law of God (or Nature); so that it is by nature that human beings are (in Spinoza's words) "led by blind desire,"[10] and equally by nature that they are rational. Human nature is twofold, and by this dual nature human conduct is conditioned.

HOBBES AND SPINOZA

Among the writers of Spinoza's day, only Hobbes is anything like as thorough as Spinoza in tracing back human nature and society to their metaphysical and psychological roots. Spinoza was strongly influenced by Hobbes, and there are similarities between their teachings, but the differences between them are more significant than the likenesses.

The contemporary dichotomy between the mechanics of the physical world and the rational consciousness of the human mind can be overcome by reducing either side to the other, resulting, on the one hand, in a materialistic monism if mind is reduced to matter, or, on the other hand, in subjective idealism if the opposite course is taken. Hobbes adopted the former expedient, as Berkeley later resorted to the latter. Thus Hobbes writes:

> ... The Universe, that is, the whole mass of all things that are is Corporeal, that is to say, Body; and hath dimensions of magnitude, namely, Length, Breadth and Depth: also every part of Body is likewise Body, and hath the like dimensions; and consequently every part of the Universe is Body; and that which is not Body, is no part of the Universe; And because the Universe is All, that which is no part of it is *Nothing*; and consequently *nowhere*.[11]

Our consciousness, therefore, Hobbes asserts is "nothing but motion," and though its "appearance to us is Fancy," no explanation is given of the precise relation of "Fancy" to motion, nor is any forthcoming of how such "appearance" is possible to body, nor to what else, if anything, it could appear. The external motion which "presseth our organs diversely" is continued within the body as sensation, and that as it decays becomes imagination. "Imagination therefore is nothing but *decaying sense*." Internal motions, reacting to these, constitute "Endeavour," which issues in "Voluntary Motions," one kind of which is speech. Speech consists in naming, and the tracing out, or adding and subtracting, of the consequences of names is said to be "Reason."[12]

It is hardly possible consistently in such a theory to derive by reason, or in any other way, normative precepts obligatory for human conduct, from what is but motion and pertains solely to corporeal beings. Yet when Hobbes turns to speak of Natural Law, he defines it as "a Precept, or general Rule, found out by Reason, by which a man is forbidden to do that which is destructive of his life, or taketh away the means of preserving the same."[13] This is the first law of nature set down by Hobbes, and the third, which is fundamental for his political theory, is "That men perform their Covenants made"[14]—an obviously prescriptive precept.

In such a doctrine the inconsistency is manifest, and Hume's accusation against deriving the "ought" from the "is" applies. Hobbes himself is partly aware of this, for he ultimately reduces all obligation to forcible compulsion, actual or threatened:

> Covenants, being but words, and breath, have no force to oblige, contain, constrain or protect any man, but what it has from the publique Sword. . .[15]

But no such compulsion can have moral validity; nobody acting under sheer duress is rightly held responsible, and no natural law, which is merely a law of fear (as a mechanistic aversion) imposes either a moral or a legal obligation.

Spinoza avoids this inconsistency by offering a more profound theory of body-mind relation and a more coherent account of the power of reason. For him, it is only under the attribute of Extension that materialism in any form prevails, and even there it is mitigated by his account of complex bodies as what we should call organic. Minds are not bodies but are ideas, albeit the ideas of the bodies which are their *ideata*; and Spinoza's universe is not restricted (like Hobbes's) to the corporeal. The more complex bodies (like our own) are, in Spinoza's world, integrated wholes (as is the world itself—*facies totius universi*) in which the principle of integration determines the nature and relation of the components. The minds of these complex bodies reflect in idea their integrated and self-dependent versatility. Their power of action, therefore, where it develops, can at least in some measure prevail over their passive subjection to external causes; and reason, or adequate thinking, can regulate the passions and mitigate their distracting conflicts by converting the resulting conduct into free (self-determined) action. The laws of reason, as we saw earlier, are just as natural as those of physics or of psychology; so that when we speak of the Law of Nature, we cover the dictates of reason as well as the regularities of the physical world and the aberrations of human greed and aggression.

It is frequently held that, despite this consistency in Spinoza's doctrine with respect to natural law, or rather because of it, all obligation is eliminated.[16] True it is that Spinoza's free man acts according to nature, no less than the passionate who are misled by *imaginatio*. But the rational person who sees his or her true advantage correctly cannot but pursue it in rational fashion. Such a person, it is alleged, does not choose freely to act, but (as Spinoza quite explicitly declares)[17] does so necessarily.

Much depends, however, on the way in which we understand the terms "freedom," "necessity," and "obligation," and how we conceive their interrelation. If one is thought to enjoy freedom of choice entirely undetermined, and is then obliged to do X rather than Y, in what sense is one obliged? If by divine command, one's obedience must still be determined by some motive such as reverence, if not by fear. But, if so, choice is no longer undetermined. If one is obliged by the requirements of some higher good for mankind, it can only be through desire for such good that one willingly complies. Spinoza denies the existence of any undetermined "free" will. He also denies that God is a supreme ruler who issues commands to be freely obeyed or disobeyed. But if the knowledge and love of God, in his sense of those words, is what is meant by one's awareness and reverence for the divine will, then obedience is nothing other than the free action (determined by one's own essence) arising from the third kind of knowledge. As knowledge of this kind is the knowledge of the true and supreme good for man, action in accordance with it is what that good requires. What "obliges" the rational man is his *conatus*, that which obliges all persons and all things. That again is always the requirement of the supreme good, for that alone is truly advantageous, and it is always what one conceives as one's advantage that one is impelled to seek. In the toils of imagination and passion, nobody by nature can live rationally and none can be "obliged" to do so,[18] except insofar as the very *conatus* that inflames desire is the same as that which, in the long run, impels to the improvement of the understanding and raises consciousness to the level of reason, *scientia intuitiva* and *amor intellectualis Dei*.

It is thus as much natural law that obliges us to virtuous action as determines us, when we fail to understand clearly and distinctly, when we give way to our passions and to vice. In showing this to be the case Spinoza does indeed derive the "ought" from the "is," but he does so without committing any fallacy. There is, moreover, no other way to derive an ought, for unless what is obligatory is good, obligation is either immorally imposed or is senseless; and nothing is good that is in nobody's interest. The criterion of value must have its roots in both the nature of the actual world and in the natural inclinations of mankind (in human nature). These may be misleading and misled, but can be satisfied adequately only if rationally ordered; and the need for rational order, the indispensable condition of attaining the true object of all desire, is what imposes obligation on the will. Because human nature is twofold, what we do viciously from passion and what we do virtuously by reason we do equally by nature.

NATURAL RIGHTS

In Spinoza's political philosophy this metaphysical and ethical consistency bears fruit; for here he is able to adopt the language of natural law and natural right while yet avoiding the difficulties in which his contemporaries became entangled. He can dispense with a presupposed, quasi-historical state of nature and (although at first he tries out the idea) with any original contract.

The law of nature is the law of God and whatever occurs or is done by nature is the expression of God's power. Whatever anything, or anybody, can do by nature, therefore, is done by natural right.[19] For human beings natural right is the right to do what human nature prompts. For Spinoza, as for Hobbes, therefore, natural rights are equivalent to natural powers; but unlike Hobbes, Spinoza considers natural powers, equally with "blind desires," to cover rational conduct characteristic of the civil condition. In Ep 50 Spinoza writes to Jarig Jelles:

> As regards political theories, the difference . . . between Hobbes and myself consists in this, that I always preserve natural right intact and only allot to the chief magistrates in every state a right over their subjects commensurate with the excess of their power over the power of the subjects. This is what always takes place in the state of nature.

When Spinoza speaks of a "state of nature" he does not refer to any presupposed societal condition of mankind, but to the natural propensities, attitudes, and emotions to which human beings are liable. He rejects the notion of a state of nature prior to the civil state, such as Hobbes and others postulate, because he views it as an unwarranted assumption of (as he calls it) "a state within a state"; that is, a kind of civil condition subject to the law of reason (which, Hobbes assumed and later Locke maintained, operates in the state of nature), before in fact civil society proper has been established.[20] Because it requires education, discipline, and practice to become virtuous and to live according to sound reason, men are by nature for the most part swayed by passion and ruled by appetite, so that they are avaricious, envious, vengeful and vindictive, often fearful, and sometimes overconfident. Consequently, if left unrestrained, they are "by nature enemies" (once again an echo of Hobbes). But they can barely survive, if at all, without mutual help, and it is accordingly obvious even to the untutored that life in society has overwhelming advantages.

In the *Tractatus Theologico-Politicus* Spinoza contends that the wretchedness of life in isolation is so great that men must have been persuaded to agree together to hand over their natural rights (or powers) to a collective body which could compel them to live according to reason.[21] No such contract, he avers, would, however, be kept unless it were of advantage to the contracting parties, and none could be trusted to observe it without further sanctions. The authority created by the contract, combining the powers of the group, must therefore enforce its observance by sanctions that leave none in doubt of the advantage of keeping its terms. Here the influence of Hobbes is plainly apparent, who had maintained that the state of nature was so intolerable that men would be induced to agree to confer their natural powers upon one man or body of men who would then enforce the observation of the contract by "the publique Sword."

In the *Tractatus Politicus*, however, the contract drops out of Spinoza's reasoning. There he argues that apart from social cooperation, the weakness and mutual enmity of men left to themselves would be such that nobody would have power to achieve anything significant, and natural right would be nil; it would exist, he says, "more in opinion than in fact." Moreover, "without mutual help it is hardly possible for men to sustain life or cultivate the mind."

Accordingly, natural rights are effectively held *only* by persons in community "enabling them together to defend the land they inhabit and cultivate, to protect themselves and repel all force, and to live by common consent." Thus they hold rights in common and are led "as if by one mind."[22]

This is the rationale of the civil condition and of political authority, and from it flow, still by the law of nature, the rights of sovereignty, the sanctions of positive law, and the duties of citizenship. All of these are natural and follow necessarily from the dual nature of human beings in their constant endeavor to persist in their own essence and increase their power of action, whether they are passionate (and require restraint) or rational (and conform to rules). The norms of morality and law, and the obligation to observe them, derive alike from that source, maintaining continuity between what is and what ought to be. The law of nature is the same whether conceived as the eternal law of God, the law of human nature, or the law of reason, and the criterion of both truth and value is one and the same, namely, what the intellect perceives as constituting the essence of Substance, through the adequate idea of which the adequate ideas of all things are conceived in *scientia intuitiva*. Such adequate ideas are at once true knowledge and the motive of free action, and although all government is not perfectly rational (for to believe that men are always ruled by reason rather than by blind desire, or that perplexed by the affairs of state they will act rationally, is to dream of a golden age of the poets), yet civil society is more rational than anarchy and civil disorder, and the more rational government becomes the more peaceful and prosperous is the life of the citizens.

So it is that Spinoza teaches a consistent doctrine of the law of nature, which bridges the reputed gulf between fact and value, commits no fallacy legitimately deriving what ought to be from what is, and is relieved of the necessity to postulate a putative state of nature historically prior to the civil condition or an Original Contract as the foundation of the civil state that cannot resolve the problem of legitimizing political power, because it provides no explanation of the moral obligation to keep promises.

Notes

1. Cf. Thomas Aquinas, *Summa Theologica, Prima Secundae*, Q XCI, A2.
2. Cf. ibid., Q I, A4, A6, A7; Q II, Q IV, passim.
3. Ibid., Q XCI, A2.
4. Cf. *De Legibus*, Bk. II, Ch. V, 2.
5. Ibid., Ch. V, 3–6.
6. Cf. *Leviathan*, Pt. I, Ch. 1.
7. Ibid., Ch. 5.
8. Cf. ibid., Ch. 14.
9. *Summa Theologica*, Ia, IIae, Q XCIV, A2.
10. TP, Ch. II, 5.
11. *Leviathan*, Ch. 46.
12. Cf. Ibid., Pt. 1, Chs. I, II, IV and VI.
13. Cf. Ibid., Ch. XIV.
14. Ibid., Ch. XV.
15. Ibid., Ch. XVIII.
16. Cf. A. G. Wernham, *Benedict de Spinoza, the Political Works,* (Oxford, Clarendon Press, 1958), p. 19.
17. Cf. TTP, note XXXIV.
18. Cf. ibid., Ch. XIV: "... *non magis ex legibus sanae mentis vivere tenetur quam felis ex legibus naturae leoninae.*"
19. Cf. TP, Ch. II, 2–4.
20. Cf. E3 Praef., and TP, Ch. II, 6.
21. Cf. TTP, Ch. XIV. Throughout this chapter the influence of Hobbes is clearly apparent.
22. Cf. TP, Ch. II, 15–16.

8

Spinoza and the Original Contract Theory

The rationale of obligation (whether moral or political) has been the central question for ethical and legal philosophy throughout history, for, apart from advantage to the agent, how or why should anybody justifiably be restrained from desired action or required to perform against inclination? The justification of any kind of obligation must embrace both moral and political, for it has long been recognized that moral obligation and political coercion cannot be divorced. Even in ancient times the Sophists sought to explain the first in terms of the second, while Socrates and Plato justified the second in terms of the first. The Middle Ages, under the influence of Christianity, found the answer in the will of God, but even obedience to divine commands requires a motive, be it reverence or fear, and that, to be philosophically acceptable as an explanation, needs rational grounds. In the sixteenth century the problem presented itself afresh with new urgency and in a new context, firstly because the Copernican revolution had introduced a new conception of nature, secondly because the authority of the Catholic Church had been called in question by the Reformation, and thirdly because the rise of national states in Europe was accompanied by the claim of their rulers to absolute power and authority.

The foundation of both Ancient and Medieval ethics and politics (as we observed in the last chapter) was the conception of Natural Law, as a facet of the eternal law of God. But when nature came to be viewed as a vast machine, and mechanical laws were found to be purely descriptive, the difficulty of deriving moral and political norms from natural laws became especially acute. The appeal to God as architect

111

of the universe and author of its laws was still available, but after the Reformation the interpretation of God's will varied with the multiplication of sects, so that resort to secular reason seemed more universally convincing. Moreover, the reformers insisted on the freedom of individual faith and conscience; so the claim of the state to derive its authority from the divine will was more easily called in question.

From the sixteenth to the eighteenth century, the main form which this appeal to reason took was enshrined in the doctrine of an original social contract by which men gave up their natural freedom and agreed to live in concert under a political superior to whom they deputed the power to enforce laws to restrain aggressive behavior, and the authority to adjudicate and settle disputes. The idea was, at least in part, derived from the conception in Roman Law of the contract of *societas*, or partnership, and in part from that in Medieval Law of obligation freely agreed upon (at least in theory) by feudal overlords with their vassals and renewed by successive generations.

The postulation of such a contract, assumed to have been entered into at some actual time in history, or regarded as tacitly presupposed in current practice, became quite general among theorists of the day, and it was often used, not merely to justify the subjection of peoples to the power of rulers, but rather (and more frequently) in the interests of the subjects, to limit the authority of princes, and to oppose the tyrannical use of their power. In short, it was made the basis of rights as well as of duties.

To this general rule two writers stand out as noteworthy exceptions in the seventeenth century. One is Hobbes, who is unique in using the contract theory to support the claims to absolute sovereignty of monarchs—although he does, somewhat reluctantly, permit the occasional substitution of a sovereign council for the rule of one man. The other is Spinoza, who first uses the contract idea as the foundation of democracy, and then dispenses with it altogether. In both these respects he is far in advance of his contemporaries; but before discussing his successive positions, it may be of interest to review the prior development of the doctrine in the previous century, by way of comparison.

The idea of contractual agreement as the explanation of moral and social regulation was not unknown in Greek philosophy. It is put forward in the second book of Plato's *Republic* by Glaucon as new support for the theory of Thrasymachus, whom Socrates had discomfited in Book I. Glaucon himself is opposed to the doctrine and calls upon Socrates to refute it. Men, it is alleged, agree to compromise between the evils suffered by the weak at the hands of their predators and the pleasures and advantages of the strong in committing injustice. Justice, then, is this compromise, by which all agree not to encroach upon the goods and enjoyments of their fellows, an agreement which anybody who is crafty and powerful enough will always seek to evade or defy.

In the sixteenth century, however, moral obligation was still almost universally regarded as originating in divine commandment, and the contract theory was almost exclusively used to explain the origin of society and to define the rights and limits of political power.

One of the earliest treatises setting out a position of this kind was George Buchanan's *De jure regni apud Scotos*, published in 1579 (but written earlier),[1] which sought to explain the political practice of the Scottish people as an example of the exercise by peoples in general of their rights against the abuse of power by kings and princes. The implicit background of Buchanan's argument is a contract or covenant made between the people and their elected king, which appears explicitly only in the oath sworn by the king on his accession to rule in accordance with recognized and acknowledged laws.

Buchanan, like most of his contemporaries and followers, presumes the existence prior to society of a natural condition of mankind, about which, however, he says little, except to draw attention to man's lack of self-sufficiency in isolation. The main cause of association, he contends, is the natural and insuperable desire of human beings for the company of their fellows, the lack of which not even the most reclusive can endure for very long. The law of association, says Buchanan, is a divine gift, which he identifies as "the natural light" and calls the Law of Nature (revealing the lingering influence of St. Augustine as it persisted in later Medieval thought). In consequence, he maintains, there is nothing of greater benefit to man than a community associated by and under law (*jure*), the parts and members of which are interrelated as are the parts and members of a living body—mutually cooperating and sustaining.

Just as conflicting principles in the body cause disease, so that its health requires the attention of a physician who prescribes a regimen in accordance with the rules of his science, so the body politic requires regulation by a king who will resolve conflicting claims among its members, administering it in accordance with acknowledged law. Kings are created and installed, not for their own sakes, but for the good of the people; their function is to preserve the good health of the society and to restore it if it relapses into dissension. Justice, which it is the king's duty to maintain, is defined as "whatever is most favourable to the common concerns of men."[2]

It follows that kingship is established by the people for their own benefit and on conditions prescribed by laws that they have promulgated, and that kings must promise to rule in accordance with these laws and to maintain them, in return for which the people promise loyalty and obedience. If this mutual covenant is broken by the citizens they may rightly be punished; if they rebel without just cause the king may use loyal forces to put down their revolt. But, likewise, if the ruler breaks the law he is as much subject to the courts as other citizens, and if he arrogates power to himself as a tyrant he may be removed from office and replaced by another. For the king is not superior in authority over the people as a united body, but is subject to them as are all their magistrates.

A much better known and more influential document is *Vindiciae contra Tyrannos,* published over the pseudonym Junius Brutus and first attributed to Languet but later, with better evidence, to Duplessis Mornay, the counsellor to Henry IV of France. This work is contemporary with Buchanan's and argues in similar vein, but it directs more attention to religion, religious toleration, and the relation between church and state. The author postulates a double contract: first, between God, the king, and the people, establishing religion, "that the people might be a people of God"; second, between the king and the people, by which the people consent to obey faithfully and the king to rule justly. The presumption is that this convention was actually entered into and was a historical event; but nobody could have believed this to be literally true (at least not of the first part) who did not accept the Old Testament with fundamentalist rigor. The contract theory, however, was seldom if ever seriously meant as a historical account of the origin of political order. It was more properly an attempt to penetrate to the logical presuppositions of the civil condition.

The author of *Vindiciae* is fully aware that kings and rulers derive their strength and authority from the people, without whose support their power crumbles. He maintains that the officers and representatives of the people are officers of the Crown (or Kingdom) but not of the king, whose power it is their function to keep within legal bounds. It is only when differences arise between individuals over property and between neighboring peoples over territory that recourse is had to a leader who can adjudicate between them and defend them against invaders; so that the only duty of kings and emperors is to provide for the people's good. The king is thus never above the laws which on his accession he receives from the people, and they (not singly, but as a body) are his superiors, not he theirs. The basis of rulership and government is thus the consent of the governed, a compact between ruler and ruled, which entitles the latter to resist all tyranny.

It is to be noticed that the tacit assumption of both Mornay's and Buchanan's argument is that prior to the contract the people is already an organized body, so the contract itself does not really mark the origin of ordered society. It is presumed that there are already laws in existence to which both people and their ruler must conform. These laws were later (e.g., by Hobbes and Locke) explicitly identified as laws of nature, without further explanation of their origin than that they were what reason prescribed.

Sentiments similar to those of Mornay and Buchanan, leading to similar conclusions, are expressed by Johannes Althaus (Althusius) in his *Politica methodica digesta*, which appeared early in the succeeding century.[3] No one, he points out, could survive if abandoned in infancy, and even an adult cannot unaided acquire the necessities of life. Therefore, society, or what Althusius calls symbiosis, is natural to humankind. But association is also voluntary, and every type of society involves a tacit or overt covenant between its members to give one another aid and support and to cooperate for common ends.

Symbioses are of two main kinds, private and public. The first are families and collegia, the second are cities, provinces, and commonwealths. Each and all rest upon covenants (*pacta*), the terms of which are fundamental laws of the society. We may pass over private symbioses, for our main interest is in the state, although Althusius reminds us that without private no public associations could exist.

The commonwealth (or state) is constituted of other public bodies, cities and provinces, and the bond incorporating them all is consensus:

> a tacit or expressed promise to communicate things, mutual services, aid, counsel and the same common rights (*jura*) to the extent that the utility and necessity of universal social life in a realm shall require.[4]

The supreme magistracy is constituted as

> a process by which the people [i.e., the representatives of the cities and provinces] and the supreme magistrate enter into a covenant concerning certain laws and conditions that set forth the form and manner of imperium and subjection, and faithfully extend and accept oaths to each other to this effect.[5]

This *contractum mandati* obliges both parties so that neither may revoke it; but the obligation of the magistrate is prior, and he binds himself to administer the realm "according to laws prescribed by God, right reason, and the body of the commonwealth." (Here the echo of the doctrine of Natural Law is plainly discernible.) By these laws the authority of the supreme magistrate is circumscribed, and he may exercise no more than is explicitly conceded to him by the associated members or bodies of the realm. For the rights of sovereignty are proper to the realm and belong to it alone; the supreme magistrate is no more than a steward and overseer of these rights, but "their ownership and usufruct properly belong to the total realm of the people" by whom they have been established, through whose members they have originated, and without whom they cannot exist.[6] So Althusius contends that

> no realm or commonwealth has ever been founded or instituted except by contract entered into, one with another, by convenants agreed upon between subjects and their future prince, and by an established mutual obligation that both should religiously observe.[7]

That the covenant creates the obligation is clearly assumed, but, as we noted earlier when discussing the law of nature, and shall have occasion to observe again, a *petitio principii* is as clearly involved.

From these original provisions Althusius draws the consequence that the people, holding the original sovereign right, appoint their own ruler and his successor when he dies; and if he breaks the contract and violates the laws, the people can annul their earlier form of polity and constitute a new one.

Vindiciae contra Tyrannos was well known in England throughout the seventeenth century, during which there were no fewer than five editions, in 1622, 1631, 1648, 1660, and 1689. The translation into English was issued anonymously, and the 1648 edition was followed immediately in 1649 by John Milton's pamphlet *The Tenure of Kings and Magistrates*, the argument of which is almost identical with that of *Vindiciae*, and the conclusion reached is the same. The style and phraseology of the translation are unmistakably Milton's, evident not only from comparison with his political pamphlet, but also from faint echoes of *Paradise Lost* discernible in it. That Milton was the translator of Mornay's treatise, therefore, is by no means an unwarranted assumption.

Man, Milton writes, is born free, in the image of God, to command and not to obey. But Adam's transgression led to sin and wrongdoing. Seeing that the resulting conflicts would lead to general destruction, men

> agreed by common league to bind each other from injury and jointly to defend themselves against any that gave disturbance or offence against such agreement.

But, he continues,

because no faith in all was found sufficiently binding, they saw it needful to ordain some authority, that might restrain by force and punish what was violated against peace and common right.

This authority, originally residing in each and every person, they then "communicate and derive" to one or to a few, not to be lords and masters, but deputies and commissioners. When these, corrupted by power, acted arbitrarily and "perverted their commissions to injustice," men framed laws by consent to confine and limit the authority of governors. Then they extracted oaths from kings and magistrates on their installment that they would administer justly and impartially, and added councils and parliaments to keep them in check. The power of kings is derivative from what is committed to them in trust from the people for the common good, and if that is betrayed, the people may reject and depose their ruler and choose another.

For all these writers some form of covenant or contract is not just the basis of ordered society but is also a fence against tyranny and a justification for revolution. They all preceded Spinoza (who was seventeen years old when Milton's pamphlet was published), and I have found no evidence that he knew of their work, although it would seem unlikely that he was altogether ignorant of Althusius, who was very popular in the Netherlands in the early part of the century and was *persona grata* with the government of the Seven Provinces which he much admired. It is hardly probable also that Spinoza knew nothing of the *Vindiciae,* for it had wide influence among Calvinistic theorists with whom he must at least have had some acquaintance. This form of contract theory, however, found its culmination after Spinoza's death in the hands of John Locke, whose *Two Treatises of Government* were completed in 1681 but were not published until 1689, and then anonymously.

The influence of all the writers so far considered is evident in Locke's account of the origins of civil society, and he reaffirms the original contract in a form similar to that proposed by Althusius and Milton. First there is an agreement between men each to give up his natural rights of executing the Law of Nature for himself and "to resign it to the public." This puts an end to the State of Nature (which Locke conceived as one of peace and order governed by Natural Law, the sole inconvenience of which is that it leaves each person as judge in his own case when disputes arise) and establishes a commonwealth. The second stage is one by which the commonwealth delegates the exercise of its sovereignty to magistrates and councils, setting up a constitution of government. The rights and powers of government, however, are limited to the requirements of the common good, and

> whoever has the legislative or supreme power of any commonwealth
> is bound to govern by established standing laws, promulgated and
> known to the people, and not by any extemporary decrees; by
> indifferent and upright judges who are to decide controversies by
> those laws; and to employ the force of the community at home only
> in the execution of such laws, or abroad to prevent or redress for-
> eign injuries and secure the community from inroads and invasion.[8]

The consent of every member of society must be given, either tacitly
or explicitly, to this social contract, although it may be originally agreed
upon only by a majority.

Locke concludes from this purported contractual origin of society
that, should the government be usurped by unauthorized persons, or
should an authorized body seek to rule in contravention of the recognized law, people would not be bound to obey. Government, but not
the commonwealth, would be dissolved, and the people would be en-
titled to constitute a new legislature. He writes:

> The end of government is the good of mankind, and which is best
> for mankind, that the people should always be exposed to the bound-
> less will of tyranny, or that the rulers should be sometimes liable to
> be opposed when they grow exorbitant in the use of their power,
> and employ it for the destruction and not for the preservation of
> the properties of their people?[9]

This is the normal form and argument of the contract theory in the
sixteenth and seventeenth centuries. It embodies what has been called
the historical theory of sovereignty and what elsewhere I have called
its ethical aspect because the sovereign is conceived as drawing its
authority from the consent of the governed. The contract idea is used
mainly to justify opposition to arbitrary and oppressive rule. But what
is overlooked is the patent fact that once the ruler has acquired supreme power, whether by delegation from the populace or by any other
means, no private person is strong enough successfully to challenge
its legitimacy. It can and must regard any revolt as subversive to its
authority, and there is no impartial superior, in Locke's words, no
indifferent and upright judge, to whom appeal can be made to decide
upon the rights or wrongs of the insurrection. Supreme power is paramount in all circumstances. The Law of Nature has not been engraved
on tablets of stone for all to read. The laws assumed by Buchanan (for
example) prior to the institution of kingship have never been promulgated, and dispute about their prescriptions can be endless and remains unresolved.

It is not surprising, therefore, that at least one attempt was made to use the device of a contract to support a doctrine of absolute sovereignty. Hobbes, writing between 1641 and 1651, draws a picture of the state of nature as one of anarchy and insecurity, in which

> there is no place for industry; because the fruit thereof is uncertain: and consequently no Culture of the Earth; no Navigation nor the use of commodities that may be imported by Sea; no commodious Building; no instruments of moving, and removing things that require much force; no Knowledge of the face of the Earth; no account of Time; no Arts; no Letters; no Society; and which is worst of all, continual feare, and danger of violent death.[10]

So grim is this prospect that men are constrained to agree to give up their natural rights (that is, their powers to acquire what they can and defend it and themselves against attack) and to confer all their power and strength upon one man or upon one assembly of men "that may reduce all their wills, by a plurality of voices, to one will."[11]

By this contract what is established is an absolute sovereign acknowledged by each of the contracting individuals as bearing his or her person and as thereby authorized to act for them all. Covenants, however, being "but words and breath," more is needed to make the agreement constant and lasting: that is, "a Common Power to keep them all in awe, and to direct their actions to the Common Benefit."[12]

Thus the contract removes men from the state of nature, establishes a commonwealth, and by the same act creates an authority to enforce its observance. But this agreement is between everyman and everyman and not between the sovereign and the people. Insurrection, therefore, is always a breach of the contract, and automatically re-establishes the state of nature. The people have no right to rebellion, no right to challenge, oppose, remove, or change their government; for the sovereign is the surrogate of the people and "beareth their Person."

Thus does Hobbes completely reverse the direction of the argument and lead it to a conclusion diametrically opposite to that of the thinkers we have hitherto considered. He is the only philosopher who succeeds in using the conception of contract in this way, preserving the element of consent implicit in political subjection while making it irrevocable short of total dissolution of the social condition.

Hobbes represents what has been called the juristic theory of sovereignty (later restated by such thinkers as Bentham, Blackstone, and Austin); juristic because in law the supreme and unchallengeable authority is the sovereign power of the realm, which is the sole authorized source of legislation. Here, however, there is no safeguard against arbitrary rule, oppression, and the injustice of tyranny, and no deference given to the fact that the power of rulers is not their own (as

Plato depicts Socrates in Book I of the *Republic* satirically asking Thrasymachus whether he means by the strongest the pancreatist in the games), but is derived from the support of the people.

Quite apart from the question-begging defect of the contract theory, therefore, neither of the two versions so far investigated is satisfactory as a theory of sovereign right and the duty of obedience. Spinoza, on the other hand, approaches the question with more perspicacity. He certainly knew the work of Hobbes and was much influenced by his thought, as he was also by Machiavelli, and that puts him, with them, in the class of political realists. But Spinoza's realism is far from cynical and does not prevent him from reaching a conclusion which is eminently liberal.[13] Clearly he has great sympathy for Hobbes's assessment of human nature, for he maintains with perspicacity that "men are led more by blind desire than by reason" and are brought by their passions, by their envy and contentiousness, into mutual hostility. In the *Ethics* he demonstrates that human beings are always liable to be overcome by passion, and that although reason can do much to counteract and control the violence of emotion, its discipline is hard and its success is rare. Nor can it ever eliminate passion altogether, for the power with which the human mind endeavors to persist in its own being is infinitely surpassed by that of the external causes to which it is subjected.[14]

Accordingly, "men are by nature enemies."[15] But Spinoza, when he speaks of a state of nature, is not referring to any presupposed historical condition prior to the civil state, but merely to human nature and its characteristics. In fact, in *Tractatus Politicus* (Ch. II, 6) he protests against those who "conceive men in nature as a state within a state." And when he resorts to the device of an Original Contract in *Tractatus Theologico-Politicus*, he does so more in deference to learned convention than from conviction. For he argues that whatever anybody does, believing it to be advantageous or disadvantageous, is done and believed by the highest right of nature (because everybody does and believes only in accordance with nature). This, if performed according to reason alone, would be a right possessed and enjoyed without hurt to anybody; but, as men are more subject to passion than led by reason, they come into conflict, even when and although they are in need of mutual help. Reason alone cannot overcome desire, so restraint can be effected only by the threat of penalties. Accordingly, men can live in peace and harmony only if they give up their natural rights of acquisition and retaliation each for himself to a society which can prescribe and enforce a common rule of life.[16] So each must contract to conduct everything by the dictate of reason alone, to do to others as he would be done by, and to defend his neighbor's rights as he would his own.[17]

Spinoza argues, however, that nobody foregoes an imagined good except for the sake of an assumed greater benefit, therefore nobody will keep a promise unless from the hope of greater good, or the fear of greater evil, much less so if the other party is liable to break his word; and for these very reasons, every party is suspect. Mutual trust is possible only between those who follow reason alone, and among the majority of people, swayed by passion, promises can be guaranteed only by the threat of a penalty for their breach. This can be ensured only if natural rights (or powers) are jointly renounced and jointly transferred to society, which, when such common power is conferred upon it by all its members, is a democracy.

In the *Tractatus Politicus*, written some ten years later, Spinoza recognizes that the natural rights or powers held by each individual would, apart from society, amount to nothing, "but exist more in opinion than in fact." For men are the less capable of action the more they are subject to fear, and are hardly at all able to sustain life and cultivate the mind without mutual help and cooperation.

> We conclude, therefore, that the right of nature which belongs to the human race can scarcely be conceived unless where men hold rights in common.[18]

This being so, man may be called a social animal, and contract is no longer necessary as an actual or assumed transaction prior to the foundation of the civil state.

Even in the earlier treatise the inessentiality of a contract is foreshadowed. There we are told that nobody can doubt the superior advantage of living by the laws and dictates of reason, which (as Spinoza demonstrates in E4PP35,36,37) aim at the true interests of all in common. For everybody wishes to live in safety and security, which is impossible if each is left to do as he pleases. Without mutual help life is most miserable and gives no opportunity or means for the cultivation of reason. Therefore, to live safely and well, men must needs join together; and, we might add in the words of the *Tractatus Politicus* (Ch. III, 7), "be led as if by one mind."

This abandonment by Spinoza of the contract as the initiating act of incorporation into civil society shows a sound philosophical insight far in advance of his time and even of such critics of the doctrine as Hume and Bentham in the next century. For the theory is at fault not simply because it is unhistorical. Few, if any, contract theorists insist upon its historicity, and lack of it is not entirely damaging. It aims rather at drawing attention to the essential element of agreement in all sociopolitical order, and the interrelation between rights and consent. But it purports to explain and to justify rights and obligations, and in doing so it overlooks two matters of vital importance. First, contract is a legal concept, derived, as we said earlier, from the doctrine of *societas* in Roman Law. Here the agreement between the parties is voluntary, and the rights which ensue derive from it. It can be dissolved as well as entered into by mutual consent, and with its revocation the derivative rights disappear. But in the case of most rights this is not so; they do not *originate* in mutual agreement even if they do imply and involve consent. Nor can they be abolished by the arbitrary withdrawal of agreement. It is upon the recognition of the rights that agreement depends: for instance, the right of property is presupposed in any agreement to recognize possession, to transfer it, or to purchase; the right of habeas corpus is prior to any agreement to refrain from arbitrary arrest or to release on bail. Secondly, and more important, whatever obligations may derive from contract, they cannot include the obligation to honor the agreement. Unless there is a prior obligation to do that, the contract is null and void.

Spinoza avoids these question-begging assumptions. He sees that rights and obligations derive from reason and the recognition of true advantage, which resides in a good common to all and in a joint will to pursue common ends.

> For it comes first to be considered that just as in the state of nature that man is strongest and most his own master (*sui juris*) who is guided by reason, so also that state will be most powerful and most fully *sui juris* which is founded on and directed by reason. For the right of a state is determined by the power of a people (*multitudo*) which is led as if by one mind. And this union of minds could by no means be conceived, unless the state does all it can to aim at what sound reason shows to be good for all men.[19]

Sound reason in politics is the capacity to organize joint action in the pursuit of the common welfare of a community. That and that alone is the root of all sociality and the source of all rights and political duties. Spinoza saw this quite clearly, and so his brief flirtation with the contract theory can be viewed as no more than the temporary influence of current ideas, in particular as developed by Hobbes. His conception of sovereignty combines and reconciles the two complementary aspects embodied in the contract theories of Locke (and his predecessors) and of Hobbes. Spinoza is, in fact, nearer in his conception of the source and justification of political power to Rousseau than to his predecessors and contemporaries. Rousseau, indeed, envisages a state of nature, as well as a social contract, but neither bears very much resemblance to those imagined by earlier thinkers. The contract, especially, is a transaction differing widely from that conceived by Mornay or Locke. It is a compact of each with all to place his person and all his power in common with theirs under the supreme direction of the general will, and one in which each agrees to recognize every other as an inalienable member of the corporate body.[20] It is the common will and the common good of the people as a whole that generate both right and duty, as well as the power to make and enforce the law. This is the case for both Spinoza and Rousseau; and at the same time, for both thinkers, the sovereign power is absolute just because, and only because, it is the power of the whole community, against which the challenge of separate individuals cannot prevail. It is, and can only be, the power of the whole people because without the support and backing at least of a considerable body no government can maintain either its authority or its supremacy. In consequence, like Rousseau's theory, Spinoza's represents a reconciliation of positions like those of Hobbes and Locke, fusing Hobbes's absolutism with Locke's popular sovereignty, coupled with the insistence of both upon the common good as the end and vindication of the exercise of power.

Notes

1. The treatise was prompted by the events of 1567 and was intended to justify the deposition of Mary Queen of Scots.
2. Cf. *De Jure Regni apud Scotos* (Edinburgh, 1579), p. 15: "... *quae in rebus communibus et hominum inter se commerciis posita est commodissime mihi nomine justiciae intellegi posse videatur.*"
3. First edition 1603, second edition 1614.
4. Op. cit., trans. F. S. Carney (London, 1964), p. 62.
5. Ibid., p. 117.
6. Cf. ibid., Preface to the first edition.
7. Ibid., p. 117.
8. *Treatise of Civil Government,* § 131.
9. Ibid., § 229.
10. *Leviathan,* Ch. 13.
11. Ibid., Ch. 17.
12. Ibid.
13. Cf. L. S. Feuer, *Spinoza and the Rise of Liberalism* (Boston, Beacon Press, 1964, 1966); and Jan den Tex, *Spinoza over de Tolerantie,* Mededelingen XXIII vanwege het Spinozahuis, 1967.
14. Cf. E4PP2,3,4.
15. TP, II, 14.

16. Cf. E4P37S2.
17. TTP, XVI.
18. TP, II, 15.
19. TP, III, 7.
20. Cf. *Du Contrat social*, Ch. IV.

9

Is There an Esoteric Doctrine in the *Tractatus Theologico-Politicus?*

THE POSITION OF LEO STRAUSS

That Spinoza wrote with double intent, especially in the *Tractatus Theologico-Politicus*, is an opinion strongly and insistently maintained by Leo Strauss, whose influence upon more sober and unbiassed thinkers seems to me to be excessive. For the view goes beyond, and frequently misrepresents, the evidence, which rightly understood supports more strongly the opposite position. Of course, Strauss is not the first to have held this opinion, for Spinoza was accused in the nineteenth century, by Jacobi and Carl Thomas, even of using the name of God, let alone attributing to him infinite attributes, as an accommodation to the common sentiments of the pious and as a cover to shield his true heterodoxy from the scrutiny and censure of the Church. Why he should have done this in his written works, when his refusal to simulate Jewish orthodoxy had already cost him his membership of the Synagogue, it is difficult to see; unless one is to argue that the consequences of his youthful frankness had taught him caution which dictated duplicity and deviousness in later life. If this were so, however, we should either have to interpret his ethical teaching as hypocritical, or to believe that he failed to practice what he preached.

In the final essay of his book *Persecution and the Art of Writing*, Strauss maintains that there are two distinct teachings in the TTP, and, indeed, in the *Ethics* itself (if not in all Spinoza's writings): an exoteric teaching which appears on the face of the text, and an esoteric one which is addressed to an entirely different audience. The former is what the average, superficial, or unitiated reader would naturally gather from the explicit statement; the latter is what the initiated or the perspicacious student will discover by careful comparison of different passages, by inference from obvious inconsistencies, and by reading judiciously between the lines.

The exoteric teaching, according to Professor Strauss, is used as a cloak to veil the true beliefs of the philosopher, and in Spinoza's case Strauss takes these beliefs to be always theologically heterodox—in fact, atheistic and antireligious. The exoteric doctrine makes apparent concessions to popular opinion and orthodox requirements, while it goes as far as prudence dares to suggest (often by innuendo) a hidden meaning, which contradicts and is to be substituted for the apparent and explicit statement.

The plea is dismissed that what is known of Spinoza's character, even through tributes paid to him by those, like Colerus, who thought his doctrine pernicious, is inconsistent with the kind of dishonesty and prevarication implicit in any such practice as Strauss alleges. Spinoza, we are told, would not have considered it reprehensible to propagate his true beliefs in this disingenuous manner; for, although he says in the *Ethics* that the free man will never act *dolo malo*, "he does not mean that the wise man will never employ any ruses; for he explicitly admits that there are good or legitimate ruses"[1] in several passages of the TTP. Nor did he accuse the biblical writers of duplicity because they wrote *ad captum vulgi*. Moreover, the standard and example had already been set by such distinguished precursors as the philosopher Yehuda Halevi's *Kuzari*, taken as a model by Maimonides and the Arab philosopher Al Farabi. Even Descartes and Bacon among Spinoza's immediate predecessors are said to have behaved in this way and to have advocated a similar practice. This moral judgment on Spinoza, whether it be censure or exoneration, I do not intend to discuss. Our estimate of his character comes largely, though not wholly, from our understanding of his writings, and our assessment of it would be different if we thought they had a *double entendre*, from what it would be if we thought they meant frankly and straightforwardly what Spinoza intended. Had he believed it morally acceptable to insinuate his true beliefs under a mask of appeasive presentation, that in itself would affect our judgment of his integrity.

What I propose to do is to examine Professor Strauss' thesis in the light of the truth or falsity of what Spinoza has written. If what is alleged to be his exoteric doctrine is demonstrably true, there would be no point in his using it as a stalking horse for a hidden teaching which must, in the circumstances, be false. And if we should find that what is alleged to be the esoteric meaning of the text is, after all, not divergent from its exoteric purport, then the whole hypothesis of ambiguous foundation (*"dubbele bodem,"* to quote Dr. den Tex)[2] falls to the ground.

It is improbable that Strauss himself would have admitted the force of any such test of his hypothesis, for he adopts a historical relativism which would not admit of any claim to truth. Spinoza, indeed, he acknowledges, believed that his own teaching was *the* truth and never considered

> the possibility which to us is so obvious: the possibility that the whole orientation of a period may give way to a radically different orientation, and that after such a change has taken place one cannot bridge the gulf between the thought of the later age and that of the earlier age but by means of historical interpretation.[3]

Which of the two alleged doctrines that Spinoza taught he considered *the* truth we can decide by applying rules of interpretation, which, Strauss claims, Spinoza himself provides. But to judge whether indeed it is the truth, or which doctrine objectively considered is to be preferred, would (presumably) be to fall into the error of thinking that the orientation of one's own period was final and must take precedence over, and must be used as a standard to judge, all others.

But if this attitude to truth were correct and justified, could we not convict Dr. Strauss of committing this same error? It is surely merely the orientation of our period that dictates historical relativity, and we have no right to impose that upon other periods in our assessment of the value of their beliefs. In fact, this very doctrine of the sole way to bridge the gulf between one period and another must become suspect, as a merely temporary belief typical of a particular age, and not generally applicable. That the age happens to be the present does not give the belief any special force, for if we adopt it, we must hold that it will in all probability be radically modified in the future. In short, we must recognize relativism of any sort as a form of scepticism—as a denial of any ultimate truth. And the answer to scepticism we have already learned from Spinoza is that the consistent sceptic can but remain silent.[4]

It may, however, unfair to accuse Strauss of taking this relativistic position wholeheartedly, for he does say that the incentive to read and to try to understand Spinoza is "the suspicion that Spinoza's teaching is *the* true teaching."[5] And he does conclude his discussion of the function of historicism and his account of the modern coalescence of history with philosophy, with the judgment:

Historical understanding lost its liberating force by becoming historicism, which is nothing other than the petrified and self-complacent form of the self-criticism of the modern mind.[6]

His main position is that we may not judge Spinoza's claim until we have properly interpreted his teaching, and that interpretation (which must be mainly historical) precedes explanation. Further, he is prepared to adopt, and even advocates, the principles which Spinoza himself lays down for the interpretation of the Scriptures, justifying the application of them to Spinoza's own writings, with Spinoza held were exempt from them, by the historical considerations to which allusion has been made. Why Spinoza exempted his own writings from interpretation, as he maintained we should interpret the Bible, is that the Bible is a hieroglyphic corpus unintelligible scientifically, whereas his own works are philosophical, and their meaning must thus be apparent on their face and from their argument as a product of the natural light of reason. This is Strauss' statement of the matter rather than my own, and I shall seek to qualify it in what follows; but supposing it to be accepted, it has rather different consequences from those that Strauss wishes to draw.

For, if we may adopt Spinoza's own principles of interpretation, we should attend not only to what he writes in TTP but also elsewhere, in TdIE and in the *Ethics*. Then we should extract his meaning solely from his own writings and judge of their validity by their own consistency and coherence. Perhaps in the end we shall be able to say that we know whether they are true, because to have a true idea is to know that it is true, the truth being the standard both of itself and of falsehood.?[7]

Strauss, however, is not wholly consistent on this matter, for first he argues that we need to interpret Spinoza by his own hermeneutic rules for historical reasons (as indicated above), although Spinoza himself asserts that he is writing philosophy for philosophers,[8] and classified philosophical argument with those simple and clear writings (such as Euclid's) which do not require the sort of interpretation he recommends for the Bible. Yet again, Strauss also contends that Spinoza inserted Chapter VII, on biblical interpretation, into the TTP deliberately, as a guide to the interpretation of his own work for the astute and observant reader and a cryptic indication of his own *irony* (or what one might be tempted to call his own insincerity). If that were true, no historical predicament facing the modern reader need be invoked to serve as a pretext for applying Spinoza's rules to his own work against his own explicit directions. On the other hand, if this historical predicament is the real ground for the procedure Strauss adopts, and if its incentive is (as he says) the suspicion that Spinoza's doctrine is *the* truth, it would, to say the least, be disconcerting to find that Spinoza did not mean what he professes, or meant only some statements, or only their implications, to be taken seriously. Moreover, if this really were the case, we could hardly treat the arguments by which Spinoza supports his position with respect, nor regard them as cogent. But that again is virtually what Strauss asserts, for he maintains that Spinoza contradicts himself in numerous respects, so that his book is well-nigh unintelligible. If Strauss ever suspected that Spinoza's teaching was *the* truth, this essay indicates that he has been disillusioned, and, if we have a similar suspicion, agreement with Strauss would go far to dispel it. But in that case we should hardly be inclined to adopt Spinoza's recommended rules of interpretation, whether of the Scriptures or of his own works.

SPINOZA ON BIBLICAL INTERPRETATION

To make anything of Strauss' thesis, and to judge either its soundness or Spinoza's sincerity and credibility, we must begin by considering just what Spinoza does write about biblical interpretation. The right method of interpreting the Scriptures, he tells us, differs little from that of interpreting nature, that is, it proceeds by first deducing definitions of terms and subjects from their histories, as from certain data (*ex certis datis*). Just as we gather from the facts of natural phenomena what natural objects are and how to define them, so we should gather from the actual statements of the biblical writers how we should define the subjects of which they write and the meaning of their terms. Spinoza's primary precept is that the Scriptures themselves and alone should be the source of evidence for our interpretation of them, and we should not import into them philosophical opinions that cannot be derived from their own pronouncements. The legitimate evidence, however, includes the history of the writings and of their authors, and we mistake Spinoza's intention if we understand this primary precept (as Strauss persistently does) to mean that the only admissible evidence must be derived from the written text. Strauss, however, accuses Spinoza of inconsistency because he admits evidence extraneous to the Bible in order to determine the character and intention of the biblical writers, or the circumstances and language in which they wrote.[9] This is clearly either misrepresentation or misunderstanding of Spinoza's hermeneutical method, for Spinoza's actual words are:

> ... si nimirum nulla alia principia, neque data ad interpretandam Scripturam et de rebus, quae in eadem continentur, disserendum,

admiserit, nisi ea tantumodo, quae ex ipsa Scriptura *ejusque historia* depromuntur...

[... if indeed no other principles should be admitted for the interpretation of the Scripture, nor data for examining the matters contained in it, except those which are produced from the Scripture itself *and its history*... (my emphasis)][10]

For this purpose we need knowledge under three heads: (1) the nature and properties of the language (namely Hebrew) in which the Scriptures were written (the New Testament, he says, although published in Greek, was written by Hebrews who "hebraize" in their expression); (2) an analysis and systematic arrangement of subjects treated in each book, giving correlation and synoptic comparison of passages treating of like matters; (3) the history of the books; the circumstances in which they were written; to whom they were addressed and for what purpose; who their actual authors were, their temperaments, opinions, and beliefs; in what language they were written and whether the writings as we have them are translations; what happened to them, whether and by whose hand additions or alterations may have been made, and by whom they were selected for inclusion in the canon.[11]

Next, Spinoza insists, the object of our interpretation is to discover the intended meaning, *not the truth,* of the Scriptures; and for this the only legitimate evidence is what the scriptural writers themselves say, understood in the light of their history.

Spinoza freely admits that much of the requisite evidence has been irretrievably lost and that we lack much of the knowledge necessary for adequate and reliable interpretation of many parts of the Bible; so that frequently we can only guess or suspend judgment concerning their intended meaning.[12]

None of this would be rejected today by any sound biblical scholar, quite irrespective of his belief about the sanctity and divinely inspired nature of the Scripture. What in it is authentic could be determined only by applying methods and principles such as Spinoza advocates, and what is chiefly remarkable about them is that they are here enunciated in a work written at least a century before they became generally recognized as the basis of biblical scholarship and criticism.

It is important to understand precisely why Spinoza considered it necessary to use the method which he prescribes to interpret the Bible; and, as we shall see, this is not understood, nor fully appreciated, by Strauss. In the first place, a large part of the Bible is history and only incidentally "theology." It must therefore be treated as a historical document and must be interpreted by scientific historical methods.

Spinoza is perhaps the first thinker to develop and elucidate such a method, for his principles are an advance upon any contemporary writer, even including Giambattista Vico. His insight anticipates modern writers like Collingwood and Marc Bloch, who have scarcely improved upon it. But what is perhaps still more important for Spinoza's purpose, in the second place, is that the Bible makes certain theological statements about God and his relation to nature and to man, and these are not scientifically demonstrated or, with some exceptions, philosophically argued, but are presented in the form of prophecy; and that as literally stated is not straightforwardly intelligible by the natural light of reason. It therefore requires interpretation in the way that Spinoza recommends. He frequently says that it surpasses the human understanding:

> ... Scripture very often treats of matters which cannot be deduced from principles known by the natural light; for part of it is composed of histories and revelations: and the histories especially contain miracles, that is (as we have shown in the last chapter) narrations of things of unusual character, adapted to the opinions and judgments of those who have written them; but the revelations are also accommodated to the opinions of the prophets ... and indeed they themselves surpass human understanding.[13]

What Spinoza meant by this is a matter of consequence yet is subject to some dispute. He could mean that the biblical revelations surpass the capacity of human reason in principle, but that is very improbable for reasons shortly to emerge. He could mean, on the other hand, that they surpass the intellectual capacity of the historians who recorded them or even of the prophets themselves who expounded them; and there is much to support this interpretation. He might also mean, not only this, but that with the knowledge at our disposal we cannot give a rational explanation of the matters reported. Or, finally, he may mean that what the prophets say and some of the events the historians relate are, as they recount them, scientifically unintelligible. It is for this reason that the Scriptures are described as "hieroglyphical" as is apparent from Spinoza's remark that difficulties of interpretation arise

> when we try to follow the meaning (*mentem*) of the prophets about things which are inconceivable (*imperceptibiles*) and which are only imagined,

and from his note to this passage:[14]

> Otherwise hieroglyphics and narratives which seems to exceed all belief I call inconceivable (*imperceptibiles*).

Strauss assumes only the first of these possible meanings of Spinoza's phrase and never seems so much as to consider the others. Yet it is the least plausible in the light of what Spinoza has written elsewhere and of his general philosophical position. Strauss maintains that the position is inconsistent, but his grounds for doing so depend to a significant extent on this interpretation of *captum humanum superare*, for he asserts that the TTP is a hieroglyphic document, in need of interpretation by Spinoza's own prescribed method because of its internal contradictions, of which the chief and most persistent is Spinoza's claim that the Bible and its prophecies surpass human understanding, while at the same time Spinoza holds and asserts that there can be no such thing as supernatural knowledge. If, however, Strauss is wrong in his reading of *captum humanum superare*, Spinoza may well be consistent, and if he is, the whole of Strauss' thesis collapses.

We must note further that the criterion adopted by Strauss for classifying the TTP as hieroglyphical is not that offered by Spinoza. It is not because there are contradictions in the Bible that it "exceeds all belief." In fact, Spinoza maintains that the Bible in its chief and only essential doctrine is wholly consistent and perfectly clear. What are hieroglyphical are certain *historiae*, because they are incredible, or incomprehensible scientifically, or both. And these, he contends, may well be false without affecting the validity or the sanctity of the central doctrine.

Alleged Contradictions

We may now turn to Strauss' main theses. They are that because the TTP is hieroglyphical, it requires interpretation, and that it is hieroglyphical, or unintelligible as written, because it is full of contradictions; that the key to its interpretation is the method Spinoza himself advocates, the deliberate purpose of which is to direct the wary reader and apprise him or her of the true meaning of the doctrine. At the same time, what Spinoza says of the prophets and prophecy is to be taken as equally applicable to his own writing.

The contradictions are as follows:

(1) The TTP begins and ends with the implicit assertion that prophecy, or revelation, is in fact possible, and defines it as certain knowledge of truths which surpass the capacity of human reason.[15] Strauss gives numerous references to support this statement, but the support they give to it is dubious. It is unclear on what evidence he says that the TTP ends with any such implicit assertion, and the statement with which it begins is certainly very different. However, it would be excessive and

tedious to comment on every reference given by Strauss, who seems to operate on the assumption that scholarship consists in listing numerous passages without due regard to their relevance or appropriateness. I shall therefore confine myself to those instances where the references are germane to the argument, whether favorable or otherwise, and only to the more important of them. The assertion, says Strauss, is repeated, explicitly or implicitly, in a number of places throughout the book. Yet in other contexts Spinoza denies the possibility of any supra-rational knowledge. This, moreover, is the central topic of the work, and on it Spinoza contradicts himself. A sincere believer in the possibility of supra-rational knowledge, says Strauss, would not declare, as Spinoza does, that man has no access whatever to truth except through sense-perception and reasoning, that reason alone, as distinct from revelation and theology, justly claims and possesses truth, that belief in what cannot be demonstrated by reason is absurd, and that teachings claiming to be "above reason" are dreams and fictions "far below reason." Where and whether Spinoza says these things I shall consider presently.

(2) Spinoza asserts that theology (or faith) and philosophy are radically separate. The first aims only at obedience, the second only at truth. He also maintains that theology rests on the fundamental dogma that obedience without knowledge suffices for salvation and that this is a supra-rational truth. But he also asserts that supra-rational truth is impossible. It should follow that theology and philosophy contradict one another and are not (as Spinoza maintains) in perfect accord.[16]

(3) Theology, or the Bible, or prophecy, so Spinoza is said to maintain, is not authoritative regarding speculative matters. But he also asserts that with regard to some speculative matters, e.g., divine providence, it is in agreement with philosophy. Yet again it is not, because only philosophy and not the Bible teaches that God cares equally for all men, meting out the same fate to the just and the unjust (in other words, that there is no divine providence at all).

(4) For Spinoza the Bible and prophecy are virtually synonymous, and he asserts that the Bible is the sole source of our knowledge of prophecy. Yet he also argues that pagan augurers and soothsayers were true prophets.[17]

(5) Spinoza avers that the mind of Christ was superhuman and is prepared to acknowledge that in him divine wisdom assumed human form. Yet again he denies the possibility of supernatural phenomena since the laws of nature, particularly human nature, are never violated and are always the same.[18] In effect, the doctrine is that Jesus was the greatest of all philosophers, a view corroborated by what is said elsewhere in the TTP. But if this were true it would conflict with the main

contention that philosophy and theology (the Bible) are radically separate. In fact, Spinoza also praises Solomon as a philosopher (despite his ignorance of mathematics). Yet, again, he asserts that the Bible teaches only "simple things" and not "philosophic things."[19]

(6) Ostensibly the TTP demonstrates that there is one fundamental moral teaching throughout the Bible, in the Old and New Testaments alike; yet Spinoza admits, while he explains away, the difference between the Mosaic injunction "hate thine enemy" and the exhortation of Jesus to "love thine enemy."

(7) Spinoza's arguments concerning Christ and Christianity are in fact complex and devious. In contrast with what is said above, he implies that Jesus' teaching, like Solomon's, was only popular wisdom and rational morality, and yet that it was more than that (being the immediate revelation of the mind of God). He also implies that both Old and New Testaments present moral precepts as commands of God (as a ruler and judge)—and so conflict with philosophical demonstration. They also teach that God is merciful in contradiction to philosophical teaching. It would follow that the New Testament is not more rational than the Old, and the apostles in their belief in the resurrection were under the spell of popular prejudices (Epp 75, 77). Yet, as argued earlier, the New Testament is held to teach a universal doctrine in agreement with philosophy including the views of many of the Ancients.[20]

(8) The TTP argues that the Bible teaches a simple doctrine and that, throughout, if we understand its language and interpret it by the right method, it is easily intelligible. Yet it is also maintained that the Bible is hieroglyphical. In his letters Spinoza admits that he does not understand the Bible, which implies that it is rich in mysteries and supra-rational illumination, but this he also denies, and, in any case, it runs counter to the meaning and purpose of the TTP, which contends that no supra-rational knowledge is necessary for biblical interpretation (nor, in fact, possible).[21]

Consequently Strauss considers it necessary and permissible to use Spinoza's own hermeneutics in order to interpret the TTP. Spinoza maintains that the prophets adapted their message to the opinions and understanding of their audience,[22] and in the TdIE the first rule of conduct he prescribes is *ad captum vulgi loqui* ("to speak in accordance with the capacity of the vulgar"). We may assume then, Strauss holds, that Spinoza himself speaks in this way. He believed that it was the philosopher's duty to observe caution and to conceal the truth if it endangers piety.[23] His private motto, inscribed upon his signet, was *Caute* ("Be careful"). Accordingly, Strauss avers, Spinoza purposely al-

ternates between orthodoxy and heterodoxy. In each chapter he re-
futes some orthodox doctrine while he supports or allows the rest.
The intention is that the lay reader will not add up the refutations
and so will not convict Spinoza of atheism, while the perspicacious
will see that Spinoza's real aim is to deny the supernatural, under-
mine the authority of the Bible, and repudiate the need for religion
(which, as Strauss has maintained elsewhere,[24] Spinoza identified with
superstition). By this device Spinoza reveals his serious views to the
attentive reader, while he conceals them from the vulgar. He

> addresses potential philosophers while the vulgar are listening. He
> speaks therefore in such a way that the vulgar will not understand
> what he means. It is for this reason that he expresses himself con-
> tradictorily: those shocked by his heterodox statements will be ap-
> peased by more or less orthodox formulae.[25]

SUPERNATURAL KNOWLEDGE

The primary premiss upon which Strauss rests his case is the bewilder-
ing (or hieroglyphic) character of Spinoza's treatise consequent upon
its numerous contradictions, and almost all of these depend upon the
key question whether or not, in Spinoza's view, supernatural knowledge is possible; for if it is not, he cannot consistently allow exceptions in the case of prophecy, the mind of Jesus, or the fundamental
dogma of theology; nor should he allege that the Bible is hieroglyphical as surpassing the grasp of human reason. We must, therefore, consider first what Spinoza meant by *captum humanum superare.*

If supernatural knowledge is taken to mean knowledge involving
contravention of the laws of nature, Spinoza leaves us in no doubt
that he rejects its possibility. The laws of nature are universal, eternal
and inviolable, and nothing can exist or occur that is not in accordance with them. But this, he maintains, is because the laws of nature
are the laws of God, who does not and cannot contradict himself. It
does not, therefore, follow from the denial of supernatural knowledge,
in this sense, that no legitimate meaning can be given to divine inspiration. In fact, Spinoza regards all natural (philosophical) knowledge
as divine, so far at the very least as it is knowledge of the third kind,
scientia intuitiva, for that consists of adequate knowledge of individual
things derived from adequate ideas of God's attributes—that is, ideas
as they are in the divine intellect. So he says in Chapter 1 of TTP:

> For those things which we know by the natural light, depend
> solely on the knowledge of God and his eternal decrees; but ordi-

nary knowledge is common to all men as men, and rests on foundations which all share. . . . Yet nevertheless by equal right with other
knowledge, whatever that may be, it can be called divine, for God's
nature, in so far as we share in it, and God's laws, dictate it to us . . .

Natural knowledge, then, is not improperly described as *rei alicujus
certa cognitio a Deo hominibus revelata* ("the certain knowledge of some
things revealed by God to men"). But this is the definition of prophecy with which the TTP opens, and Spinoza does say almost at once
that from this definition it follows that natural knowledge could rightly
be called prophecy, and it is only the vulgar preference for the un-
usual that excludes it from the common connotation of that term.

The difference between natural, or philosophical, knowledge (what
we know by "the natural light") and what is commonly called prophecy is not the source of the revelation but the medium. The source of
both (as of all truth) is the divine intellect; but whereas rational knowledge is revealed to human beings through the intellect, prophecy is
revealed to the prophet through his (or her) imagination.

The pertinent question of consistency that Strauss never raises is
how it is possible for *certa cognitio* to be revealed through the imagination; for Spinoza has said in the *Ethics* that *imaginatio* is the sole source
of error (E2P41). He does not say, however, that it necessarily gives
rise to falsehood; on the contrary, he allows that the mind does not
err because it imagines, but only insofar as it lacks ideas of what excludes the existence of things imagined to be present. Error and imagination are not, therefore, identical nor even coincident, for in its
positive content *imaginatio* is not false;[26] so the possibility of the revelation of truth through its means is left open.

In the TTP Spinoza asserts that this does in fact occur. Is he then
committing himself to the admission of supernatural knowledge? Certainly
not in the sense in which he denies it (as contravening natural laws),
for he says that prophecy is a special gift enjoyed by some persons.[27] It
is a gift of the same general kind as the gift of poetry, or music, or
any other artistic talent. We do not regard these as supernatural, although
we frequently describe them as inspired. Yet we cannot explain them
psychologically, that is, on rational scientific principles, not because
they are in principle inexplicable, but simply because of our lack of
knowledge. In *this* sense, *limites nostri intellectus excedunt* (they exceed
the limits of our understanding). Likewise prophecy is a special gift,
for which, Spinoza admits, we can give no explanation (except to say
that God is its cause, which is no explanation, because God is the
cause of everything).[28]

Spinoza, certainly, in several places does say that what is revealed to the prophet through his imagination exceeds the limits of the intellect,[29] or surpasses human apprehension, and what exactly he means by these phrases is not immediately obvious. It is well-nigh impossible that he means by them what his principles exclude—namely, that prophecy is the revelation of what in principle is inaccessible to reason. He says:

> I go on to treat more fully the other causes and media by which God reveals to men those things which exceed the limits of natural knowledge, and also those which do not exceed them (for nothing prevents God from communicating to men by other means those things which we know by the light of nature).[30]

First, this statement strongly suggests that Spinoza considers the contents of prophecy to be *the same things* as we know by the light of nature, a suggestion confirmed by his later contention that the central revelation of prophecy is a moral truth to which we are also led by reason. Secondly, "the limits of natural knowledge" cannot mean here the limits of the intellect as such, for the intellect as such is strictly God's intellect, and so far as, in *scientia intuitiva*, the human intellect coincides with God's, nothing revealed "by other means" can surpass it.

Rebus limites nostri intellectus excedentibus, concerning which we must consult the Scriptures, are such things as we cannot deduce from first principles because they are either historical or such as lie beyond the scientific and empirical evidence at our disposal. Among the latter are future events, the prediction of which, although in principle not impossible by reason if our knowledge of all the relevant facts were sufficient, is nevertheless not deducible because we rarely if ever do know sufficient beforehand. Yet matters such as these may be revealed to prophets through dreams, or visions, or other imaginative means. If there is such a phenomenon as extrasensory perception, we cannot with our present knowledge explain it rationally, but it does not follow that it is supernatural in the sense excluded by Spinoza.

Spinoza, in fact, makes it quite clear that he does not regard prophecy as supernatural knowledge, for he explicitly states in the opening chapter of the TTP:

> With respect to the certainty it involves, and the source from which it is derived (that is, God), ordinary knowledge is by no means inferior to prophetic, unless indeed we believe, or rather dream, that the prophets had human bodies, but superhuman minds, and that therefore their sensations and consciousness were entirely different from our own.

In the instances in which prophets have extraordinary imaginative experiences that reveal to them matters which neither they nor we could have deduced from first principles, the revelation, of course, exceeds the capacity of the intellect of the prophet himself to whom it is made; and in most contexts where Spinoza uses such phrases as *captum intellectus superare* this seems to have been uppermost in his mind, for he is emphatic in his declaration that the prophets were not learned, or wise, or intellectually outstanding. Some were soldiers, some politicians, some craftsmen, others were simple rustics, or even servants, but they were not scholars, scientists, nor philosophers.

Not merely was the prophets' intellectual capacity surpassed by the revelations they received, however, but the revelations were of matters which are not susceptible of demonstration *geometrico ordine*, and if they are to be made intelligible they must be interpreted by a different method. That this is what Spinoza has in mind is born out by what he says in Chapter 7 in the passage already quoted:

> But that it may be clearly established that this way of interpreting is not only certain, but also the only way, and that it agrees with the method of interpreting nature, it is to be observed that Scripture most frequently deals with matters that cannot be deduced from principles known by the natural light, for the greatest part of them consists of histories and revelations: and the histories for the most part contain miracles, that is (as we have shown in the previous chapter), stories of events of unusual character accommodated to the views and opinions of the historians who wrote them.

It is hardly likely that Spinoza would have aligned his method of interpreting the Bible with that of interpreting nature had he believed that the matter to be interpreted was supernatural. But historical events and extraordinary occurrences recorded unscientifically by unlearned chroniclers cannot be deduced from first principles and must be understood by other methods. The one recommended by Spinoza is the method of scientific history, as it has been set out in our own day by such writers as R. G. Collingwood, E. H. Carr, and Marc Bloch, whom Spinoza anticipates by three centuries.

A further reason for the necessity of interpretation by a systematic hermeneutic is that prophecies are "hieroglyphical." Strauss invariably understands this word to imply an incomprehensibility by the natural intellect that implies a supra-rational source. But this is not at all what the contexts in which it is used require. "*Repraesentationes propheticae, et hieroglyphica, quamvis idem significarent, variabat tamen . . .*" writes Spinoza,[31] and he follows with examples of various visions and images in which the prophets Ezekiel and Isaiah express their prophecies. *Hieroglyphica*

here obviously means symbols or imagery. We do not regard the meta-
phors of poetry as supernatural, sublime and transcendent though they
may be. They are the creatures of the imagination, and so likewise,
according to Spinoza's teaching, are the prophetic visions of the Scriptures. Hence they require interpretation; and Spinoza means no more
than this in the passages to which attention has been drawn above.

It is for the same reason that the prophets "could perceive many
things beyond the limits of the intellect." They did so with the aid of
the imagination, which is far more prolific in ideas than the intellect,
if only because it does not recognize the same restraints, "for from
words and images far more ideas can be put together, than from those
principles and concepts only on which the whole of our natural
knowledge is founded."[32] Clearly, then, a prophet can imagine much
that he cannot understand, although it may well be true; and we can
understand it (if at all) only by interpreting it historically on the evidence
of what the prophet actually said and in the light of the circumstances
in which he said it.

We can see now why Spinoza could say quite truthfully and consistently in his letter to van Blyenburgh[33] that he does not understand
the Holy Scripture. For so far as it reports visions and images, and
teaches *parabolice et aenigmatice*, it is opaque to the understanding. But
he also consistently maintains that these hieroglyphical portions of the
Bible, as well as the speculative views expressed by its writers, are not
germane nor relevant to its universal teaching. They vary in character
and import from one writer to another.[34] But there is one central and
universal doctrine that appears throughout, from the Pentateuch to
the New Testament: that salvation depends upon love of God and one's
neighbor. In effect, Spinoza maintains that in these two precepts are
contained all the law and the prophets. It is this doctrine which is
divine and this doctrine alone that makes the Scripture sacred. This,
moreover, is taught straightforwardly and simply and is comprehensi-
ble equally to the learned and to the ignorant.[35] There is therefore no
conflict between Spinoza's assertions, on the one hand, that the Scriptures are (or contain) hieroglyphical writings which surpass the limits
of the intellect and which he does not himself understand, and, on
the other, his claim that the central and only essential teaching of the
Bible is simple and intelligible to all.

This central doctrine is, moreover, true, for it accords with the dictates of reason as demonstrated in the fourth part of the *Ethics*. There
is only one feature of the biblical doctrine that here diverges from the
rational. The prophets and evangelists teach that obedience to the
precepts to love God and one's neighbor is sufficient for salvation *without*

knowledge, whereas reason deduces it as a conclusion from first principles and finds salvation precisely in knowledge—in the *amor intellectualis
Dei.* We cannot elicit from first principles that obedience without understanding effects salvation and this has to be accepted on faith as an
act of divine grace.[36] Is Spinoza inconsistent in this account of the
nature of faith?

The notion of divine grace is an imaginative idea, picturing God as
a ruler dispensing salvation as a reward for obedience; and the pious
who believe in the doctrine of grace observe the precepts to love God
and their neighbors. The rational conception of salvation is the blessedness, the peace of mind, that supervenes upon the true knowledge of
God and his attributes and accompanies the free action that such
knowledge occasions. The conduct is the same in both cases (for behavior
prompted by passion may coincide with genuine action),[37] and so likewise is the peace of mind. Further, very few are capable of acquiring
virtue purely under the unaided guidance of reason, so that, apart
from faith, salvation would be beyond the reach of the vast majority.[38]
Accordingly, although nobody has ever succeeded in proving by reason that salvation can be achieved simply by obedience and faith in
God's grace, we may be *morally* certain, as were the prophets, in the
truth of their message.[39] This moral certainty, however, is anything
but supernatural cognition. It is not in conflict with reason, for even
though the imaginative idea were false, its truth or falsity is irrelevant
to its moral effect, and that coincides with the moral effect or practical expression of reason. No contradiction, therefore, is involved in
Spinoza's exposition of this matter.

Another important issue, not unconnected with what we have so far
discussed, is Spinoza's view about Christ and his attitude to Christianity. To this we must next turn our attention. We now see what Spinoza
means, and to what he is referring, when he speaks of that which is
not contained in or deducible from the foundations of our natural
knowledge. It is no supernatural cognition but is a belief the purport
of which is not absurd, and of which we can be morally certain, although we cannot deduce it from first principles—namely, the belief
that salvation is attainable, not only through comprehension of God's
divine nature and the love and blessedness that that entails, but also
through faith and devotion to moral principles prompted by the imagination. The first is revealed to man immediately in *scientia intuitiva*
(which, in principle, has as much right to be called prophecy as any
other form of cognition). The second is revealed through *hieroglyphica*
in the pronouncements of the prophets, to whom it was imparted by
way of the imagination. The one exception, as appears from the Gos-

pel record, is Jesus, who was immediately aware of the truths of faith without the intermediation of visions or signs. Thus, *sola mente*, he perceived what is not contained in the first principles of natural knowledge nor can be deduced from them.[40] Such a mind, says Spinoza, is superior to, and far more excellent than, human.[41] Accordingly, we may say that in Jesus the wisdom of God assumed human form. Spinoza's statement here is precisely in agreement with what he writes to Oldenburg in Ep 73:

> ... it is not entirely necessary for salvation to know Christ according to the flesh; but we must think far otherwise of the eternal son of God,[42] that is the eternal wisdom of God, which has manifested itself in all things, especially in the human mind, and most of all in Christ Jesus.

There is no more admission here of supernatural knowledge than in the case of what is known by the natural light, of which Spinoza says likewise that

> we may clearly understand that God can reveal (*communicare*) himself to men immediately, for he communicates his essence to our minds using no corporeal media.[43]

Nor does it necessarily follow that Jesus must have been the greatest of all philosophers, for what was directly revealed to and in him was the truth of faith, which is not philosophically demonstrable.

REFUTATION OF STRAUSS

Enough has now been said to demolish the central pillar of Strauss' argument. There is no contradiction in the TTP on the issue of the possibility of supernatural knowledge. What "surpasses the capacity of the intellect" is the deduction of historical fact and the demonstration of the truth of what is expressed in symbols and imaginative visions. No supernatural knowledge is involved in faith nor even in its direct revelation in the mind of Christ—except, of course, in the sense that all knowledge of truth, whether by reason or by faith, may be called divine revelation.

With the removal of this contradiction most of the others that Strauss claims to detect disappear:

(1) Spinoza nowhere says that man has no access to truth except through sense-perception and reasoning. Sense-perception he includes under *imaginatio*, and, as has been shown, while that is the sole source of error, it can also be the medium of revelation. He does not say that

whatever cannot be demonstrated by reason, only that whatever is contrary to reason, is absurd.[44] And he castigates what *claims* to be above
reason as "far below reason" only on the demerits of the doctrines
which make the claim.[45]

(2) In his assertion that theology and philosophy are separate and
have no mutual interconnection (*commercium*),[46] as is now fully apparent, Spinoza is wholly consistent. Strauss confuses the issue by using
"theology," "the Bible," "prophecy," and "faith" as interchangeable.
Spinoza himself frequently substitutes the first for the third and the
last, but, as I shall presently show, he does not use "the Scripture" as
synonymous with "prophecy." At all events, what theology is concerned
with in his view is obedience and piety, which depend on faith, and
that (we have seen) is not a philosophically demonstrable doctrine.
Philosophy is concerned solely with truth and the perfection of the
intellect. Its practical concomitant coincides with that of faith; but neither
can theology dictate its conclusions to philosophy, nor can philosophy
prescribe the requirements or the effects of faith.

(3) Spinoza certainly denies that the prophets (not the Bible) are
authoritative in speculative matters. They are not scientists or learned
men. But some of their pronouncements agree with the conclusions
of reason. Moreover, it is only reason, in the last resort, that can judge
of their authority in matters of faith. For if they teach an immoral
doctrine their prophecy is to be declared spurious. It is only reason
that can judge of the genuineness of prophecy, even though it cannot
prove the fundamental thesis of faith.

(4) Spinoza does not say that the Bible is the sole source of prophecy but only that it is all the evidence that remains to us of the nature
of prophecy.[47]

(5) We have seen that Spinoza's opinion about Christ is in keeping
with his philosophical position. He alleges no violation of the laws of
nature, either in this connection or in the case of prophecy generally.
For what in fact we cannot in practice explain scientifically does not
necessarily violate the laws of nature in principle. As there is no necessary implication that Jesus was the greatest of philosophers, the rest
of Strauss' objection falls away; but even if there were, it would not
involve Spinoza in any contradiction. He does not equate the Bible
with theology and admits that some of the Scriptures are philosophical—
Proverbs. Ecclesiastes and the Wisdom of Solomon, for instance.[48] The
separation of theology from philosophy occurs in the Bible itself, and
it is only the commentators who confuse the two.[49]

(6) The moral teaching which is pervasive throughout the Scriptures, Old Testament and New, is indisputably the paramount precept

to love God and thy neighbor. This is Spinoza's contention, and it is true. The quibbles concerning it indulged in by Strauss are therefore futile.

(7) The alleged confusions about Christ and Christianity we have already dispelled. Spinoza's remarks to Oldenburg in Epp 75 and 78 are to the effect that the disciples' main teaching would not be vitiated even had they been mistaken in their (admittedly sincere) beliefs about the resurrection of Jesus, as the errors of so many other prophets on speculative matters do not affect the validity of their fundamental message. Again, Spinoza's consistency is fully maintained.

(8) The simple doctrine that the Bible teaches is now plain. That is not hierogyphical, and it is discernible by the use of the method of historical interpretation prescribed for the reasons given. What is hieroglyphical mostly concerns speculative matters which Spinoza says are more curious than useful.[50]

IF NOT SPINOZA, WHAT PRICE STRAUSS?

As Spinoza's theory turns out to be consistent throughout, there can be no pretext for seeking a second and hidden doctrine beyond that which is expressly stated. And if the exoteric theses are true, there could be no reason for Spinoza to insinuate another doctrine for more perspicacious readers to winkle out. And Spinoza's assertions about the Bible are true. Its moral teaching from beginning to end is substantially one, even if in the course of its development its emphases change in detail. The distinction Spinoza makes between divine law and ceremonial law has a sound basis in the text, and the exhortation of the later prophets to the genuine practice of righteousness in preference to sacrifices and ceremonies is obvious and widely recognized. That the New Testament develops this same theme further is beyond controversy. Again, the prophets were the sort of people Spinoza says they were. Their message was revealed to them as Spinoza alleges, through the imagination in symbolic forms, and is expressed in poetic language. They were not learned persons, and their beliefs about nature were for the most part false. Yet, for all that, their spiritual and moral teaching is clear and unassailable.

The Bible, moreover, is for the most part historical, and even its prophetic and moral teachings are conveyed through historical narrative. To be understood properly, therefore, it requires interpretation by historical methods, whether or not we believe it to be divinely inspired, and in order to establish whether and in what sense it was so inspired. The method of interpretation set out by Spinoza is, by and large, that which has quite independently come to be recognized by competent historians as appropriate to their subject. There are, then, no grounds to suggest that Spinoza inserted the seventh chapter into the TTP as a cryptic guide to the interpretation of his own writing.

In these circumstances, why should a commentator make any such allegation? If Spinoza's main theses are patently correct, the representation of them as cosmetic to appease vulgar prejudices and to disguise a hidden and more unorthodox opinion would appear to spring from a somewhat perverse interpretation prompted by some ulterior motive.

Strauss persistently contends that Spinoza adopted his own rule, as enunciated in the TdIE: *ad captum vulgi loqui*. But it is first to be noted that the rule is stated there only as a temporary practical precept to be observed until the correct method of discovering the truth has been found. Secondly, *ad captum vulgi loqui* in no sense means that one should deceive people, or hide the truth from them. On the contrary, its meaning is (and it is always used by Spinoza in this sense) that one should express the truth in such language and by such means as the vulgar can understand. For instance, if one wants to persuade the masses that they should act justly and be charitable, it would be futile to recite to them geometrical proofs that such conduct is in their best interests. It would be far more effective to teach them that God, an almighty judge and ruler of the world, commands the practice of justice and mercy and will reward men accordingly.

It is far from plausible to suggest that Spinoza intended this precept, in accordance with his motto "*Caute*," to mean "be careful to conceal truth that might be dangerous." He did insist on care in two respects: the first is not to advertise arguments to those who are likely to misunderstand and misrepresent them, and the second is to exercise great caution in developing one's own position, so as to argue always validly and fall into no inadvertent error. Thus he writes:

> Indeed . . . to deduce things solely from intellectual concepts most often requires long chains of insights (*perceptionum*), and, besides, the greatest caution, penetration of mind (*ingenii*), and the highest self-restraint (*continentia*).[51]

"Caute," therefore, as likely as not, refers to meticulousness and care in reasoning aright rather than to any craven concealment of beliefs one holds to be true lest they prove socially or politically dangerous.

It is Strauss then, rather than Spinoza, whose argument is marred by inconsistencies, inaccuracies, and misrepresentations. He alleges that Spinoza wrote *ad captum vulgi*, yet acknowledges that in the preface to the TTP the vulgar are urged to leave the book alone and not to read it because it is intended only for philosophers.[52] This, says Strauss, is not sincerely meant, because Spinoza says in the same context that he writes for those who would philosophize more if only they did not believe that reason must be subordinated to theology; so, in fact, Spinoza wrote for "potential philosophers while the vulgar listened"—for he knew that all educated people of his time could read Latin.[53] Yet again, Strauss says that Spinoza did not write for his contemporaries but for posterity.[54] Strauss asserts also that Spinoza despised the ancients and respected only contemporary writers, but admits that he admired Lucretius, Epicurus, and Democritus, and quotes Cicero with approval.[55] Again, Strauss acknowledges in one place that Spinoza considered his own writings clear and intelligible, in no need of historical interpretation,[56] yet he also implies that Spinoza deliberately inserted his hermeneutical instructions to enable the wary to interpret his own writings.[57] Strauss argues that Spinoza denied the possibility of miracles and would make no concessions on this point, but he allowed the supra-rational character of prophecy (to placate the vulgar) while maintaining that it was a natural phenomenon. No such doctrine, however, would make sense, for if the only natural knowledge is rational, supra-rational knowledge must be supernatural. One cannot say in defense of Strauss that the incoherence was Spinoza's, for I have shown that it is not; so this muddle is either Strauss' misunderstanding or a deliberate confusion of the issue.

With respect to miracles Strauss is undoubtedly right in his assertion that Spinoza refused to compromise. His firm doctrine is that the laws of nature are God's eternal decrees which cannot be and never are violated. For God to transgress his own laws would be for him to contradict himself, which his perfection interdicts. But Spinoza does not deny that miracles occurred and are recorded in the Scriptures. What he denies is that the miraculous events were violations of natural law. By the biblical writers they are ascribed directly to God and represented as his action, but (Spinoza explains) it is a persistent Hebrew custom to ascribe all things directly to God's will—and indeed God is the cause of all things. Further, the biblical writers were not scientists, and their object was not to explain the events they described. Nor were their descriptions always accurate, but were often based on hearsay and embellished by imaginative accretions.

Moreover, he points out, the Bible nowhere teaches that the miraculous events violated natural law, but, on the contrary, expressly states that the decrees of God are eternal. In many cases the natural causes are actually recorded. The Red Sea, we are told, parted because God blew with his wind; and Saul came to Samuel in search of his father's asses. In other cases we know what the natural causes were— of the rainbow, given as a sign to Noah, the cause was the refraction of the sun's rays—and in yet others we can imagine and hypothesize probable causes.

It is misleading, therefore, to say as Strauss does that Spinoza denied the occurrence of "miracles proper," and quite wrong to accuse him of inconsistency in departing from his own hermeneutical rules in Chapter VI of the TTP. Spinoza openly explains that here he is dealing with a philosophical, and not merely a historical, issue. Even so, he does observe his own interpretive method in quoting what the Bible actually says and in explaining the writers' forms of expression and narration on historical grounds.

It would be tedious to extend the list of inconsistencies and inaccuracies in Strauss' argument, although it would not be difficult to do so. It would be possible also to show that among his numerous references some, so far from supporting his argument, run counter to it. One example is his attempt to confirm his assertion that Spinoza thought deceptive ruses to be justifiable. He refers here to the passage in the TTP (Chapter XVI)[58] where Spinoza actually writes that nobody can promise to forego his right over absolutely everything without dishonesty, which does not mean that we may legitimately make such a deceptive promise, but that if we did we should be disingenuous. The explanatory note asserts that while deception in the civil state may be classified as good or bad because the law provides a criterion (note that this is the civil law, not the moral law), no such distinction is possible in the state of nature. These references give no support to the view that Spinoza believed deliberate deception to be justifiable, but rather the reverse. E4P72, which is listed by Strauss in the same footnote, is a flat and emphatic denial of the thesis maintained, a denial that is driven home by Spinoza in the Scholium, where he argues that it would be absurd to try to justify breach of faith even under the threat of instant death. I shall not weary the reader with a longer enumeration of similar incongruities, for we already have sufficient before us to cripple the case Strauss has tried to make out.

Our conclusion should be, if we were to accept Strauss' argument, that his essay is hieroglyphical and needs interpretation in the way he supposed Spinoza to be insinuating. We should, if we took his advice, conclude that he, Strauss, is writing *ad captum vulgi*, and that the astute and wary will discover behind his exoteric doctrine another which he really intends to convey. The esoteric argument is that Spinoza was truly an atheist, trying to justify his defection from Judaism by specious arguments[59] and to discredit traditional and orthodox Jewish theology, while at the same time undermining the authority of the Bible. The insinuation is also made that Spinoza's favorable comments about Christianity are insincere and insupportable, while his professed lack of comprehension coupled with his castigation of Church dogma as absurd are to be taken seriously.[60] In short, the esoteric argument of Strauss' essay should transpire as an advocacy of orthodox Judaism and the authority of the Old Testament against the alleged attacks of an atheist and a renegade, on the one hand, and against the superiority of Christianity, on the other. The explanation of such writing could be discovered only from historical evidence provided by the investigation of the background and circumstances of Strauss' thinking; and whether the motive was the one suggested, or some other, only historical research could ascertain.

Notes

1. L. Strauss, *Persecution and the Art of Writing* (Glencoe, Ill., Free Press, 1952), Ch. V, p. 179.
2. Cf. *Spinoza over de Toleratie,* Mededelingen XXIII vanwege het Spinozahuis, 1967.
3. Strauss, op. cit., p. 153f.
4. Cf. TdIE.
5. Strauss, op. cit., p. 152.
6. Ibid., p. 158.
7. Cf. TdIE and E2P43S.
8. TTP, Praef. Strauss, op cit., p. 162.
9. Strauss, op. cit., p. 146.
10. TTP, Ch. VII.
11. Ibid.
12. Ibid.
13. Ibid.
14. Cf. TTP, *Adnotatio* VIII to Ch. VII: *Caeterum hieroglyphica, et historias, quae fidem omnem excedere videntur, imperceptibiles dico.*
15. Strauss, op. cit., III, p. 169.
16. Ibid., p. 170.
17. Ibid., p. 171.
18. Ibid.
19. Ibid., p. 173.
20. Ibid., pp. 172–174.
21. Ibid., pp. 175–176.
22. TTP, Chs. II and IV.
23. Strauss, op. cit., p. 180. Cf. TTP, Ch. XIV.
24. Cf. Strauss, *Spinoza's Critique of Religion* (New York, Schocken Books, 1965). Translation of *Die Religionskritik Spinozas als Grundlage seiner Bibelwissenschaft* (Berlin, Akademie Verlag, 1930).

25. Strauss, *Persecution and the Art of Writing*, p. 184.
26. E2P17S.
27. Cf. TTP, Ch. II.
28. TTP, Ch. I.
29. Ibid.: "*de rebus, limites nostri intellectus excedentibus*"; "*multa extra intellectus limites percipere*"; "*de Prophetia, quandoquidem ipsa captum humanum superat,*" etc.
30. Ibid.
31. TTP, Ch. III.
32. TTP, Ch. I. By "natural knowledge" Spinoza is apparently referring here to *ratio*, scientific knowledge deduced from common concepts and principles.
33. Ep. XXI.
34. Cf. TTP, Chs. II and XIII.
35. Cf. TTP, Chs. XII, XIII and XIV.
36. Cf. TTP, Ch. XV.
37. Cf. E4P54SP58 and S, P59, and E5P4S.
38. Cf. TTP, Ch. XV, ad finem.
39. Ibid.
40. TTP, Ch. I.
41. It is by no means obvious that this means that Jesus' mind was superhuman. That it was divine, insofar as it coincided with the divine intellect, Spinoza undoubtedly held. But the sentence is "*ejus mens praestantior necessario, atque humana longe excellentior esse deberet,*" which may mean simply that Jesus' mind, though human (which, after all, is good Christian doctrine) was more excellent and admirable in its moral perfection than it was human.
42. Cf. KV, I, Ch. IX.
43. TTP, loc cit.
44. TTP, Ch. VI.
45. Cf. TTP, Ch. VII.
46. TTP, Ch. XIV.
47. TTP, Ch. I.
48. Cf. TTP, Ch. II and Ch. IV.
49. E.g., Maimonides. Cf. TTP, Ch. VII ad finem and Ch. XV.
50. TTP, Ch. VII.
51. TTP, Ch. V.
52. Strauss, *Persecution and the Art of Writing*, p. 162.
53. Ibid., p. 187.
54. Ibid., p. 153.
55. Ibid., pp. 152–153.
56. Ibid., p. 48.
57. Ibid., p. 178: "It is no accident. . . ." Cf. also p. 187.
58. Ibid., p. 179.
59. Cf. ibid., p. 164f.
60. Cf. ibid., p. 176.

PART III

Spinoza
and
His Successors

10

Spinoza and Leibniz

LEIBNIZ'S FIRST REACTION TO SPINOZA

At first sight the metaphysical positions of Spinoza and Leibniz appear poles apart; Spinoza is inveterately monist and Leibniz professedly pluralist. Spinoza insists that there is only one Substance; Leibniz declares that there are innumerable substances. Yet when one examines Leibniz's system more closely, one discovers a holism that is closely akin to, and in all probability directly derived from, Spinoza's, of which the pluralistic vesture is no more than a development of some of the implications of Spinoza's theory.

A few years before Spinoza's untimely death, Leibniz visited him, and the two philosophers discussed points of mutual interest. There was also some correspondence between them on optics. It seems that Spinoza was somewhat suspicious of Leibniz and must have sensed that (at that time) he had no clear grasp of his meaning. Spinoza's motto was "*Caute,*" and he counseled caution in imparting his ideas to others who might misunderstand, or fail to make good use of them. He urges the friends for whom he wrote the *Short Treatise on God, Mankind, and Human Well-being* "to be careful about imparting these matters to others" unless for the sole purpose of "the welfare of your neighbor, as one on whom you are unmistakably assured that the reward of your labor will not be lost." For much the same reason he asks his friend, Schuller, to be careful about transmitting his ideas to Leibniz (Ep 72).

It is fairly clear from what Leibniz writes in his notes on Spinoza's *Ethics* (1678) that he did not properly understand Spinoza, and the criticisms he offers are for the most part rather captious, indicating a hasty and somewhat superficial reading. Nonetheless, Leibniz was already thinking along Spinozistic lines, and as he matured he must

150

have made use of Spinoza's ideas in order to reach his own conclusions. In 1669 he had written to Jacob Thomasius, grouping Spinoza with Clauberg, Reay, Clerselier, and other Cartesians, with the remark that none of them had added anything significant to the thought of their master, Descartes.[1] Nobody who had reflected at all deeply on Spinoza's writings could have passed such a judgment; but at that date Leibniz probably knew nothing of the *Ethics*, which had not yet been published.

Some years later, in 1676, Leibniz wrote:

> There seems to be a certain center to the whole universe, and an infinite general vortex, and a most perfect mind, or *God*. And this mind is a whole in the whole body of the world; to it is due also the existence of the world. In itself is its own cause. . . . Furthermore, since some things exist, and certain things do not exist, it follows that there must exist most perfect *Elements of a Secret Philosophy of the Whole of Things*, geometrically demonstrated. . .[2]

Were these ideas inspired by what Leibniz knew, or had heard, of Spinoza?

LEIBNIZ'S EARLY CRITICISM OF SPINOZA

In 1678 Leibniz received a copy of Spinoza's *Opera postuma* from G. H. Schuller, and apparently read it with some attention. He then set down critical notes on Part 1 in some detail.[3] These notes may be no more than hasty jottings on first impressions, for the critique is far from weighty or perspicacious, and answers to the points raised are easily forthcoming from anybody who really understands Spinoza's thought.

Leibniz begins by complaining that to define a thing as finite if it can be limited by another of the same nature (E1D2) involves obscurity, because it is not clear how one thought limits another. For anybody of Leibniz's acuteness of mind this should surely offer no difficulty. One thought can limit another in various ways: by mutual exclusion, as the thought of duality excludes and limits that of unity, or the thought of a wood excludes and so limits (and is limited by) that of a desert; or by mutual contradiction, as affirmation contradicts negation; or by complementation, as with the ideas of whole and part. Further, if he had read the second Part of the *Ethics*, Leibniz should have realized that Spinoza held that *idea* and *ideatum* are identical in substance, so that one idea can limit another just as one body can limit another. Spinoza, however, is here much more concerned about the mutual exclusion and individual self-containedness of the attributes, for he asserts that "a body is not limited by thought, nor a thought by body." What he is anxious to avoid is any suggestion that ideas are caused by physical impress upon the bodily sense organs, as had been maintained by Hobbes and was later alleged by Locke. Spinoza was careful not to get ensnared in any causal theory of perception, or correspondence theory of truth. The relation between *idea* and *ideatum* is not correspondence but identity.

Next Leibniz objects to Definition 3, which states that substance is in itself and is conceived through itself; for, he says, it is not stated whether these two characteristics are assigned to substance disjunctively or conjunctively. If the latter is meant, he contends, it must be proved that what is in itself is also conceived through itself. In a footnote, here, Loemke points out that this distinction is important for Leibniz because he intended to maintain of monads that while they existed in themselves they could not be conceived through themselves, but only through their relation to God. To Spinoza, however, it was evident that nothing could be in itself unless it were conceivable only through itself, for what requires something else for its conception must be somehow dependent also for its existence on that through which it is conceived (e.g., color is not conceivable without extension, and likewise cannot exist unless extended); and vice versa what is in itself, independent of all else, can be conceived only through its own nature or essence. For this reason, anything like the Leibnizian monad could not, for Spinoza, be a substance, but, at most, an "affection" of that upon which it depended for its existence. We shall see later that the monads of Leibniz's system are, after all, not as different from Spinoza's finite modes as they seem to be, or as Leibniz himself believed.

Leibniz admits that substance is usually conceived in this way; but he finds a further difficulty in the definition of attribute, which, he says, is perceived, according to Spinoza, as belonging to substance and as constituting its essence, so that the concept of attribute is necessary to form the concept of substance; in other words, substance must be conceived through its attributes rather than the other way round. What Spinoza actually says is that attribute is the way in which the essence of substance is perceived by the intellect. Now, the essence of substance, is what substance is in itself. That, indeed, is necessary for the intellect to form a conception of it, but it is nothing other than substance itself—its own essence—through which it is conceived. So the objection is unfounded and ill conceived.

Leibniz shows in his demur against Definition 4, complaining that it too is obscure, that he does not understand what Spinoza means by attribute. He complains that Spinoza does not say whether by attribute is understood every reciprocal predicate, or every essential predicate (reciprocal or not), or every primary essential or indemonstrable predicate of substance. It is, however, a grave mistake to confuse an attribute with the predicate of a subject (presumably Leibniz is thinking of Aristotle's definition of substance). If one bears in mind what Spinoza says of the eternal things in TdIE, one will realize that this is very far from what he means by attribute, which is rather what gives sense and purport to any and every predicate applicable to finite and mutable things. We may assume that Leibniz had read the *Tractatus*, so he should have known better. He does, however, withdraw his objection after considering the purport of Definition 5.

Commenting on E1D6, Leibniz asks whether "these two definitions" (presumably of substance and of attribute) are equipollent, by which he means each substitutable for the other. If this is considered important, it can certainly be shown. But his main misgiving is that the *definiendum* might not be possible. Is there really no self-contradiction in the notion of an absolutely infinite substance with infinite attributes? It was Leibniz's condition for accepting the ontological argument that the idea of a perfect being, including all possible perfections, should be shown to be possible (i.e., not self-contradictory). That a perfect being should be self-contradictory, however, would itself be a contradiction. This Spinoza demonstrates in the second proof of Proposition 11, so Leibniz's fears should have been allayed. His own proof of the compossibility of all perfections in a single subject depends on the posit that each and every perfection is simple and unanalyzable. But that would make it undefinable and strictly inconceivable, which is hardly compatible with the idea of perfection. Later, we shall find, what Leibniz conceives as simple is really very different from this, and is much more like what Spinoza calls a whole, in the proper sense of that word.

He doubts, further, whether the same simple essence can be expressed through many different attributes; again, an ill-directed misgiving, for Spinoza does not say that God's essence is simple. He says it is infinite and eternal, and argues that what is absolutely infinite must have infinite attributes; in other words, God's essence must be infinitely complex—must be expressed through infinite attributes. Presumably what is simple would have only one attribute, as Leibniz says here, "its essence can be expressed only in one way."

The axioms give Leibniz little trouble, except for the phrase "to be in itself" which obviously means to be entirely self-dependent. He also takes exception to Spinoza's assertion that every idea agrees with its *ideatum* because, he says, that would eliminate false ideas. Spinoza had explained fully what he meant by such agreement and what constituted false ideas in TdIE and again in E2P7PP11–13 and S, and L7S, and in E2PP33–35, and Leibniz could hardly have raised this objection if he had attended sufficiently to these passages.

His refinement of the concept of "prior by nature" in his comment on E1P1 has the merit of noticing that implication can be, and usually is, a reciprocal relation, and Leibniz astutely adds that what cannot be conceived without what it implies is posterior to what is implied, but what can be conceived without that which it implies can be said to be prior by nature. Spinoza would probably have agreed. But then Leibniz qualifies his submission by introducing several rather dubious mathematical examples which are hardly relevant to Spinoza's proposition.

In his comment on Proposition 2, Leibniz shows that he does understand the force of Spinoza's argument, but then he rejects it on the ground that two different attributes cannot express the essence of the same substance, showing once again that he does not understand what Spinoza means by attribute. This misunderstanding resurfaces in the comment on Proposition 4, where Leibniz expresses surprise at Spinoza's statement that nothing exists (outside the intellect) except Substance and its modes, apparently forgetting the attributes. In terms of Definition 4 this ought not to have been surprising, but more important, what Leibniz has failed to notice is that Spinoza identifies reality, perfection, and power of existence (E1P11Dem3 and P2D6), and that God's essence is the same as his power; accordingly, the attributes are God's powers (not merely predicates or categories) identical with *Natura naturans*, and this exists formally along with *Natura naturata*: God-or-Substance and its modes.

The comment on Proposition 5 is both captious and confused, revealing failure to grasp Spinoza's meaning of "Nature" (the nature of things is in the last resort God-or-Substance; that is why there cannot be more than one), as well as of attribute, repeating the error noted above.

Proposition 6 is accepted; Leibniz offers an abbreviated proof, which Spinoza would probably not have rejected.

With respect to Proposition 7 Leibniz objects to the use of *causa sui* as ambiguous, but he does not explain why. Spinoza, he says, gives it a special meaning in Definition 1, but uses it in its popular meaning, although what this is Leibniz does not specify. The need to show that Substance, as conceived, is possible, before one can prove that it exists, is restated here, and a proof is given, which is, in effect the cosmological argument for the existence of God. But then Leibniz introduces a new doubt based on the two meanings of possibility, logical possibility and what seems to be his later notion of compossibility. As here stated in terms of causality, this simply leads him back to the Cosmological Proof, which is really not called for in this context, as what Spinoza is stating is, in effect, the Ontological Proof. Leibniz ends the comment by wondering if his strictures are really necessary.

Proposition 8 and especially its Scholium are approved, with the caveat that the notion of limitation is obscure, and this we have dealt with already.

Proposition 9 is again subjected to difficulties arising from Leibniz's confusion over the concept of an attribute, although he accepts the proof in terms of Spinoza's Definition 4. The same confusion infects the brief statement about Proposition 10. The next proposition depends on the seventh, and Leibniz repeats his objections to that and again stresses the need to show that substance is a possible concept; hence, in Spinoza's third demonstration, the argument that the infinite would have less power of existence than the finite if the latter exists and the former does not is countered by saying that if the infinite is self-contradictory it will have no power of existence at all, and that existence is not a power. Here Leibniz falls into more confusion and obscurity. Infinity, in Spinoza's sense, is self-completeness and self-dependence (not endless finitude). To suggest that this might be a self-contradiction is to invert the facts. It is always the finite which is in contradiction with itself (although Spinoza implies this in his account of finite modes, it had to wait for Hegel to state it explicitly), for the finite depends for its being and nature on what lies outside it, yet claims both as belonging to itself exclusively. This contradiction can be remedied only by continuous supplementation of the finite (such as Spinoza describes in E2L7S) until eventual complete totality is reached: that is, the infinite, in which all negation is negated and all contradiction is resolved. Spinoza understood this, and it is foreshadowed in his exposition, but here at least Leibniz does not seem to. To contend that existence is not a power runs counter to Spinoza's (not to mention Plato's) dynamic conception of being, and in his later work Leibniz himself implies, if he does not actually state, a similar view.

Proposition 12 to 20 are simply summarized, with a doubt expressed in relation to Proposition 14 whether bodies are substances (although with minds, Leibniz says, the case is different). However, Spinoza denies that bodies are substances, so the relevance of the parenthetical remark is not obvious. Objection is made to Corollary 2 because Spinoza has not yet shown that Extension and Thought are attributes or can be conceived through themselves. But all the Corollary states is that they are either attributes or affections of God; that they are, in fact, attributes of God is proved in Part II, Propositions 1 and 2.

The next major criticism is of Proposition 20, the demonstration of which is said to be circular and unnecessary after the proof of Proposition 19. That there is some redundancy here in Spinoza's demonstrations may be conceded, but what he is striving to emphasize is that, in the case of God, necessary existence, eternity, and essence are all one and the same (probably he had Aquinas in mind), and that they are all identical with power, or action.

While accepting Proposition 24, Leibniz rejects the demonstration as fallacious, because, he says, Spinoza uses the phrase "cause of itself" in its common meaning whereas he assumes the meaning arbitrarily assigned to it in Definition 1. It is untypically obtuse of Leibniz to insist on this difference of meaning, for surely what causes itself, in the ordinary sense of the words, is not caused by another and, if it exists at all, must exist of necessity through its own essence, or what it is in itself. Spinoza's definition, therefore, is not merely stipulative or arbitrary. In a marginal note, Leibniz points out that this proposition proves, contrary to Spinoza's claim, that not all things are necessary, foreshadowing Leibniz's own distinction between necessary and contingent truths. But, of course, Spinoza holds that all things are necessary, not because their existence is involved in their essence, but because God's nature is necessary and he is their necessary cause. Leibniz's own mature theory involves much the same conclusion, if consistently thought through, although Leibniz insisted that God's will was free, more as Descartes had maintained than as Spinoza held (that God was free because wholly self-determined). Yet because God always chooses the best possible (according to Leibniz), the assumption must be that he acts rationally, which is precisely what Spinoza asserts.

The proof of Proposition 25 is said to be invalid because it does not follow, as claimed, from Axiom 4, which does not say that the cause of a thing is that without which it cannot be conceived, and even if Proposition 15 is admitted (that nothing can be conceived without God), the conclusion of Proposition 25 would not follow. The reasoning here seems quite perverse. Leibniz says that it is false that things cannot be conceived without their causes; yet of finite things it is surely true that to be adequately conceived, their dependence on their causes must be included in the conception. He gives the example of a circle, saying that it cannot be conceived without its center, but its center is not its cause. In some sense its center is its cause (for its circumference is defined by its distance from the center), and even if the point were conceded, it would not follow that the circle could be conceived without its cause (the movement of a point equidistant from another point).

Leibniz says further that to involve something is not the same as to be inconceivable without it, and he gives as example the parabola, knowledge of which involves knowledge of its focus, yet which can be conceived without it. How a parabola is to be conceived without a focus is difficult to understand, especially if the knowledge of one involves that of the other. But to go back to Proposition 25, the proof is a *reductio ad absurdum*: if God were not the cause of the essence of things, they could be conceived without God, which is absurd according to Proposition 15. This is quite straightforward, sound, and involves none of the defects detailed by Leibniz.

The somewhat arrogant and disdainful statement of Leibniz's dissatisfaction with the corollary (which anyhow he accepts) shows that he understands neither what Spinoza intends by modes nor what is meant by attribute; for he says that the ways in which we conceived particular things (modes) are the determinate ways of conceiving the divine attributes. This is quite wrong. The attributes are determinate ways of conceiving God's powers, and the modes are determinate ways in which those powers are exercised. Once again, Leibniz is thinking of attributes as general terms.

The comment on Proposition 28 is more promising. This is Spinoza's proof that finite modes are caused by other finite modes regressing back indefinitely, because they cannot follow from the absolute nature of any attribute of God unless they are infinite and eternal. Leibniz sees, as have later commentators, that this seems to leave an unbridgeable gap between the infinite attributes and modes, on one side, and the finite modes, on the other. Spinoza here says that a finite thing must follow from some attribute of God insofar as it is in some way modified, and as this cannot be by a modification that is infinite and eternal, it can only be by one that is also finite. Hence the infinite regress results. What is not made clear is how an attribute of God can be modified to produce a finite mode, and the impression is left of a hiatus yawning between God's absolute nature and the finite modes of Substance.

This Leibniz sees, and he offers his own solution, to be developed later, that God determines things prior to their efficient causes and determines them to be connected with the efficient causes according to certain rules of divine wisdom, so that the posterior things are the final causes of the prior. We shall find much significance in this resolution of the matter when we come to consider Leibniz's mature position. But concerning Spinoza we must note that he suggests a similar solution in E2L7S and in the 32nd Letter (to Oldenburg), from which it transpires that the infinite mode (*facies totius universi*, of the attribute of Extension) is the structural principle determining the existence, interrelation, and interchange among finite modes, all of which are differentiations of the primary infinite mode (Motion-and-rest), that is, bodies. The infinite mode thus becomes the final cause of changes among finite modes, which are nevertheless caused efficiently by other finite modes.

There is also some wisdom in Leibniz's remarks on Proposition 29. He accuses Spinoza of failing to define "contingent," then gives his own definition, which is a good one and is clearly what Spinoza means by the term. He rightly rejects the idea of contingent events as uncaused and as occurring in spite, and in defiance, of established conditions. The hint is also given that what is properly called contingent is the result of the deficiency of our knowledge—Spinoza's view—when Leibniz says: "Everything is defined and determined by its own nature, even though this nature may be unknown to us." With all this Spinoza undoubtedly would agree. Leibniz, however, dismisses Spinoza's demonstration of the proposition as obscure and abrupt. Why he should think so is far from apparent.

Proposition 30 is significant for Spinoza. It states that the intellect in act (*intellectus actu*), whether finite or infinite, must comprehend the attributes of God and the affections of God and nothing else. It will be remembered that in TdIE Spinoza stated that it was of the nature of the intellect to frame true ideas. In the proof of this proposition he repeats that a true idea must agree with its object. The reason for this we already know; but Leibniz again expresses disbelief in its self-evidence or even in its truth, though how an idea could be true if it did not agree with its object he does not reveal. The rest of Spinoza's proof is perfectly straightforward and clear; yet, for unstated reasons, Leibniz condemns it as tortuous, disconnected, and circuitous, although he accepts the proposition itself as clear. What Spinoza seeks to establish is that the intellect, unclouded by imaginative ideas, comprehends the truth, whether it be God's intellect (as one must expect) or the human intellect, whose nature it is to frame adequate ideas. All this is further demonstrated in Part II of the *Ethics*, but to this Leibniz pays no heed.

With Proposition 31 Leibniz declares he does not agree. He states the proposition and disagrees with it, but gives no reason. What it says is that intellect, will, desire, love, etc., belong to *Natura naturata* and not to *Natura naturans*. Spinoza gives good reasons for this statement, and Leibniz's crass disagreement has no clear warrant.

Surprisingly, Leibniz states Proposition 32, denying the freedom of the will, without comment. Then he gives the next proposition qualified approval depending on how it is interpreted. His own interpretation is that the world could not have been produced by God otherwise than it has been, because God would (must?) choose the best possible world, although he could if he wished produce some other. Clearly this is not Spinoza's understanding of the proposition. For him, God is absolute perfection in the only sense that he deems legitimate: that is, totally self-complete. And God's creation is what proceeds necessarily from his nature: that is, everything that can fall within the scope of an infinite intellect. There can be no question of other possible worlds, for Spinoza holds that nothing is contingent, except in relation to the deficiency of our knowledge, and that if things could have been produced by God otherwise than they have been, that would imply that God could have had a different nature from what he actually does have, which is absurd; and as God is supremely perfect, he has brought everything into being in the highest perfection. Anything different could only have been imperfect.

Leibniz approves Proposition 36, but says that it does not follow from Proposition 34 as Spinoza claims in the proof. What Spinoza seems to be implying is that whatever expresses God's power in a conditioned manner must have further consequences, for God's power is infinite, and what is conditioned is finite. This has important consequences involving the *conatus in suo esse perseverandi* in all finite things, but we cannot enter here into the details.

Leibniz notes that the first Part of the *Ethics* ends with an Appendix attacking those who believe that God acts with a purpose. This, he says, is a mixture of truth and falsehood, for although it is true that not all things happen for the benefit of mankind, it does not follow that God acts without will or knowledge of the good. Spinoza, however, does not deny that God acts with will or knowledge; in fact, he identifies God's will with his intellect, so that he must act with both; but the will is no "free will" in the sense of arbitrary or indeterminate, and how one is to understand "the good" is not a simple matter. For God, all things are good. His thought is always adequate and his eyes are too pure to behold evil; for evil is only privation, which is the negation that God excludes. But for man, when he thinks inadequately good is simply what he desires and imagines will be to his advantage, and when he thinks adequately it is what he knows for certain is to his advantage: that is, the most adequate knowledge he can attain of God and the blessedness that results from *amor intellectualis Dei*. As this is identical with God's own knowledge and love, it would seem that Leibniz should have no reason to demur; and as we go on to examine his more mature doctrine we shall find that there is less difference between him and Spinoza than he himself perceived at the stage when he wrote these notes on the *Ethics*, or than he was ever prepared to admit.

LATER LEIBNIZ

In his maturer period, Leibniz turned again to comment on Spinoza, in notes that he made on a book by Johann Georg Wachter in which the author claimed to demonstrate agreement between Spinoza and the Cabbala.[4] Leibniz is here more critical of Wachter than of Spinoza, to whom he is now more conciliatory and sympathetic, showing better understanding than in earlier years. He is, however, still anxious to affirm God's freedom in the act of creation, both of the universe as a whole and of individual things, assuming that Spinoza would have denied this. What Leibniz seems to miss is Spinoza's contention that the opposite of freedom is not determination but compulsion. Spinoza fully agrees that God creates freely, that is, he is not compelled by any external restraint, but he insists that God's will is determined, although only by his own nature; he is self-determining. In effect, Leibniz admits this for he says:

> He [Spinoza] correctly denies that God is indifferent and that he decides anything by an absolute [exercise of the] will; he decides through will based on reasons. (*Op. cit.*, p. 278)

But then Leibniz objects to Spinoza's claim that things follow from God's nature in the same way and with the same necessity as its properties follow from the nature of a triangle. This, says Leibniz, cannot be proved. Yet he himself declares that God decides on rational and moral grounds (moral grounds for both philosophers are essentially rational); and God's will and his intellect (his rationality) are, for Spinoza, the same thing. Leibniz too believed that it was God's nature to choose the best, for otherwise, he could not be God, the most perfect being. Accordingly, it follows irrefutably that things must follow from God's nature by the same rational necessity as the equality of the angles of a triangle to two right-angles follows from the nature of the triangle.

Leibniz is shocked by Spinoza's doctrine of human immortality as consisting in the idea *sub specie aeternitatis* of the human body in God's mind, the human mind being nothing other than the idea of its body. He apparently fails to notice that Spinoza is not maintaining the everlasting endurance of the human mind, but only its eternal being and blessedness in *amor intellectualis Dei*. The sensuous mind, Spinoza held, terminated with the finite body, as it obviously is dependent upon bodily functioning; and here Leibniz disagrees. The soul, he holds, is immortal and, as reason is no more than the conclusion of which memory and imagination are the premises, the soul must retain its memory and imagination after the death of the body. In Leibniz's doctrine the body is, in effect, as immortal as the soul, for all that is real is the monad, its body being simply its confused perceptions. It follows that memory and imagination (the confused perceptions) will persist as long as the monad itself exists. We have observed the parallel in Spinoza's teaching, but he takes the human individual to be one finite "thing" (*res*) viewed under two attributes. As finite, it ceases to be in the order of time; but in God, *sub specie aeternitatis*, it is eternal, and the idea of the body, so understood, involves all its relations to other finites and their effects upon it; so in some sense, imagination and memory will still be preserved.

To what extent Leibniz was acquainted with Spinoza's correspondence is not clear. He had certainly read some of it, but he does not seem to have understood the implications of the letter to Oldenburg on wholes and parts (Ep. 32), for he complains that Spinoza fails to show how finite modes arise from God, for they are each and all produced only by finite causes, and it is not shown that they arise even mediately from God:

> Therefore, it cannot be said that God acts by means of secondary causes, unless he produces these secondary causes. (*Philosophical Essays*, p. 281)

In his criticism of Spinoza's doctrine of immortality, Leibniz objects that the idea of the body (or, for that matter, any idea) is a mere abstraction, which defines the possibility of its object, but in no way determines its existence. Spinoza, of course, would have agreed, in the case of finite things. But this applies only to imaginative ideas, not to ideas *sub specie aeternitatis*, which are not abstract, but are concrete systematic concepts determining all the relations of the thing with the rest of the universe. It is odd that Leibniz seemed to miss this distinction, for later he himself says,

> However, it is true that there are certain things in the soul that can only be explained in an adequate way through external things . . . insofar as, in creating the mind, God took things other than the mind itself into consideration to a greater extent, for in creating and conserving each and every thing, God takes all other things into consideration. (Ibid., p. 279)

We shall recall that Spinoza explains the difference between adequate and inadequate ideas precisely in this ways, that the former, in God's mind, involve other things, whereas the latter are isolated from their true context and, so to speak, truncated (cf. E2P11C).

WHOLE AND PARTS, MONISM AND PLURALISM

Irrespective of the various interpretations, naturalistic, deterministic, or materialistic, as well as atheistic, which have been offered of Spinoza's system, there can be little question that its predominant character is its essential and profound holism. Spinoza's Substance is one, self-complete and self-sustaining, indivisible, and combining innumerable "affections" systematically into an integral unity. The 32nd Letter makes all this quite clear. On the other hand, Leibniz professes a pluralism which, at least at first sight, looks thoroughly radical. On closer scrutiny, however, this pluralism is so qualified that the difference between the ideas of the two philosophers tends, in large measure, to evaporate.

Early in his career, Leibniz's thought was dominated by the concept of a universal harmony. In the period between 1671 and 1676, the idea surfaces continually in the papers that he produced, and it pervades all his thinking. "*Harmonia id est unitas plurimorum seu diversitas identitate compensata*," he wrote.[5] Unity in diversity is the typical definition of a whole. He equates it with God, who, he says, is perfect intellect, and whose will is "merely a certain aspect of his intellect";[6] of this divine intellect every simple idea is a mode and so harmonizes with every other, reflecting all possible entities as in a mirror. And God, Leibniz asserts, must be an infinite mind such as alone is capable of grasping the universal law of intelligibility under which all existence (subject to the universal harmony) must fall. Furthermore, God is cause of himself. Although these ideas had been germinating in his mind long before he could have known much about Spinoza, by 1676, when he wrote them down, Leibniz had already been in touch with Spinoza; and although Spinoza's God is much more than a perfect intellect, the Spinozistic ring of Leibniz's thought at this time, and the echo of Spinozan terminology, are unmistakable.

From these beginnings, as well as in later developments of his philosophy, it is clear that Leibniz's thinking is as holistic as Spinoza's. In fact, his assumed pluralism is only the result of his attempt to avoid the atomism and genuine pluralism prevalent in his day.

There are two labyrinths in which the human mind is caught. One concerns the composition of the continuum; the other concerns the nature of freedom. And both arise from the same source, namely, the infinite.

This he wrote in 1679 (or thereabouts),[7] and the first of these two labyrinths arises when one tries to determine how movement can begin, or occur at all, in the continua of space and time, which are infinitely divisible. In *Theoria motus abstracti* he writes:

> *There are indivisibles or unextended beings,* for otherwise we could conceive neither the beginning nor the end of motion or body. The proof of this is as follows. There is a beginning and an end to any given space, body, motion, and time. Let that whose beginning is sought be represented by line *ab,* whose middle point is *c,* and let the middle point of *ac* be *d,* and of *ad* be *e,* and so on. Let the beginning be sought at the left end, at *a.* I say that *ac* is not the beginning, because *cd* can be taken from it without destroying the beginning; nor is it *ad,* because *ed* can be taken away, and so forth. So nothing is a beginning from which something on the right can be removed. But that from which nothing can be removed is unextended. Therefore the beginning of body, space, motion, or time— namely, a point, conatus, or instant—is either nothing which is absurd, or unextended, which was to be demonstrated.[8]

This is the problem that had been set for the Ancients by Zeno in his paradox of the dichotomy, and Leibniz seeks to solve it by postulating an unextended yet real being as the substantial origin of all extension. Being unextended, this cannot actually be spatial, temporal, or bodily, and so must be spiritual, of the nature of thought. This is the source of Leibniz's theory of monads, which he says are substances, but are souls, not bodies, and the latter are but confused perceptions of the relations between the monads, represented as spatio-temporal. As the relations are real, and are defined by Leibniz in terms of obscure and distinct perceptions, passivity and activity, space and time are not illusory, but are *phenomena bene fundata.*

The theory of monads, therefore, is Leibniz's device for avoiding the atomism of the contemporary scientific conceptual scheme; for atoms are supposed to be the minimal parts of matter having volume and extension, yet are indivisible—in Leibniz's view, a contradiction. So he sought a minimal entity that was indivisible and could be the original source of all extensional relations. As he says in the opening of the *Monadlogy:*

> 1. The *monad* which we are to discuss here is nothing but a simple substance which enters into compounds. *Simple* means without parts. (*Theodicy,* Sec. 10) 2. There must be simple substances, since there are compounds, for the compounded is but a collection or an *aggregate* of simples.

That the monads are not internally simple will presently become apparent, and that word will assume a new meaning of some moment. Certainly they are not aggregates, or collections, and some doubt may be entertained whether they can be elements of aggregates or collections. Whether bodies can rightly be considered aggregates is a further question into which we shall not enter at this stage.

In the *Discourse on Metaphysics* (Para. 12), Leibniz identifies what in bodies "is related to souls" with substantial form, denying that bodies can be explained in terms of extension alone. This he also identifies with entelechy and holds to be the source of *conatus* and motion in bodies, as souls are in intelligent beings. In the *New System* he writes:

> ... it is impossible to find *the principles of a true unity* in matter alone or in what is merely passive, since everything in it is but a collection or aggregate of parts to infinity. Now a multitude can derive its reality only from the *true unities*, which have some other origin and are entirely different from points, for it is certain that the continuum cannot be compounded of points. To find these *true unities*, therefore, I was forced to have recourse to a formal atom. ... It was thus necessary to restore and as it were to rehabilitate the *substantial forms* which are in such disrepute today [his italics].[9]

Substantial forms thus prove to be principles of unity and indivisibility, and, as will presently appear, of unity in difference (i.e., harmony). They are, apparently, the unifying principles of monads, those formal atoms which are the elements of all combinations.

Because the monads are simple, they cannot act on one another or transmit influences one to another. So they are said to be windowless. Yet they must differ one from another, for otherwise they would be indistinguishable. Their mutual differences, Leibniz says, are constituted by their differing qualities, which are due to an internal principle of change among the detailed variety united in the monad. These details are innumerable perceptions, which taken together represent, or mirror, the entire universe, and as the only realities or substances are monads, it would seem that these perceptions are of other monads, for Leibniz says that each reflects the universe from its particular viewpoint, as a city may be viewed from different angles, so that the views differ although the city is the same in each. Accordingly, each monad is a whole of diverse elements (perceptions), its unique character being expressed by its substantial form.

In Spinoza's system every finite mode (as we learn from the 32nd Letter) is adapted and adjusted to every other in the structured whole of *facies totius universi*, so there is a sense in which it too will register every change and every other mode that occurs under the governance of the infinite mode, and its mind will similarly reflect, in varying degrees of obscurity and clarity, the entire universe. Between the two doctrines the similarity is significant.

From what has been said, it is clear that the simplicity of the monad is not just blank unity. It is explicitly stated that it is a unity of differences, that its unity enfolds a multitude (*Monadology*, 13), and this multitude is subject to gradual alteration according to a principle of change. In short, the monad is a whole of interrelated states (perceptions), distinguishable but not separable, and its so-called simplicity is nothing other than this indivisible wholeness.

Perceptions are not necessarily conscious, and those that are consciously perceived are distinguished as apperception. The unconscious perceptions are obscure, while those that are consciously perceived are more distinct. The more confused perceptions are said to be passions, for the monad is passive so far as it has confused perceptions, while it is active in its clear and distinct perceptions. Accordingly, perceptions are ranged in a series of degrees of confusedness and clarity, and monads differ according to the extent that they perceive clearly or obscurely.

Confused perceptions represent the relations between monads as extensive and their qualities as physical, so they appear as bodies in space and time. Thus the passive level of the monad is its body, while its clearer apperception constitutes its mind. It will be remembered that for Spinoza every body is beminded, for of each there is an idea, and that whatever occurs in the body is reflected in its idea, or mind, but (at least in the first instance) only confusedly; so, as presented under the attribute of Thought, each individual mode is much the same as the Leibnizian monad.

The principle of change in the monad is said to be appetition, an endeavor to increase its power of action, that is, to clarify its perceptions, or alternatively, to move up the scale along which monads differ from one another. The *conatus*, for Spinoza, serves precisely the same function, for in its endeavor to maintain itself in its own being, the essential activity of the finite mode is to free itself from external causes, its body becoming more self-sufficient and its mind becoming more capable of perceiving many things together—more clearly and distinctly. Increase of its capacity so to do proportionately augments its power of action, of which it is itself the adequate cause.

At the upper end of the scale the monad whose perceptions are all perfectly clear and distinct is the Monad of monads, namely God, the supreme substance. In Paragraphs 40–41 of the *Monadology*, Leibniz writes:

We may conclude . . . that this supreme substance, being unique, universal and necessary, and having nothing outside of it which is independent of it, and being a simple consequence of possible being, must be incapable of limits and must contain as much reality as is possible. It follows from this that God is absolutely perfect; *perfection* being nothing but the quantity of positive reality taken strictly, when we put aside the limits or bounds of the things which are limited. But where there are no bounds, that is, in God, perfection is absolutely infinite.[10]

Quantity of positive reality is (presumably) the same as action (for "what does not act does not exist"[11]), and action is clear and distinct perception. In God the entire universe is perceived clearly and distinctly; he is *actus purus*. Hence, he is the sufficient reason for everything in the universe.

Now this is very much the way in which Spinoza talks about perfection and about God. For him, perfection is the same as reality or power of existence; action is what is caused solely by the essence of the agent, as is everything accomplished by God, who is the absolutely infinite Substance, and indeed the sufficient reason for everything in the universe.

Sufficient reason is the condition that an entity or event is compossible with all others, and compossibility is the mutual adjustment of things and events to constitute a coherent system. In short, it is the submission of the individual to the order and structure of the whole. Leibniz's well-known dictum that God chooses to create the best of all possible worlds means, in effect, that God creates that total system which is most coherent and harmonious. And this is the final cause, which governs and determines all efficient causation. The final cause is thus the harmonious structure of the whole universe, and final causation is strictly nothing more nor less than the governance of the part by the whole to which it belongs. From what we already know of Spinoza's *facies totius universi*, this is as true of his doctrine as it is of Leibniz's.

That the universe is a coherent whole, which could not be other than it is, Leibniz is convinced (whatever he may say elsewhere), for he writes to Count Ernst von Hessen-Rheinfels, "The universe is a whole, which God sees through and through with a single glance," and in reply to a letter from Arnaud he says:

> . . . in reality because of the interconnection of things, the universe with all its parts, would be wholly different and would have been wholly different from the very commencement of it if the least thing in it happened otherwise than it has. . . . The slightest movement is communicated as far as matter extends.[12]

In what sense other worlds are possible, and how their events and entities would be compossible, he never explains; and since only what are compossible can exist, it is equally unclear how other worlds might have been viable options for God. But it will not serve our present purpose to pursue this particular issue further.

That the universe is a coherent and harmonious whole is guaranteed by the pre-established harmony between the monads, so that each reflects all and is a microcosm from its own point of view of the macrocosm; and as all this is clearly and distinctly perceived by God, it is plain that God comprehends the whole, that he is in fact the whole, not only culminating the series, but also including it as a whole in his own adequate apperception, with all the degrees of imperfection and perfection that characterize finite beings. He is, as Leibniz has declared, the supreme substance.

In fact, the pre-established harmony cancels out the windowlessness of the monads, because it ensures that they are mutually internally related and together constitute a single indivisible system comprehended within the nature of the Monad of monads. Leibniz's supreme substance, declared to be absolutely infinite, is much the same as Spinoza's, at least under the attribute of Thought; but Leibniz makes no provision for any other attribute and reduces extension to *phenomena bene fundata*. That would put it more or less on a par with the common order of nature, for Spinoza, which is largely a congeries of confused perceptions, although they are *bene fundata* so far as they reflect the actual causes affecting the human body. Spinoza does not volatilize bodies away into minds or souls, but he does assert that they are all in varying degrees *animata*, and Leibniz is convinced that all organisms are made up of lesser organisms, equally *animata*, if not all consciously enjoying apperception. Also, as we have seen, each of Spinoza's attributes expressing the divine essence is, not unlike the Leibnizian scale of increasingly active monads, a hierarchy of modes progressively increasing in degree of perfection up to that of the infinite mode.

To what extent did Leibniz, after later and more careful study of Spinoza's work, model his own system on that of his immediate predecessor? It is difficult to say, for he had powerful political and religious reasons for concealing any agreement he might otherwise have acknowledged with the much-maligned Jew (and reputed atheist) of the Paviljoensgracht. Judging from the final result, however, and following out the unavoidable implications of Leibniz' contentions, we find so much similarity with what Spinoza taught that it is difficult not to conclude that the debt owed to him by Leibniz is not inconsiderable.

Notes

1. Cf. Gottfied Wilhelm Leibniz, *Philosophical Letters and Papers*, ed. L. E. Loemke (Dordrecht, D. Reidel; Atlantic Highlands, N.J., Humanities Press, 1970), p. 94.
2. Ibid., p. 158.
3. Ibid., pp. 196–206.
4. Cf. G. W. Leibniz, *Philosophical Essays*, translated by Roger Ariew and Daniel Garber (Indianapolis and Cambridge, Hackett Publishing Co., 1989), pp. 272–281.
5. Quoted by Georges Friedmann, *Leibniz et Spinoza* (Paris, Gallimard, 1962), p. 32.
6. C. I. Gerhardt, *Leibniz, G. W., Philosophische Schriften* (Berlin and Halle, 1875–1890), 7 vols., I, 257, No. 16.
7. "On Freedom," in Loemke ed., p. 264.
8. In Loemke ed., p. 139f.
9. In Loemke ed., p. 454.
10. In Loemke ed., p. 646f.
11. *De vera methodo Philosophiae et Theologiae* in G. W. Leibniz, *Opera Philosophica*, ed. J. E. Erdmann, Faksimile der Ausgabe 1840, p. 111: "*satis autem ex interioribus metaphysicae principiis ostendi potest, quod non agit nec existere, nam potentia agendi sine ullo actus initio nulla est.*"
12. Correspondence between Leibniz and Arnaud, May 1686.

II

Fichte and Spinoza

THE ROLE OF THE EGO

The philosophy of Fichte, in an important sense, brings to a climax the developed implications of the modern philosophical revolution initiated by Descartes. The Ancients and the Medievals had conceived the universe as a living, teleological system, hierarchical in structure, which culminated in God, who as the immanent principle of its continuing being was its original cause, and as the pinnacle of its perfection was the goal of its internal striving. But the Aristotelian form of this system, which Aquinas had accommodated to Christian theology, was shattered by Copernicus. The removal of the Earth from the center of the universe and its revolution around the Sun, with the consequent displacement of the outer heavens, irretrievably broke the chain of causation from God to sublunar creatures. The Greeks had regarded the human soul as a local manifestation of the world soul, separable from other matter, of which some thought it was a more rarefied form, or, as others held, in which it had become embedded as a distinguishable substance. The medievals thought of it as created by God in his own image, or (where Neoplatonic influence prevailed) as an emanation, or a falling away from the infinite, effulgent, and all-embracing divinity. But after Copernicus and Galileo, the material world came to be conceived as a machine moving according to its own laws independently of any spiritual agency, except insofar as one cared to assume that the mechanical structure had been created by a celestial artificer, who had ordained the laws of its operation.

Within this machine no place was left for consciousness or thought, and the human mind inhabited a body within the material world (itself a part of the machine) as an alien spirit which had nothing in common with its corporeal housing. Whereas the human soul had earlier been conceived as belonging integrally to the living world-system and intimately related to the Godhead, it had now become a creature separated from the material universe, a visitor, as it were, from another sphere temporarily sojourning in a foreign element. It was still directly related to God, created in his image, and so immaterial, a being apart and set in this world only in stewardship, but not as an integral member.

The problem for Descartes and his successors, therefore, was to account for human experience of a world which in its own nature excluded consciousness. It was tempting, and some (like Hobbes and Gassendi) yielded to the temptation, to assimilate the mind to the mechanico-material system. So Hobbes declares:

> . . . qualities, called *Sensible,* are in the object that causeth them, but so many several motions of the matter, by which it presseth our organs diversely. . . . Neither in us that are pressed, are they any thing else, but diverse motions; (for motion produceth nothing but motion).[1]

But Hobbes did not, and could not, in mechanical terms, account for "its appearance to us [which] is Fancy" and which remained inexplicable.

Descartes, however, established irrefutably the existence of a self-conscious subject, whose undeniable being was manifest in its own awareness: *Ego sum cogitans.* The problem set for the ensuing centuries was that of relating this self-conscious subject, both in knowledge and in practice, to the material, mechanical, unconscious world, with which as its object it was confronted. The conscious subject, being self-revelatory, inevitably becomes the epicenter of knowledge and of action. The reality of the material world, in contrast, can be established only inasmuch as it is revealed in consciousness, and only through the agency of thought. Without these we remain oblivious even of its resistance to possible action. Yet the extended world, as inert object, as unconscious matter, dead and purposeless, is alien to consciousness, and presents itself to the mind as an external other. The embodiment of the self in a material part of that objectified world encloses the Ego in a tegument subject to foreign influences and surrounds it with an obstructive environment. Both in knowledge and in practice the Ego's endeavor is to overcome this obstruction and to subject the object to its own domination. The aspiration of the thought of the Enlightenment, accordingly, was to establish the supremacy of the Ego over, and its freedom from, all external restraints.

The radical objectification of the material world enabled empirical science, with its experimental method, to progress with enviable rapidity, but the attempt which this progress prompted to pursue investigation of the mind by similar methods turned that also into a mere object obedient to mechanical laws (e.g., of association) and imprisoned within a completely determined causal system. Pursuit of this line of investigation led first to incoherence, because it represented perception as the result of a causal process that was in the nature of the case imperceptible (as in the theories of Hobbes and Locke), and thus unobservable and unknowable, and thence to scepticism, which, in the writings of Hume, demolished as illusion all belief both in the existence of an external world and in the reality and identity of the self. Yet, at the same time, it was the mind of this very self which, as the subject of knowledge, advanced so spectacularly in its scientific research and progressively acquired greater power and control over external nature. If the results of investigation of human mentality by "the empirical method" were true, this could hardly be, and the impasse is reached that if science is valid no human mind could acquire it, for in order to do so the mind must be exempt from the laws of nature that science discovers and to which it makes mentality subject.

Kant sought to overcome this impasse by demonstrating that the prior condition of any coherent experience and of all objective science was the self-identity of the conscious subject, and its spontaneous a priori synthesis of the presented manifold of sensations. But the objectivity thus validated was bought at the cost of restricting knowledge to phenomena and excluding from it the intrinsic being of things in themselves. The autonomy of the practical subject was also established only at the price of its incessant failure to realize empirically what it categorically demanded. Theoretically and practically the ideal of all activity is a goal the attainment of which is indefinitely deferred and never actually achieved. It ought to be, but never is. And in the theoretical sphere even the goal is only putative and inapplicable to things in themselves.

Fichte goes a step further by declaring the *Ding-an-sich* to be itself a postulate of the Ego, and the object to be a product of the Ego's absolute activity. The self, thus totally free, self-determining, and autonomous, posits itself as limited by the non-Ego and realizes itself by subordinating to its own ideal requirements the non-Ego so posited. The contradiction involved in this antithesis of the self and its other, posited by the absolute Ego, Fichte strives to overcome through a dialectic based on the formula that there can be no antithesis without synthesis and no synthesis without antithesis. Both must, and can only be, posited by the Ego, so that the inevitable check (*Anstoss*) which it suffers in confronting an object, has to be attributed to its own activity and is somehow self-administered. In the last resort we are left with unresolved contradiction, the apparently inescapable price of ultimate freedom.

That it is inescapable follows from the transcendental method instituted by Kant and its inevitable result. That method is to inquire into the conditions of experience before pronouncing upon the status of its contents; and the condition of any experience whatsoever proves to be the integrity and absolute priority of the subject's activity. To that all objective determination is posterior, and any determinate system transcendent beyond the Ego could only be dogmatically postulated and ipso facto self-contradictorily.

A philosophy setting out an all-inclusive transcendent system in which the human mind is but one finite factor wholly and completely conditioned from without is what Fichte calls Spinozism. He held it to be the only possible alternative to the transcendental philosophy he himself advocated, and an unacceptable one because dogmatic. It is so, Fichte considers, because it uncritically asserts the existence and nature of Substance without inquiring first into the conditions of any knowledge or experience of objective reality. The implications of an objective system consistently followed out lead to unrelieved determinism in which the finite self has not the slightest autonomy. Our sense of freedom is no more than the absence (when it occurs) of external interference with a natural propensity itself conditioned in minute detail. Our finite consciousness is at best but a mode of an original power of thinking, and, from the limitations upon us which we experience directly, we infer both to external objects and to that of universal being.

My object in what follows is to show that Fichte misunderstood Spinoza, and that the account he gives of Spinozism (as in Book 1 of *Die Bestimmung des Menschen*) is a misrepresentation; that Spinoza, in fact, succeeded in solving a problem which to the end defeated Fichte; and that transcendental idealism is impaled on the horns of a dilemma which only Spinozism, rightly understood, can escape. This is not to say, of course, that Fichte was not profoundly influenced by Spinoza in the development of his own system, in effect substituting the absolute Ego for Spinoza's Substance.

FICHTE'S REPRESENTATION OF SPINOZISM

In *Grundlage der gesamten Wissenschaftslehre,* Fichte contrasts critical with dogmatic philosophy, defining the first as that which establishes the Ego as sheerly unconditioned and determined by nothing higher, and which derives everything from that postulate. He defines dogmatism as the philosophy which sets a thing-in-itself over against the Ego-in-itself as equal and opposed to it and then arbitrarily elevates the thing into the highest reality. So far as dogmatism can be consistent, he says, the most consistent dogmatism is Spinozism (*Sämtliche Werke*, Vol. 1, p. 120).

Spinoza, he had already told us, rejects completely pure consciousness, though he does not deny the unity of empirical consciousness. Pure consciousness is the transcendental subject's inevitable awareness of itself as existing. It is the consciousness of Descartes's *cogito*, which is not a presentation and must be prior to and involved in any and every presentation of empirical consciousness. Fichte admits, however, in the same passage, that Spinoza attributes pure consciousness to God, who, he asserts, never becomes aware of himself, because pure consciousness never attains to consciousness. (Does this mean God's or ours?) The Ego (yours and mine) exists for Spinoza because something else exists; it is for something else (as well as for itself), and, as posited self, is a modification of God's intellect. This means, presumably, that Spinoza's God posits the human mind but not the infinite intellect, and that the human intellect (according to Spinoza) does not posit itself absolutely.

Fichte complains that Spinoza had no right or ground to go beyond the pure consciousness given in empirical consciousness, although his reason for doing so was the necessity of establishing the most complete unity in human knowledge—a legitimate and inevitable urge. His error, in Fichte's view, was to imagine that this unity could be deduced theoretically, whereas it is no more than a practical regulative requirement.

The type of system dictated by this regulative demand is outlined in the first part of *Die Bestimmung des Menschen*, and that is, therefore, what we must assume Fichte took Spinoza's doctrine to be. There he gives a sketch of a completely determinate universe in which every detail is fixed both by concurrent circumstances and by prior causal conditions:

> I enter into a closed chain of appearances, since every member is determined by its predecessor and determines its successor; in a rigid interconnection, for I can discover at any given moment all possible situations in the universe by pure reflection, backwards if I explain the given moment, forwards if I deduce from it; backwards if I seek out the causes through which alone it could become actual, forwards if I seek out the consequences that it must necessarily have. In every part I acquire the whole, because every part is what it is through the whole; but through this it is of necessity. (*SW*, Vol. 2, p. 174)[2]

This description almost exactly echoes Laplace's declaration that a sufficient intelligence aware of the position and velocity of every particle in the universe at any one moment could calculate precisely the entire state of the universe at any other moment, earlier or later. Fichte adds the Spinozistic touch that this is because every part is necessarily determined to be what it is by the whole—a conception the implications of which he does not develop and which he does not seem properly to have grasped.

It does not occur to him that the account of the world he has given is one in which every detail is determined by its predecessor and its immediate neighbor, rather than by the whole. For Fichte (and Laplace) the whole is woven out of these causal chains, which determine its character, rather than the organizing principle of the system determining them. The reason why Fichte finds the whole in each part is that each part is the precipitate of all prior and the cause of all subsequent parts; not because the organizing principle governing the structure of the whole molds every particular detail and dictates its nature and behavior. The determinism contemplated by Fichte and attributed by him to Spinoza (wrongly, as I hope to show) is Laplacian mechanical determinism, in which intrinsic properties (e.g., position and velocity) of the parts determine their interrelations and not vice versa. It is not a holistic determinism in which the comprehensive character of the totality generates the properties of the parts.

Consequently the free spirit of Fichte's Ego is dismayed at the apparently unanswerable argument which he has unfolded, and appeals to his guardian angel for enlightenment. This comes with the realization that only in and through self-consciousness can any such knowledge of an objective causally determined world be constituted, and that the very determining relations between the parts of that world and their qualities depend on principles supplied a priori by the cognizing subject. (Clearly the "Spirit" in the dialogue of Book 2 is the spirit of Kant.)

The Transcendental Subject, the Empirical Subject, and Holism

In relation to mechanical determinism of the Laplacian kind, the transcendental turn taken by Kant and Fichte is of the utmost importance, establishing as it does the prior agency of the self-conscious subject as the unifying source and origin of all principles of order in knowledge. Both Kant and Fichte recognize that it is the unity of experience that is fundamental to knowledge ("Knowledge," says Kant, " is a whole of related and connected representations"),[3] and that this depends upon and derives from the allegedly analytic unity of the transcendental subject. But for both of them the importance of the analytic unity of the ego takes precedence over that of the synthetic unity of the object, so that the validity of experience is seen by Kant as subjective in relation to an unknowable *Ding-an-sich*, and by Fichte as necessarily and exclusively derivative from an absolute Ego.[4] For both, the unified completeness of the object of experience is theoretically unattainable and ranks only as a regulative principle: for Kant, because it is not empirically given; for Fichte, because the antithesis between subject and object can never be completely overcome in experience.

In Kant's case the insistence upon the reality of things-in-themselves as external and inaccessible to human consciousness keeps experience finite and the understanding limited to the confines of the sensuously given. Fichte dispenses with things-in-themselves; but then an ambiguity arises with regard to the status of the Ego. For human understanding it is and must be the finite subject, yet its absolute priority to all objective reality forbids it to accept any limit that is not self-imposed. Limited it must be, if it is to be presented with an object, yet whatever is posited beyond that limit can be posited only by itself. Otherwise the indispensable unity of experience is broken, and the conditions of the possibility of knowledge are violated. To account for this self-limitation Fichte can appeal only to a mysterious *Anstoss* for which his principles give no warrant. Apart from this "shock," the Ego is absolute, omnicompetent, and Godlike; but subject to it, it becomes no more than a self-posited object, the empirical ego, included within experience as a whole, and as such it is subject to natural laws and is as determined as any other empirical object. Everything said of it in Book 1 of *Die Bestimmung des Menchen* remains true, and in the light of transcendental criticism it is revealed as incapable of systematic knowledge. It would at most be a subject of sensations and feelings if even these had not been preempted by the transcendental Ego. This ambiguity of the ego is endemic in all transcendental idealism, and it vitiates Fichte's metaphysic.

On the other hand, if we transfer our attention from the unity of apperception, however rightly insisted upon by Kant, to the synthetic unity of the whole which its spontaneity effects, as not only what makes experience possible, but also what implies the organizing principles that are provided by the categories and give every object its intrinsic character, we see first that no such unity can be purely analytic, because no purely analytic unity is or can generate a genuine whole, and next that synthetic unity which is all-embracing must be dialectically structured in continuously graded phases of completeness.

The general nature of this dialectic Fichte had already grasped in his recognition that there could be no synthesis without antithesis and no antithesis apart from synthesis. Hence a synthetic unity must be built up out of a series of antitheses, each of which generates a synthesis of wider scope. It was later Hegel who worked out this dialectic systematically and in detail, and based upon it both epistemology and ontology. But in doing so he made the totality absolute and prior—"the truth is the whole"—and in the generation of the dialectic the finite subject proves to be, not the Absolute itself, but a provisional manifestation of it, a self-transcendent phase in the dynamic. It is, as Kant and Fichte required, a unity expressing and embodying the unity of the whole (what Hegel calls the Concept), yet opposed to a genuine other—an object posited by the absolute Idea which, though immanent in the ego, is transcendent beyond it, and is the source and unification of both self and other.

My purpose in this chapter is not to expound Hegel, so we may leave the matter there, for the moment. My aim so far has been merely to show that Fichte's critical idealism is but a halfway house, and is encumbered with a problem that it is powerless to resolve. The next question is whether the alleged transcendent dogmatism of Spinozism really has the faults of which Fichte complains, or if Spinoza did not in significant measure anticipate the solution that Hegel developed.

NATURALISM

There is indeed a type of transcendent dogmatism which falls into hopeless incoherence, and against which Fichte's strictures are entirely justified. Naturalism which attempts to give a "scientific" account of subjectivity, the materialist theories of the mind, which today are still being advocated, and even immaterialist theories which shift the locus of objectivity to a different "substance" while they conceive the mind as a *Seelending* set in an alien surrounding of material reality. Such theories can give no coherent account of conscious experience. The first can give no intelligible explanation of any appearance to a subject—that representation (*Vorstellung*) without which the comprehension by a finite material entity of an indefinitely extensive surrounding world becomes inconceivable. Even less intelligible, on such theories, are misperception and error. The second variety, insisting on representation, can give no explanation of the possibility of recognizing it as such, or of deciding of what it is a representation, because it is cut off from its supposed original (or archetype), the only access to which available to the mind is the representation itself.

These incoherencies have often enough been exposed and castigated, and Fichte's insight in rejecting the dogmatism that gives rise to them is thoroughly sound. At the same time, they lead either to a self-contradictory doctrine of determinism which eliminates the possibility of judgment by an individual enmeshed in causal chains (and so incapable of acknowledging the truth of the theory itself), or alternatively to an untenable notion of indeterminate freedom which would render all judgment and all action entirely arbitrary. But Spinoza was far from committing these errors and was careful to avoid the pitfalls of such theories, although he is often misinterpreted as advocating one of similar character; and Fichte is certainly one who is guilty of such misinterpretation.

TRUE SPINOZISM

The *Substantia-sive-Natura* that Spinoza identifies with God is often criticized as a blank unity absorbing into its seamless and indivisible identity all apparent differences. The differences are supposed to be the product of the human imagination, which apprehends as diverse what is really simply and singly one. This is a travesty of Spinoza's doctrine and is utterly incoherent. The human imagination is, on his theory, characteristic of finite minds, finite modes of Thought, the existence of which already presupposes differentiation within Substance, thus the modes cannot themselves be the product of imagination. Diversity cannot, therefore, be a mere appearance attributable to *imaginatio*. So gross a misunderstanding is presumably not worth further discussion.

More plausibly, Spinoza has been accused of providing no principle of differentiation to explain the multiplicity which he postulates within the nature (or essence) of Substance. But neither is this criticism just. The principle is stated by Spinoza, if somewhat obliquely, in Epp 9:

> *quo plus realitas aut esse aliquod ens habet eo plura attributa ei sunt tribuenda.*[5]

Hence an absolutely infinite being must have infinite attributes. In short, what is absolute and infinite cannot for that very reason be a blank unity. As was said earlier, it cannot be an analytic unity, or in any way abstract. It is, and must be, by its very nature, the most concrete reality conceivable. "*Quo plus realitas aut esse aliquod habet . . .*" The more reality anything has, the more concrete it is, the more being it comprehends and integrates, the more attributes (i.e., the more diversity) it must include: "*eo plus attributa ipsa componunt.*"[6] Accordingly,

God-or-Substance has infinite attributes, and "from the necessity of the divine nature infinite things follow in infinite modes (that is, everything that can fall under an infinite intellect)" (E1P16).

Spinoza conceived Substance as a genuine whole, and that, as is apparent from what he writes in Epp 32, is one of which the parts are mutually adapted and internally related one to another. It is a structured whole the differences within which are interdependent and are governed in their nature and interrelations by a single principle of order (or organization). This, in the case of Spinoza's Substance, we have already shown, is the divine essence, as it is expressed in each of God's attributes. And, as he tells us in the contexts to which reference has repeatedly been made, it regulates the mutifarious changes among the finite modes. *Facies totius universi*, for example, the infinite mode of Extension, "compels" the innumerable changes of motion and rest that occur among bodies, its finite modes; and the order and connection of modes is the same under all attributes. The principle of differentiation is thus clearly established.

God is the whole, and the whole (as we are assured in TdIE)[7] is the truth. This we must bear in mind throughout, and we see here Spinoza's anticipation of Hegel's dictum. For our purpose, however, what is more important is the structure of the whole, and that it is dialectical in form appears in Spinoza's exposition by implication, if not explicitly. Several features of his system give evidence of this structure, which is that of a scale of forms, sequentially overlapping, and progressively increasing in degree of concreteness or integral wholeness. The first evidence of this is Spinoza's assertion in the Appendix to Part I of the *Ethics* that God did not lack material for the creation of all things, from the highest to the lowest grade of perfection. God, therefore, the all-embracing Substance, is thus infinitely diversified as a scale of degrees of perfection, from (to reverse Spinoza's order) the lowest to the highest; that is, as a dialectical scale.

That this is no merely fortuitous and isolated statement may be shown by pointing to certain exemplifications in Spinoza's exposition of the graded scale of forms of perfection. Perhaps the clearest is the one to which we have so often drawn attention in earlier chapters, that is, the scale of complexity (that Spinoza describes as perfection) in bodies from the simplest right up to the face of the entire universe. The order and connection of ideas, we must also remember, is the same as that of bodies, so we must expect a similar scale under the attribute of Thought. That this is so the scale of degrees in knowledge from *imaginatio* to *ratio* and *scientia intuitiva* bears witness. Another example is the scale of goods, first mentioned in TdIE, pleasure, wealth, honor, and ultimately blessedness. In this *Treatise* Spinoza does not represent these as a scale, but merely lists the first three as supposed goods commonly sought by men, all of which have proved unsatisfying. Instead of seeking satisfaction in these objects, Spinoza offers the search for an infinite and eternal object the possession and love of which is accompanied by no pain. He does, however, say in this work that, while the terms good and evil are merely relative and no more than aids to the imagination, men do form an ideal of human nature, and that whatever helps them to achieve it they call truly good, and the actual achievement is the supreme good. In the last three Parts of the *Ethics* it becomes clear that a scale is involved. There are emotions that lead to hatred and conflict; there are emotions that lead to love and mutual admiration, and there are emotions that accompany free action, that calm the passions and lead to concord and mutual cooperation. Most judgments of value are said to be purely imaginative, corresponding to nothing in reality; some point to goods that are only relative; others refer to conditions that are fortuitously advantageous; but the true good is what we know for certain to be useful to us.

These are only indications of the structure of the real, and most of them are mainly incidental to Spinoza's argument; but the whole structure of Substance as he sets it forth consists of a scale of forms. At the lower end are simple modes; these increase progressively in degree of perfection to the level of infinite modes; these follow immediately from the relevant attributes, which together express the essence of the one absolutely infinite Substance.

The dynamic that drives the dialectic of the system upwards along the scale of degrees is the *conatus*. This has been identified as the essence of the particular mode which it energizes, and also with the essence of God. Because every attribute of Substance is one of God's powers, the infinite modes are dynamic principles (e.g., Motion-and-rest and the infinite intellect). These regulate the nature and behavior of the finite modes, whose essences are, accordingly, also dynamic and express themselves as the *conatus in suo esse perseverandi*. But Spinoza also maintains that action from one's own nature alone is free action—true action, of which the agent is the adequate cause. What is only the effect of external causes is passion, not action. Although it too is the expression of the *conatus*, it amounts rather to a limitation and a constraint upon the essence of the patient, who suffers in consequence a diminution in his or her power of action (i.e., suffers pain). To that extent, passion is a failure to persevere in one's own being (or essence). The *conatus*, therefore, is a striving towards free action, or power properly so-called. In the case of simple entities this can be achieved by combination with others to constitute what, as Spinoza describes it, is clearly an organic body, one the action of which is more dependent upon itself alone and less on the "concurrence" of others.

In the case of humanity the essence of the human being is the intellect concomitant with a state of the body which makes free action possible; and Spinoza tells us in the TdIE that it is of the nature of the intellect to frame true ideas. True ideas, moreover, are adequate ideas grasping the nature of things through an adequate conception of one of God's attributes (E2P40S2). That is to say, they are concrete ideas which contain objectively more reality than inadequate ideas, so that human action is free when the intellect comprehends the greatest amount of perfection or reality and its *ideatum* is a body of the highest possible organic integrity.

The tendency up the scale of degrees of perfection is thus the immanent power of the whole expressing itself as the *conatus* and impelling the more imperfect or inadequate forms towards a fulfillment that supplies in successive stages what is lacking or deficient in them. This is no mere addition of new parts, but is at the same time reorganization and integration of parts to constitute a whole on a higher level of being, or perfection. Yet it is also plainly implied that every level of the scale, however lowly, is an essential stage and element in the totality which is Substance or God. All are parts in one whole which determines, as it were, from above, the nature and conduct of each and all.

The system is thus dialectically structured; and it now clearly transpires that although everything in it is determined, and, as Spinoza puts it, necessary, there are differing kinds and degrees of determination. There is geometrical determination, then there is causal determination, then psychological determination (by passion), then rational determination (action). The last, being self-determination, is free. Spinozistic determinism, therefore, is something quite different from and other than Laplacian determinism, which it tolerates only at a specific and appropriate level in the scale.

SPINOZA AND FICHTE RECONCILED

We are now in a position to see how far Fichte's conception of Spinozism succeeds and how far it fails to do justice to the real Spinoza. Certainly Spinoza's world is thoroughly determined. Necessity reigns, and contingency is only an appearance resulting from deficiency in our knowledge (E1P29 and P33S1). But it is not throughout *mechanically* determined. It is determined by God dialectically and organismically.

Mechanical determination is characteristic only of the lower orders of perfection, but as we go up the scale the kind of determination changes. At a higher level it becomes physico-chemical,[8] and higher still it is determination by the laws of psychology governing the passions, and beyond that again, at the level of adequate thinking, it is self-determination or free action, which is ultimately the action of God by which everything is determined. Determinism itself is specified in a scale of forms interrelated dialectically, through which the free power of God, determined by nothing but itself, is manifested as much in mechanism as it is in intelligent action.

How then must we conceive human freedom? For Spinoza human beings are finite modes under the attributes of Extension and Thought, and as such they are parts of nature, subject to external influences, a prey to passions by which they are tossed hither and thither "like waves of the sea driven by contrary winds." To that extent they are determined from without. But they are also capable of understanding clearly and distinctly, of framing adequate ideas the physical counterparts of which are free actions, determined indeed, but rationally, not by external causes. Minds capable of such thinking are the ideas of bodies capable of doing and suffering many things together and of maintaining themselves by their own action independently of the concurrence of other bodies. They are organismically, or holistically, determined, which, for all that Spinoza says about teleology (a polemic justified with respect to its popular and illegitimate use), is teleological determination in its proper meaning. Such action is rational; it ensues when the mind grasps the essences of things through the common properties inherent in the attributes of God and their infinite modes—what in TdIE Spinoza calls the eternal things, which

> though they are themselves individuals (*singularia*), nevertheless because of their ubiquity and power will be for us as universals or genera of the definitions of changeable and particular things.

Better still, in *scientia intuitiva* we proceed from an adequate idea of one of God's attributes to adequate ideas of the essences of individual things. In short, when we comprehend things in the light of the whole, we are free both in thought and in action.

Such thought and action, however, is identical with God's so far as it is adequate, and our free action is, in consequence, God acting in and through us more fully than he does in our unfree behavior. In our *imaginatio* and passion God expresses himself through us only so far as he also expresses himself through other things, whereas in our adequate ideas and actions we reflect his own, and we express his nature truly. Consequently, in such thinking and action we are autonomous or self-determined.

But the awareness of things in the light of the whole is precisely the sort of self-conscious experience that Fichte envisages for his absolute Ego; though Fichte, as we have seen, never succeeds in reconciling this with the finite self, who is palpably in much of its life subject to external determinants, is inevitably limited by the non-ego and submitted constantly to *Anstosse.*

Spinoza saw that the two were related as different degrees of perfection in a dialectical scale, in every phase of which the infinite totality or absolute Substance is immanent but which is expressed in each in differing degrees of adequacy. It is because of this immanence and its operation through the *conatus* that the finite mind can transcend its limits and become aware of the whole. It is the priority of this whole which, for Spinoza, is the condition of there being any objects of experience. Everything is and is conceived only in and through God, and nothing can be or be conceived except through God. And this in effect is the same condition as Fichte postulates, for his prior condition is an integral subject for whom all experience is one interrelated system, an original unity of apperception which demands a self-contained, unconditioned ideal whole.

In attributing pure consciousness to God, therefore, as Fichte alleged, Spinoza did not go amiss; and God in his system is par excellence the *res cogitans.* It is also true that the finite ego exists for Spinoza because God exists. But it is not wholly true that God is "something else," nor that the ego is only *for* something else. The human intellect is the immanent power of God, the *conatus* working in and as the essence of man; and human knowledge is brought to fruition in *scientia intuitiva,* in which it is coincident with God's consciousness—but it is God's consciousness expressing itself through his attribute (of Thought) in his own self-differentiation. God's intellect is the condition and source of all consciousness, just as, for Fichte, the absolute Ego is the absolutely prior condition. And we have already seen that, for Fichte, the absolute Ego assumes the place of the deity. Why Fichte should have alleged (if that is what he means) that Spinoza's God never becomes aware of himself is obscure—and surely false; for Spinoza's God, as surely as Aristotle's, is *noēsis noēseōs.* His is the active intellect "without which nothing thinks."

In later life Fichte came to recognize the transcendent nature of his own position, without, however, revising his judgment of Spinozism or admitting his own change of outlook. In 1810, when he wrote *Die Wissenschaftslehre im allgemeinen Umriss,* he almost echoed Spinoza:

Only one is absolutely through itself: God, and God is not the dead concept, of which we have just spoken, but he is in himself pure life. Also this cannot in itself change and determine itself, and make itself another being; for through its being all being and all possible being has been given, and neither in him nor outside him can a new being come into existence. If now there is to be knowledge … it can, since there is nothing but God, be only God himself, yet outside of himself … his utterance.[9]

He struggles to find a way of conceiving a knowing which is not God himself, yet, since nothing but God is, must be God himself; and he concludes that it is God, but paradoxically outside of himself, and therefore an image or schema of God. This is declared to be a self-determinate capacity, which, as the theory develops, is seen to differentiate itself into finite subjects, each under the obligation, and subject to the drive, to see and to realize itself as the divine totality. Here indeed we find Spinozism in Fichte: the primordial absolute and all-inclusive unity of God expressing itself as a power or pure *Vermögen*, self-differentiating into finite modifications or expressions of itself in which its power (capacity) becomes a *conatus* (*Trieb*) to actualize that free activity which is the comprehension of the whole.

Not merely is the doctrine Spinozism, it is also an adumbration of Schelling's and Hegel's Absolute. For Hegel it becomes the absolute Idea, differentiating itself in indispensable embodiment, in and as a vast dialectical system of Nature and Spirit. It is to Fichte as much as (or rather more than) to any other thinker that Hegel owed the structure of his dialectic, and the realization that without antithesis no synthesis is possible, however much antithesis itself depends on prior synthesis. But that is another story and is not prominent (although latent) in Spinoza. In Giordano Bruno, however, whom Spinoza must surely have read, the *coincidentia oppositorum* explicitly emerges.

Notes

1. Thomas Hobbes, *Leviathan*, Pt. I, Ch. 1.
2. "Ich trete ein in eine geschlossene Kette der Erscheinungen, da jedes Glied durch sein vorgehendes bestimmt wird; in einen festen Zusammenhang, da ich aus jedem gegebenen Momente alle möglichen Zusstände des Universums durch bloßes Nachdenken würde finden können, aufwärts, wenn ich den gegebenen Moment erklärte, abwärts, wenn ich aus ihm ableite; wenn ich aufwärts die Ursachen, durch welche allein er wirklich werden konnte, abwärts die Folgen, die er notwendig haben muss, aufsuchte. Ich empfange in jedem Teil das Ganze, weil jeder Teil nur durch das Ganze ist, was er ist; durch dieses aber notwendig das ist."

3. Cf. *Kritik der reinen Vernunft*, A47.
4. In his late summary outline of the *Wissenschaftslehre* (1810) he modified his position significantly, and to this we shall return.
5. Cf. also E1P9.
6. Ibid.
7. "... *perfectissima ea erit Methodus, quae ad datae ideae Entis perfectissimi normam ostendit, quomodo mens sit dirigenda.*"
8. Cf. Ep 56, and my *Salvation from Despair*, pp. 124–5.
9. "Nur Eines ist schlechthin durch sich selbst: Gott, und Gott ist nicht der todte Begriff, den wir soeben aussprachen, sondern er ist in sich selbst lauter Leben. Auch kann dieser nicht in sich selbst sich verändern und bestimmen, und zu einem andern Sein machen; denn durch sein Sein is alles Sein und alles möglich Sein gegeben, und es kann weder in ihm, noch ausser ihm ein neues Sein entstehen. Soll nun das Wissen dennoch sein ... so kann es, da nichts ist denn Gott, doch nur Gott selbst sein, aber ausser ihm selber ... sein Äusserung."

12

The Spinozism of
F. W. J. Schelling

In the last chapter we examined the relation between Spinoza's philosophy and that of one of the major figures in the development of early nineteenth-century German Idealism. I now want to consider the influence exerted by his thought upon the next great thinker in that development. In order to do so it will be helpful to retrace our steps and to glance briefly at the transition from the Critical Philosophy of Kant to the Absolute, or Objective, Idealism of Hegel.

We have seen how Kant and Fichte became committed to subjective idealism, and when we come to Hegel, we find him repeatedly criticizing Kant, especially for his subjectivism. Kant, as we saw, had reacted mainly to the failure of Empiricism, as established by Locke and developed by Berkeley and Hume, to support and justify the objectivity of empirical science, despite the fact that it was precisely by becoming empirical, under the influence of Bacon and Newton, that science was making such spectacular progress. But Kant halted persistently between two opinions, remaining an empiricist so far as he insisted on limiting the scope of human knowledge to what was given in sense, but insisting at the same time that that knowledge was made coherent (and so "objective") through a priori synthesis of the manifold of sense-given data by unifying principles (categories). The categories are principles of organization derived from the unity of the ego, and the knowledge they objectify, therefore, is only of phenomena (things as they appear to us), not of reality (things in themselves). So Kant has one foot in the empiricist camp, while the other is planted in rationalist terrain; and he remains subjectivist, probably due to the influence of Leibniz, for whom also spatio-temporal objects were only *phenomena bene fundata*.

Fichte went a step further in the direction of subjectivism, by dis-avowing belief in any things-in-themselves, and making the transcen-dental Ego the source of all knowledge and reality. A metaphysic like that of Spinoza, accordingly, which ostensibly overlooks the necessary condition of any experience that it be subject to the unifying synthesis of the knowing subject, and envisages a world of Nature knowable by human beings who are but finite modes, becomes for Fichte an un-warranted and unsubstantiated dogmatism.

Yet the epistemological grounds for Critical Idealism seemed unas-sailable. To maintain, as Locke had done, the existence of a world of objects external to our minds, which, through the physical and physi-ological effects they cause upon our sense organs, give rise to ideas (*Vorstellungen*, as they became for Kant and his sucessors), was self-defeating. Locke himself was forced to confess that we could know only our own ideas, so that any external world, and any process of causation originating ideas, must inevitably be inaccessible to our knowl-edge, and the very bases of his theory become, on that theory, unknowable. If it were true it could not be conceived; if it can be contemplated, it must be false. Locke's immediate successors, Berkeley and Hume, therefore, were committed to a subjectivism, from which all escape was precluded and all objective scientific knowledge ban-ished, and which led inexorably to the complete disintegration of co-herent knowledge and to scepticism.

Awakened from his dogmatic slumber by Hume's scepticism, Kant strove to repair the damage that had led to this debacle, and to give the ship of knowledge a compass that would enable it to avoid the sandbank on which, Kant said, Hume had beached it and left it to rot. But even when refloated, the ship was still navigating subjective wa-ters. The real ocean in itself remained invisible through the telescope of the understanding, and the observable phenomena were the con-struct of its lenses. Under the captaincy of Fichte the telescope became both ship and ocean, and performed the ambiguous and insupport-able role of originating the world that it revealed while it remained a single item of the ship's equipment.

When we turn to Hegel we find the problem resolved. Realism and idealism have been reconciled, the existence of Nature, in its own right, as "the Idea in the form of other-being" affirmed, and the question how knowledge of the world gets into the mind answered in the dec-laration that "the mind is the truth of Nature" or Nature brought to consciousness of itself as the human mind. For Hegel, Nature is the self-manifestation of the Idea as a real external world. "The external world is implicitly the truth," he writes, "for the truth is actual and must exist." (*Enzyklopädie*, §38 *Zusatz*). Through Nature, the Idea develops itself, in a series of dialectically related forms, which, in the organism, brings it to consciousness of itself through sentience in the minds of human beings. They, on the one hand, are natural products, and on the other hand, they represent the level on which the Idea, which has been immanent throughout the dialectical process, rises to self-consciousness.

How did Hegel succeed in breaking out of the apparently inescapable circle of the pure activity of Fichte's transcendental Ego? The answer is that the trail was blazed by Schelling in his *Ideen zu eine Philosophie der Natur*, and the works immediately succeeding. Schelling was acutely aware of the problems set by Lockeian realism, as his discussion in the introduction to the *Ideen* plainly shows. But he was equally aware that Nature—especially organic nature—could not satisfactorily be disposed of simply as the product of the activity, theoretical and practical (as Fichte had maintained), of the self-conscious Ego, transcendental or other, however free and independent that activity might be. To work out a solution to his problem he sought fresh inspiration from Spinoza. But before we investigate the Spinozistic element in his thought, we must return briefly to Kant to trace the germ of Schelling's ideas in the third Critique.

Kant had already drawn attention in the Critique of Teleological Judgment to the problematic nature of organization as a natural phenomenon. With unerring insight he saw that purposiveness and wholeness were inseparably connected. He writes:

> It is requisite to a thing as natural end (or purpose) first that the parts (as regards their existence and their form) are possible through their relation to the whole. For, consequently, the thing itself is an end conceived under a concept or an idea which must determine a priori everything that is to be contained in it. (*Kritik der Urteilskraft*, §63)

If the thing is simply thought of as possible under these conditions, it is an artifact. But if it is to be related to a purpose in itself as a natural product, without the intervention of an extraneous rational cause (e.g., human or divine intention), the further condition must be fulfilled that parts and whole are mutually ends and means, for only so is it possible that the idea of the whole should determine, and be determined by, the form and connection of all the parts. Each, then, is mutually cause and effect of the other(s), and only then is the thing an organized being which may be called a natural end.

There is considerable affinity between this characterization of teleology and what Spinoza writes about whole and part in the 32nd Letter (to Oldenburg), where he insists upon the adaptation of the parts one to another in determining the nature and identity of the whole, which, again, by its overall configuration determines the inter-relations and reciprocal changes among the parts, so that it would not be inappropriate to describe them as mutually means and ends. There is no evidence that Kant had this letter in mind, but it is not at all improbable that Schelling (who, as we shall presently see, builds on Kant's position) was influenced by it.

Now, according to Kant, observation of Nature, as brought under the categories of the understanding, yields only mechanical laws, by which this mutual teleology cannot be explained. There are no a priori grounds in the idea of Nature, as a complex of observed objects, for the belief that they serve one another as means and ends. Nor can we discover this from experience. To conceive natural things as teleologi-cal organisms (a notion as indispensable to biology as mechanism is to physics), we must impose upon our experience of them, not just categories of the understanding, but an idea of reason, which is not constitutively valid, but only regulative. To be constitutive the idea must be the necessary condition, not simply of our representation of the thing as organized (analogously to our own purposiveness), but of its very existence.

The effect of Fichte's abolition of things-in-themselves, however, was to make the distinction between phenomena and noumena, and so that between constitutive and regulative ideas, purely relative to the dialectical level at which the Ego was operating. Ideas of reason could now be conditions of objective knowledge as well as (or even better than) concepts of the understanding. Schelling concluded, accordingly, that objectivity and subjectivity were merely two aspects of the same reality, which itself was neither or both. Organization thus becomes, for Schelling, clear evidence of the coordinate reality of Nature, equal and opposite to that of the subjective experience of the Ego. This realization seems to have sent him back to Spinoza, who, he says in the introduction to the *Ideen,* was the first to recognize the identity of subject and object.

Organism implies, and is in itself, a whole, determined in structure and function by a holistic principle (which Schelling, like Kant, calls *Begriff,* concept), and this holism cannot be regarded merely as im-posed upon the object by our minds, because our minds are com-pelled, by the very nature and possibility of the object, to recognize the immanence in it of the concept (or principle of organization) as the very condition of its being. The entities of physical nature obeying the laws of mechanism might well be no more than the subjection of phenomena to the ordering categories of the understanding (although this is not Schelling's final view), but an organism is self-subsistent and self-maintaining, through its own life and activity, in a way which the categories do not and cannot require. It must, therefore, be an independent manifestation of the concept or idea. In effect, this is Spinoza's doctrine as set out in the epistle to which reference has been made, and in the Scholia to E2P13 and L7. Although Schelling here makes no comparison with Spinoza, he comes to the conclusion that the Idea manifests itself indifferently in two coordinate ways, as organic Nature (for he subsequently finds, like Spinoza, that all Nature is ultimately organic—compare Spinoza's account of *facies totius universi* and his assertion that all bodies are *animata*), and as subjective experience. This corresponds to Spinoza's Substance expressing its essence under the two attributes of Extension and Thought.

On the one hand, therefore, Fichte is vindicated so far as his *Wissenschaftslehre* goes, but this needs, in Schelling's view, to be supplemented, on the other hand, by a *Naturlehre*, to do justice to the objective aspect of the real. The Ego is the original act of cognition, for Schelling, in itself indifferently subjective and objective, from which the ideal world is subjectively generated (as in Fichte's philosophy), but which equally manifests itself in a world of Nature, through a series of "potencies" rising to the levels of consciousness and reason in the highest form of organism, mankind.

The metaphysical background of Schelling's *Naturphilosophie* is set out, not always in quite the same terms, in a number of works subsequent to the *Ideen*. The general outline of the system seems to have been taking shape in his mind when he wrote this book, but he seems not to have felt sure about it until later, when he came to write *Darstellung meines Systems der Philosophie*; but it also appears, with certain minor differences, in *Von der Weltseele* and in *Bruno*. He never seems to have been able to make it quite unambiguous or clear-cut, never as systematic and coherent as Spinoza's, but it has very definite parallels to Spinoza's ideas.

In Schelling's system, as in Hegel's, the ultimately real is the Absolute, corresponding to Spinoza's Substance. Schelling gives different descriptions and different names to it in different contexts. Sometimes it is the indifference point, sometimes pure Identity; at other times it is the Infinite, or "sheer Absoluteness"; then again he calls it Absolute Knowing, or the absolute act of cognition, and likewise the unity of the Absolute-ideal and the Absolute-real. Sometimes Schelling seems to identify this with the Idea, but at other times the Idea appears at a slightly lower level in the hierarchy of reality, and it is never quite clear whether it is the same as the Essence, or alternatively, what he calls the Form. Essence and Form, however, are the two opposites into which absolute Identity differentiates itself, and Spinoza's Thought and Extension as attributes identical in Substance seem to be what he had in mind, although the exact correspondence remains vague. Essence suggests the category of universality, and Form that of particularity, but both are still held to present ideal and real aspects, both are at once objective and subjective. The latter (Form) is the projection of the former in the realm of appearance to constitute what Schelling calls relative objectivity, as opposed to relative subjectivity, both uniting in the indifference of absolute Identity.

Form is the realm of embodiment (*Einbildung*), or objectification, of the infinite in the finite, and is primarily differentiated into relative identity, relative difference (or opposition), and the unity of these—the identity of identity and nonidentity. There is presumably a similar differentiation of Essence, but we are told little about it, although it ostensibly constitutes the ideal sphere set out in detail in Schelling's *System des Transcendentalen Idealismus*. Thus there are three major unities:

> that in which the essence is absolutely shaped into form, that in which the form is absolutely shaped into essence, and that in which both these absolutenesses are again one absoluteness.[1]

So are the three potencies generated that are exemplified at various levels (but never systematically expounded by Schelling) as thing, concept, and idea; or real, ideal, and the identity of the two; or finite, infinite, and eternal; or Nature, Mind, and the Absolute (indifferent, or neutral, Identity). Schelling flits from one to another of these diverse methods of expressing the triadic structure of this Absolute in a rather confusing manner, so that it is difficult to say just how they are all to be included in one system. Nor is it clear whether the absolute act of cognition (also called Absolute Knowing) is the Absolute itself, or only the second of the three major unities. At times he refers to it as if it were the latter, but at other times he seems to be insisting that this is the original and primordial unity from which the other two emerge. It was left to Hegel to weld all these representations of the Absolute and its dialectical self-differentiation into a single coherent whole by means of one consistent principle. But it was Schelling who first came to see that Fichte's transcendental Ego was really the Absolute (or God), which differentiates itself, on the one hand, as the system of Nature, through which it brings itself to consciousness in the human mind, and, on the other hand, as knowledge, in a parallel system objectively identical with the first. And this pattern is essentially Spinozistic.

Spinoza anticipated all this when, at an early stage, in TdIE, he realized that adequate knowledge can only be generated (or deduced) from the idea of the most perfect being, that this is the perfect method, and that the perfect being (God) expresses his essence in the attributes of Extension and Thought, which are identical in Substance. This God-or-Substance-or-Nature, he saw, was immanent in all its modes, of which the human body and mind are each one under corresponding attributes, identical with each other in substance as *idea* and *ideatum*. And when Schelling tells us that the Philosophy of Nature is the one essential aspect of philosophy, he may well be using the word "Nature" in Spinoza's sense of *Deus-Substantia-sive-Natura*. In fact, Schelling's thinking is so closely molded upon Spinoza's that Spinozistic terminology is frequently appropriate and is often used by Schelling himself to give it expression, as when he refers to the absolute act of cognition as *Natura naturans*, and to the natural world ("the mere body or symbol thereof") as *Natura naturata*.

I shall proceed to exemplify the echoes of Spinoza's ideas as they occur from time to time in Schelling's writings. It must be borne in mind that Schelling never really expounds his metaphysics in systematic fashion, so that one can hardly demonstrate any clear systematic parallel between his theory and that of Spinoza. All I propose to do is to point to the echoes and latent applications of Spinoza's concepts in Schelling's more poetic and somewhat fantastic speculations.

Throughout *Von der Weltseele*, in which he insists on the organic character of Nature, Schelling stresses the immanence of the whole in every part, both in general and in detail, saying at one point that the highest aim of science is to reveal the ubiquitous presence of God in all things. God, he says, is the One in the totality, in whom all things live and have their being. Although one cannot point specifically to Spinoza as the source of this sentiment, the whole passage is Spinozistic in tone, and Spinozism is its most likely inspiration. A little further on Schelling quotes Spinoza directly as saying "the more we know of things, the more we know of God," to support his own conviction that those who seek "the science of the eternal" should do so by way of physics.[2]

When we turn to *Darstellung meines Systems*, where Schelling's exposition is as systematic as he ever succeeds in making it, the evidence of Spinoza's influence is more copious. He begins by declaring reason to be absolute and indifferent to all subjectivity or objectivity. He asserts that all philosophy proceeds from the standpoint of reason, and treats things, therefore, as they are in themselves, and not otherwise. As such, he says, they are essentially infinite, and the fundamental law of reason being A = A, it posits absolute Identity, which is the absolutely

Infinite. This is clearly Spinoza's God, defined precisely in these terms in E1D6. Schelling proceeds immediately to give a Spinozistic proof of this absolute infinity, to the effect that there can be nothing to limit it either internal or external to itself, because it is all-inclusive and self-identical. The absolute Identity, he asserts, does not emerge or proceed out of itself, and true philosophy consists in proving this—namely, that all things in themselves are infinite and are the absolute Identity itself (in short, it is all-inclusive). Only Spinoza, he says, among previous philosophers, had recognized this truth, although even he (Schelling contends) did not carry through the proof completely, nor state it with sufficient clarity to prevent misunderstanding.[3]

Schelling goes on to tell us that there is a primordial knowledge of the absolute Identity, posited with the proposition A = A; and because there is nothing external to the absolute Identity, this knowledge is in the absolute Identity itself. But it does not follow immediately from its essence, from which only its being follows. The knowledge, therefore, belongs to the form of its being, and that is as original as the being itself. Thus there is an original knowledge of the absolute Identity belonging to the form of its being. It is, Schelling avers, an attribute of the absolute Identity itself.[4]

It is fairly obvious that what he has in mind here again is Spinoza's Substance with its attribute of Thought, the infinite modes of which are the infinite intellect and the idea of God. Also, Schelling is recalling Spinoza's doctrine that because Substance is *causa sui*, its essence immediately involves its existence. Spinoza says that an attribute is what the intellect perceives as the essence of Substance, and Schelling seems to be trying to convey something of the sort by saying that the original knowledge of the absolute Identity belongs to the form of its being and is posited with it as following immediately from it, just as the attributes and their infinite modes follow immediately from Spinoza's Substance. For Schelling, Essence is the dialectical opposite of Form, but just what he means by either term is far from clear.

In §31 he says that the absolute Identity *is* (exists) only under the form of indifference of the subjective and the objective (and thus also of Knowing and Being). Schelling speaks of this indifference as "quantitative." He maintains that there is no qualitative difference between the subjective and the objective, and that they can be differentiated only quantitatively. Probably here he is thinking of Fichte's assertion that contradictory opposites are reconciled when treated as mutual complements.[5] Further, when Schelling uses the word *Differenz* (as he does here in the negative) what he means is complementary, rather than (or as well as) difference. So if absolute Identity exists only under the form of "indifference" of Knowing and Being, the indication is that these two complementary opposites are united in it much as Thought and Extension are united in Substance for Spinoza.

Schelling goes on to explain that the absolute Identity is the universe, and vice versa, because it *is* only as universe, and can be treated in accordance with essence and form only under limitation (*Einschränkung*)—again, reminiscent of Fichte (not to say Spinoza). It follows that it is the same in essence in every part, and so is indivisible (§§33, 34). Spinoza, it will be remembered, insists that the essence of Substance, as expressed in each attribute, is indivisible, for much the same reason. Then, Schelling continues, no limited individual has its ground of being in itself, for all are equal in essence (the absolute Identity is the same in each) and the being of every limited individual derives from the Absolute. Here, once more, we have pure Spinoza. Next we are told, almost in Spinoza's own words, that every individual thing is determined by another individual thing, and that by another, ad infinitum, the reason being that the existence of none is determined by itself, and the absolute Identity encompasses the ground of the totality (§§35, 36). In short, only Substance is in itself and is conceived through itself, while its finite modes are all in it and are conceived through one or other of its attributes, each being an effect of a finite cause, itself a similar effect of a finite cause, and so on ad infinitum. So Spinozan is §38 that one is tempted to quote it in toto:

> *Every individual being is, as such, a determinate form of the being of the absolute Identity, but not its being itself, which is only in the totality.* For every individual and finite being is posited through a quantitative difference of subjectivity and objectivity, which again is determined by another individual being, that is, through another determinate quantitative difference of subjectivity and objectivity.—Now, however, subjectivity and objectivity as such is form of the being of the absolute Identity, the determinate quantitative difference of both, therefore, is a determinate form of being of the absolute Identity, but for just that reason not its being *itself*, which is only the quantitative indifference of subjectivity and objectivity, i.e., only in the totality. So the statement can also be expressed thus: Every individual being is determined by the absolute Identity, not insofar as it is absolutely, but insofar as it is under the form of a determinate quantitative difference of A and B (subjectivity and objectivity), which difference, again, is determined in like manner, and so on *in infinitum.*

With the substitution of a few Spinozan terms for Schelling's somewhat convoluted language, this passage could almost have come straight out of the *Ethics.* What it says in effect is: Every individual thing is a determinate mode of Substance. For every individual finite mode is a finite affection of Substance through one of its attributes (e.g., Thought or Extension). Each is determined by another such finite mode, and that by another, and so on. However, Thought and Extension are alternative expressions of God's essence but are identical in substance. In other words, every individual thing is determined by God, not insofar as he is infinite, but insofar as he constitutes a finite mode of one of his attributes, each caused by another such finite mode, and so on ad infinitum.

Spinoza, when he discusses space, time, and number (or quantity), as he does in the 12th Letter (on the Infinite), as well as in the *Short Treatise* and the *Ethics*, insists that quantitative division is only conceivable when Substance is considered as affected in specific ways: only in terms of finite modes. And here Schelling is echoing very closely the Spinozan doctrine. In the remark appended to §44, Schelling expressly states that his "A and B" (subjectivity and objectivity) are precisely Spinoza's attributes of Thought and Extension, except that, so he says, "we never think of them as one merely *idealiter* (as one generally understands Spinoza), but *realiter*." Whether one generally understands Spinoza as identifying the attributes only ideally, Spinoza himself is quite clear that they are really, substantially, one and the same.

In §53 Schelling tells us that through the absolute Identity subjectivity and objectivity are immediately posited as being, or as real, just as Spinoza tells us that from eternal things, from Substance and its attributes, eternal and infinite modes follow immediately (E1PP21, 23). And just as Spinoza asserts that from the necessity of the divine nature infinite things follow in infinite ways (E1P16), Schelling proceeds to "deduce" from his absolute Identity and its two "attributes" A and B the two fundamental attractive and repulsive forces which, for him, together constitute matter, and thence the entire physical world (as he deduced the ideal world from the absolute identity of the Ego in *System des Transcendentale Idealismus*). He also speaks in Spinozan language of gravity striving to maintain the product(s) of the two forces in being. According to him, light is the ideal or inner aspect, while gravity is the real or outer, of matter as such; thus to say that gravity strives to maintain bodies in being is much the same as what Spinoza maintains when he says that everything, so far as it is in itself, strives to preserve itself in its own being (E3P6).

We have already noted that Spinoza's conception of *facies totius universi* was of a universal organic whole made up of subordinate organisms at different levels of "perfection." That is exactly how Schelling conceives Nature, both in *Von der Weltseele* and in *System des Transcendentale Idealismus*

(Teil III, ii, D.iv). He could as well have gotten the idea from Leibniz, but the source in Leibniz is surely Spinoza. In the *System of Transcendental Idealism*, Schelling defines freedom exactly as Spinoza does: the absolute act of will is free, simply because it is determined by the necessity of its own nature. However, Schelling's argument here is as much Kantian as Spinozan, although there can be little doubt that the influence of Spinoza persists.

In *Bruno*, in an extraordinary sort of amalgam of Plato's *Timaeus* and Spinoza's *Ethics*, an account is given of the relation of soul and body which is, in all essentials, Spinozan. The universe is said to be a vast immortal animal, so well ordered that it can never die. Organisms, we have already seen from *Ideen* and *Von der Weltseele*, are unified and organized in accordance with a principle identified by Schelling as the concept. So the universe unites a vast multiplicity; as in a living animal each individual organ is both distinguished from and united with every other, each having, as it were, its own soul, yet all bound together, in the unity of the whole. The soul is the concept, and that of which it is the concept is the body. Thus all things are, each in its own degree, animate, and the soul (or mind) of each, being the idea of its body, contains only what is expressed in the particular thing of which it is the idea. Schelling's reasoning to demonstrate how the body can contain within its concept the possibility of, and relation to, innumerable other things, is much vaguer and looser than Spinoza's, but the general doctrine is the same.[6]

There is no need to give further examples to show that Schelling's speculation is saturated with the thought of Spinoza. What, you may ask, is the historical and philosophical significance of this fact?

The problem set for Western philosophy in the seventeenth century by Descartes and Locke, each in his own peculiar way, was: How do ideas of the external world get into the human mind? Reflection on this question led all their successors, except Spinoza, into an incurable subjectivism, liable to the most serious objections. Berkeley became committed to a criterion of truth that was unviable, and Hume was led in consequence into a scepticism that undermined all science. Leibniz produced a more promising theory, but it required a miraculous pre-established harmony between windowless monads (whose common reflection of the rest of the universe was, in effect, left unexplained), in order to give it at least the appearance of consistency. Kant developed Locke and Berkeley, with the help of some Wolffian Leibniz, only to restrict human knowledge to phenomena, with no theoretical bridge to the real world of things in themselves; so that Fichte had to resort to a transcendental idealism which was again inescapably subjectivist. Spinoza was the one philosopher of the era who was able to recognize that ideas of an external world did not, and did not need to, "get into the mind": that the mind and physical things were not entities of the same type, related one to another in space and by causation, but were two different aspects of the same thing (or the same thing under two different attributes). Ideas, for him, were simply the self-awareness of the bodies whose minds they constituted, and the more complex and organically self-complete those bodies were, the more adequate and comprehensive were their ideas. Both bodies and minds were ranged in an ascending scale of "perfection" culminating in an all-encompassing whole, or infinite mode, that was the direct outcome of the necessary nature of an absolutely infinite Substance.

Thus, by relating everything to the whole, to what he called appropriately "the most perfect being," Spinoza avoided a causal representative theory of perception and knowledge, what Professor Philippe Muller has felicitously termed the *pons asinorum* of modern philosophy.[7] It is the bridge that leads either to realism and a theory of knowledge which, if it can be framed by the human mind, must be false, and if it were true could not be humanly known; or to an idealism committed (by implication) to equate the human mind, or make it privy, to the divine, and prone to a solipsism which contradicts itself and fails to resolve the problem originally posed of how a finite member of a surrounding world can become aware of that world and of its own relation to it.

Fichte accused Spinoza of similar failure, because, he alleged, Spinoza made an unwarranted leap from his own consciousness to a transcendent God. But Fichte failed to notice that Spinoza's Substance is an absolute whole, immanent in all its parts, and thus also in the human body, of which the idea is its mind. It was only when Schelling, who was very clearly aware of the original problem, recognized that Spinoza, in unifying Thought and Extension in one Substance, had pointed the way to a solution, that he and Hegel were able to develop a dialectical conception of the universe, at once both realistic and idealistic, that could account satisfactorily for human perception and knowledge. The key influence in this liberating advance was Spinoza's. Little wonder that Hegel called him the philosopher's philosopher, and declared that the first essential step in philosophy was to be a Spinozist.[8]

Schelling's position is, in a way, even nearer to Spinoza than Hegel's, for he envisages Nature as the coordinate objective counterpart of knowledge, differentiated from it within an Absolute, which is, as he calls it (among other epithets), "the indifference point" neutral between objectivity and subjectivity. He never makes clear satisfactorily the dialectical relationship between them. Nevertheless, in Schelling's speculative system, there is an implicit dialectic, vaguely following Fichte's successive syntheses of antitheses, and proceeding by way of the three potencies (again never clearly explained) of infinite, finite, and eternal. Through these potencies, repeated at successive levels, of which Schelling's various accounts are rather confused and his deduction rather far-fetched, Nature on the one hand and cognition on the other develop towards the absolute Identity; yet this takes us back to the original act of cognition, of self-consciousness in the Ego, whose position in the general scheme, as related to its own self-objectification, as Nature and as human experience, remains ambiguous.

It was left to Hegel to weld all this into a coherent and dialectically consequent system. His Absolute is no mere indifference point, no blank unity, but is a definite, absolute, whole, which could not be a whole if it were not the unification of infinite differences; just as Spinoza's Substance depends for its absolute infinitude on the possession of infinite attributes. And just as for Spinoza the attributes are powers and Substance is dynamically active, so for Hegel the Absolute is an "infinite restlessness" perpetually differentiating and specifying its organizing principle, the Concept, in avatars of dialectical forms constituting Nature and Spirit. They range from space and time (united as motion) up to organism, in which the concept immanent throughout the process comes to consciousness of itself in human experience. That again develops through its own appropriate scale of forms to absolute knowing, or philosophical science (*Wissenschaft*), which culminates in the absolute Idea. Thus an objective realism is intelligibly reconciled with an absolute idealism, and the problem set by the reflective understanding, from which Schelling begins in his introduction to *Ideen zu einer Philosophie der Natur*, is solved.

It is no very wild conjecture to suggest that in all this Hegel followed the lead of Spinoza's gamut of increasingly complex and individuating bodies, with their increasingly perceptive and intelligent minds, up to the *facies totius universi* under Extension, paralleled under Thought by the order and connection of ideas. Schelling, with whom I have been primarily concerned in this chapter, thought constantly in Spinozistic terms, and Fichte, whom he closely followed, was hardly less influenced by Spinoza, recognizing Spinoza's philosophy as the only consistent alternative to his own, and constructing his *Wissenschaftslehre* always with one eye on Spinoza, even if he kept the other steadily on Kant. There can be no dispute about the dialectical character of the thought of these three thinkers. Overlooking what Plato and the Ancients had to say about dialectic, and regarding Kant as providing, as it were, negative suggestions about the place and function of dialectic in philosophy, one might say that Fichte was the initiator of the dialectical method, Schelling an inspired if somewhat confused developer, and Hegel its consummate master. But the contention, which I have consistently made, that Spinoza is a dialectical thinker, when it has not been simply disregarded, has been hotly disputed and denied. Yet it seems clear that all the major dialectical thinkers of German Idealism have, in one way or another, cast their thought in a Spinozistic mold, while strenuously repudiating the kind of empirical naturalism so often attributed to Spinoza.

It would hardly be justifiable for me to repeat at length here what I have written elsewhere. The kernel of my argument in other contexts has been that every genuine system is dialectical, that is, a structure determined by an organizing principle, that specifies itself in a scale of forms related as distinct but interdependent instantiations of the holistic principle in progressive degrees of adequacy.[9] Spinoza gives repeated evidence that he conceived God-or-Substance-or-Nature in just this way, although he tends to view the system from the top down rather than from the bottom up (as does Hegel). The scale, as it is for Spinoza, runs from Substance to attributes, from attribute to infinite modes, from infinite to finite modes, and so on through the entire range of complex individual body-mind combinations down to the very simplest.

Spinoza maintains that all things are determined by the necessity of the divine nature (the fundamental organizing principle). But, as I have argued above, not all forms of necessity are the same, and at different levels the type of necessity varies, so the concept of necessity itself is specified in a scale of forms, from mathematical and causal, through psychological to rational. The last, being determination solely by the nature or essence of the agent, Spinoza declares to be free (self-determination). Each of these is a specific expression of the divine nature and an exemplification of its necessity; but as we proceed through the series, each successive form is a more adequate manifestation of that nature, until finally we reach the free action of God himself.

In partial association with this series, there is the scale of forms of human knowledge. In TdIE there are four grades: hearsay, vague experience, inference from the essence of one thing to that of another, and, finally, the perception of the thing through its essence alone or through its proximate cause. In the *Ethics* there are three: *imaginatio*, *ratio*, and *scientia intuitiva*. Here again, the series satisfies the conditions I have laid down for a dialectical system; and we have seen that the continuous range of individual bodies with their correspondingly competent minds, each under its appropriate attribute, fulfils the requirement of a graded approach to the self-sufficiency of the infinite mode, and so of Substance itself. It is a scale of overlapping, mutually complementary, forms, increasing as it progresses in adequacy to the holistic nature of the total system. Thus it is entirely fitting for Spinoza to declare in the Appendix to Part I of the *Ethics*:

> *Non defuit materia ad omnia, ex summo nimirum ad infimum perfectionis gradam, creanda.*

In effect, there is no lack of material for the creation of a complete system expressing itself in forms of every grade of perfection—what I have claimed to be a dialectical system.

Notes

1. *Ideen zu einer Philosophie der Natur, Einleitung, Zusatz*; English translation by Errol E. Harris and Peter Heath, *Ideas for a Philosophy of Nature* (Cambridge, Cambridge University Press, 1988), p. 48.
2. *Von der Weltseele, Sämmtliche Werke*, IV p. 378.
3. Cf. *Darstellung meines Systems der Philosophie*, §§1–14, *Sämmtliche Werke*, Vol. IV pp. 114–120.
4. Ibid., §17.
5. *Grundlage der gesamten Wissenschaftslehre, Erste Teil*, §3.
6. Cf. *Weltseele, Sämmtliche Werke*, Vol. IV, pp. 278ff. The parallel with Spinoza is recognized by Michael Vater in his translation of *Bruno* in footnote 88.
7. Cf. *Dialectic and Contemporary Science: Essays in Honor of Errol E. Harris*, ed. Philip Grier (Lanham, Md., University Press of America, 1989), Pt. III, pp. 185ff.
8. Cf. *Lectures on the History of Philosophy*, trans. E. S. Haldane and Frances H. Simson (London, Routledge and Kegan Paul, 1896, rpt. 1955, 1963, 1968), Vol. III, p. 257.
9. Cf. *Foundations of Metaphysics in Science*, Ch. 13; *Formal, Transcendental, and Dialectical Thinking* (Albany, State University of New York Press, 1987), Pt. III; *Cosmos and Anthropos*, Ch. 2.

13

The Concept of Substance in Spinoza and Hegel

THE HERITAGE OF THE EIGHTEENTH CENTURY

THE HERITAGE OF THE EIGHTEENTH CENTURY

The conception of substance has a history that goes back to Aristotle, whose doctrine on the subject is multiply ambiguous. From what Aristotle tells us it is difficult to decide whether substance is simply what is always the subject of a proposition and never a predicate, or is the indestructible and eternal unity identical with all being, or is God and efficient reason exclusive of all else, or what is embodied in *infimae species*, or is finally restricted to sensible singular individuals each of which is a "this somewhat" (*todé tí*). The concept with its ambiguities descended through the Middle Ages to the seventeenth century, when we find one aspect adopted by Locke and his empiricist successors: that of a permanent underlying substratum of all apparent and variable accidents; and another adopted by Descartes and the Rationalists, of a being that is dependent for existence on itself alone, whose existence is, in fact, involved in or identical with its essence.

Spinoza accepts this latter from Descartes and develops to the full its logical implications; but the Lockeian version passes over to Kant, who elaborates the idea of it in his exposition of the dynamic categories under Analogies of Experience. It is this Kantian version that is Hegel's immediate heritage, and is the category (or concept) which emerges in the dialectic as the first phase of absolute relation under Actuality in the Doctrine of Essence in the second part of the Logic.

Hegel maintains that every category is a provisional definition of the Absolute and that in the history of philosophy each in succession has been adopted by some thinker or school. Substance, he alleges, is the conception of the Absolute adopted by Spinoza, which, he says, is true, but not the highest, not the final, concept of the Absolute. That is absolute Spirit, of which substance (presumably as Spinoza conceives it) falls short.

It is clear that what falls short of absolute Spirit is the Kantian category of substance, that which comes in the Hegelian logic at the stage of Essence, which is not yet the Concept, although it is near the point of transition from Actuality to the Concept. A case might be made for the position that this is also the notion of substance in Aristotle and Aquinas (but that would be subject to some qualification), as well as in Locke; but whether it is Spinoza's idea of substance is a further question, which I am more inclined to answer in the negative.

True it may be that every category is a provisional definition of the Absolute; but it is not so much that Spinoza defines the Absolute as substance as that he defines Substance as absolute. He elevates the conception to the highest grade of reality and (like Descartes) identifies it with God. But, whereas Descartes conceives God as one substance among others, differing from them only in that they are dependent upon it for existence while it exists of necessity through its own essence, Spinoza's substance is unique. For him there is only one substance, which is God or Nature, the whole of reality, an absolutely infinite totality the essence of which is infinitely expressed in infinite attributes. It is, in short, the absolute Substance.

Now this is just how Hegel himself conceives absolute Spirit. In the introduction to his *Lectures on the Philosophy of World History* he writes:

> ... reason ... is substance and infinite power; it is itself the infinite material of all natural and spiritual life, and the infinite form which activates this material content. It is substance, i.e., that through which all reality has its being and subsistence; it is infinite power, ... and it is the infinite content, the essence and truth of everything, itself constituting the material on which it operates through its own activity.[1]

For Hegel, reason is the activity of absolute Spirit, as for Aristotle it is the activity of God. Here Hegel and Aristotle are at one. And the above description of reason as substance and infinite power, creating the material on and in which it works by its own activity, is an almost exact description of Spinoza's *Substantia-sive-Deus-sive-Natura*.

That it is so, however, Hegel, despite his undoubted and proclaimed admiration for Spinoza, fails to see, because he seems to have missed something at least of Spinoza's expressed and implicit meaning. So he downgrades Spinoza's concept of God to the substance of Kant and

Locke, failing to notice that Spinoza is doing much what he, Hegel himself, professes—that is, upgrading the conception of substance to the level of reason or spirit. It is, however, just this that Hegel accuses Spinoza of failing to achieve. It will therefore be my task in this chapter to show how and where he is mistaken.

HEGEL'S CRITICISM OF SPINOZA

In what way, then, does Hegel consider Spinoza's theory to be deficient? In the *Lectures on the History of Philosophy*, Hegel sets out his criticism of Spinoza at length, and he repeats the main points in the *Enzyklopädie* and in the *Science of Logic*. While he praises Spinoza's philosophy as the high point of modern thought and especially applauds his declaration that *determinatio negatio est*, he complains that the conception of substance, to which everything else is made subordinate, remains abstract and never attains to self-consciousness or the concrete activity of living and thinking. Spinoza's Substance, Hegel avers, is fixed, rigid, and petrified. It is the abstract universal into which all determination (just because it is seen to be negation) is absorbed and extinguished. Spinoza, he says, falls short of the negation of negation because he lacks the principle of subjectivity. Moreover (and this is just another aspect of the same alleged defect), Spinoza is said to provide no principle of differentiation to diversify the unity of Substance on which he insists. He declares that infinite things follow necessarily in infinite ways from the nature of Substance,[2] but he does not explain how. He says that God has an infinity of attributes, but he gives an account of only two, Thought and Extension. In fact, Hegel goes so far as to allege that Spinoza's Substance consists of only two attributes. Why only two? Why just these two? How does the divine nature necessitate these two attributes specifically? he asks. As Spinoza defines "attribute" it is the way in which the intellect perceives the essence of Substance, but the intellect is a mode, belonging to *Natura naturata*, and modes are modifications of Substance, which have no reality in themselves, Hegel contends; in fact, they are simply the product of the human imagination, itself alleged to be due to the affections of the human mind, which is also a mere mode. How does the intellect come by the ideas of the two attributes, Thought and Extension? Spinoza, he maintains, does not explain. In general no intelligible way is provided to proceed from substance to attribute and from attribute to mode, although all three (corresponding to universal, particular, and individual) are essential to Spinoza's system.

Hegel criticizes further Spinoza's account of individuality. He quotes the definition (preceding E2A3 and L4) in which Spinoza says:

> When any bodies of the same or different magnitude are pressed together and lie one upon another or if they are moved with the same or different degrees of velocity, so that they communicate their motion one to another in a certain fixed *ratio* [here Hegel misquotes, writing "in some way or other" for "a certain fixed ratio"], we say that those bodies are united with one another and all at the same time [Hegel writes *zusammen*] compose one body or individual which is distinguished from others through this union.[3]

Here, Hegel tells us, we see the limitations of Spinoza's system: individuation is mere juxtaposition (*Zusammensetzung*) or aggregation, as opposed to the integrated unity of the ego, of self-consciousness. Consequently, all differentiation is left to the understanding and is not "deduced" (i.e., is not self-generating). It belongs, says Hegel, to *Natura naturata*, not to *Natura naturans*.

"The essence of man is constituted by a modification of the attributes of God," Hegel quotes further from E2P10C (Spinoza's words are *"Essentiam hominis constitui a certis Dei attributorum modificationibus"*). But modes are mere appearances, at best modifications of Substance; they are nothing in themselves, but are only appearances relative to our understanding, and so, along with the attributes, all of which are the same in substance (each being merely a different way in which the intellect views it), are absorbed into, and nullified by, the featureless abyss of the unity of Substance. Thought and Extension are taken merely as given (*vorgefunden*) in common experience; they are not deduced either from first principles as defined by Spinoza, or through their own dialectical development.

In short, Spinoza's conception of substance, although it is a premonition of the concrete whole of the Concept (or reason), is not the absolute Idea. It is stated to be the unity of Thought and Being (or rather Extension), but this is not demonstrated, and no explanation emerges of how or why the intellect comes to attribute these forms to absolute substance.

For the rest Hegel's critique is directed to the unsuitability to philosophy of Spinoza's geometrical method, in which the existence of the matters discussed is merely presupposed or taken from common knowledge, not deduced; terms are dogmatically defined, not critically examined, and no inner dialectic develops itself. It is remarkable that Hegel says nothing in this connection about Spinoza's attack on teleological thinking, although (or perhaps because) it has much in common, at least so far as it castigates the shallow conception of a world created entirely to serve the purposes of mankind, with Hegel's own. Followers of Hegel, however, have attributed Spinoza's ostensible rejection of teleology to his adoption of the geometrical method, with a consequent mechanization and rigidification of his system, giving no place to freedom of the will and human responsibility.[4]

HEGEL'S MISCONSTRUAL

Now this account of Spinoza's doctrine is far from justified and contains considerable misrepresentation. Hegel is not himself guiltless of misquotation and innaccuracy (some of which we have already noted), whether deliberate, in order to emphasize differences from his own position, or inadvertent, is not always clear. For instance, he says (in *Enzyklopädie* §50) that Spinoza defines God as "the unity of Thought and Extension (the material world)" but, as Hegel well knew, this is not Spinoza's definition, for in the *Lectures on the History of Philosophy* he quotes E1D6 (which he numbers *siebente*)[5] as "Gott ist das absolute unendliche Wesen oder die Substanz die aus unendlichen Attributen besteht, deren jedes eine ewige und unendliche Wesenheit [essentiam] ausdruckt." The importance of this definition and its accurate interpretation cannot be overemphasized, yet it seems altogether to have been misconstrued by Hegel, who repeatedly asserts that Spinoza presents us with only two attributes. It is indeed the case that the most puzzling features of Spinoza's system, and the problem that he left unsolved, is that of the relation between the infinite attributes, and in particular the relation between the attribute of Thought and the rest; nor does he ever adequately explain why the human mind is restricted to the knowledge of two attributes only, although he does give cogent reasons for assigning infinite attributes to God, and a good, but insufficient, reason why we are aware, at least primarily, only of Thought and Extension. I have dealt with these difficulties in previous chapters and elsewhere, but Hegel does not address them at all.

EXAMINATION OF HEGEL'S CRITICISMS

Let us consider each of Hegel's complaints against Spinoza in turn:

(1) The first is that substance or God, for Spinoza, is not spirit—"*Gott* hier ist nicht *Geist*." We may remind ourselves that, for Hegel, *Geist* is ambiguous. It may be *der endliche Geist* or *der absolute Geist*. God, of course, is absolute Spirit, and that sums up the whole system of the dialectic, encompassing the absolute Idea, Nature, and finite spirit. But the Idea manifests itself equally in Nature and in the gamut of

conscious forms of finite spirit, the essence of which is self-consciousness, or reason; and this is what is alleged to be lacking from Spinoza's
substance.

Yet quite obviously there is no such deficiency in Spinoza's God. He
is the absolutely infinite Substance, with infinite attributes, every one
of which expresses the infinite essence of God. One of these is Thought
(and another Extension). Thought with its infinite modes obviously
corresponds to Hegel's Idea, in spite of his protests to the contrary;
and in denying self-consciousness to Spinoza's finite modes of thought,
Hegel ignores the doctrine of *idea ideae*, which precisely posits the self-
reflective or self-conscious character of thinking. As an attribute, Thought
expresses the infinite essence of God, who must therefore be conceived
as possessing, among other powers, that of self-conscious thinking. And
as the Idea in Hegel's system is deployed in the form of otherbeing,
or externality, as Nature, so Substance in Spinoza's system expresses
itself under the attribute of Extension under which the modes are the
same in substance as those under Thought. The status of the other
attributes is similar, even if we are left with the problem of understanding their exact relation to Thought, and in particular to human
knowledge.

At least we cannot say, as Hegel does, that Spinoza's *Substantia-sive-
Natura* lacks self-consciousness, for one of its attributes is Thought, in
which every idea (or mode) involves *idea ideae*, the idea of itself, and
that again the idea of itself—infinite self-awareness. The difference from
Hegel is that, at least prima facie, the attributes of Spinoza's God are
all mutually coordinate, whereas in Hegel's absolute syllogism, comprising
the subject matters of the three major philosophical sciences, these are set out seriatim as a *Stufenfolge*. But this difference
also is only apparently the case, because Hegel insists that the dialectic is circular and that the end is as much presupposed in the beginning as the beginning is actualized in the end. Thus the major phases
of absolute Spirit (Idea, Nature, and Spirit as such) are related in
much the same way as the attributes of Spinoza's Substance: each expresses the essence (or Idea) of the whole which is, for Hegel as for
Spinoza, the truth.

(2) Next, Spinoza's Substance is castigated as rigid, ossified, and devoid
of life and living awareness. Now we see that this is not the case; but
of further importance is Spinoza's insistence that the attributes are
powers, not just assigned predicates. Essence and power are one and
the same, hence God's essence, his existence, his intellect, and his will
are all one.[6] For reality, or perfection, is nothing other than the power
of existing and acting, and action is that of which the agent alone is

the adequate cause.[7] Consequently, God-or-Substance, which is absolutely infinite, has infinite power of existing and of acting, so that infinite powers (or attributes) belong to it, and infinite things follow from its nature in infinite ways. This "following from" is being actively produced, for God is *actus purus*, and his essence must be conceived dynamically, not statically. To say, therefore, that the Substance of Spinoza is rigid and petrified is as great a misunderstanding as it would be to say this of Aristotle's *energeia*, or of efficient reason.

Likewise, Spinoza declares that *idea* is not "a blind picture on a tablet"[8] but is an activity, in some degree even when it is inadequate (for it involves affirmation, and qua appetite is an expression of the *conatus in suo esse perseverare*) and when it is adequate it is action *par excellence*. Not even Extension is passive and inert. Its primary infinite mode is Motion-and-rest (today we should say "energy"), and it is of this that all bodies are constituted.[9] Spinoza's Substance, therefore, is essentially dynamic, and its nature or essence is expressed in its attributes as its powers. Thus, being absolutely infinite and having infinite perfection or realty, it must possess infinite attributes, both in number and extent: "The more reality, or being, any entity has, the more attributes must be assigned to it (*ei tribuenda sunt*)."[10]

(3) Here, indeed, we have the rebuttal of yet another of Hegel's objections, and what in his eyes is the most serious; for here we find, at least implicitly, a principle of differentiation. Substance is completely perfect and possesses the fullest reality; it cannot, therefore, be simply a blank unity (a "night in which all cows are black"), but *must* be an infinitely differentiated totality. In Spinoza's words: "Infinite things in infinite ways *must* follow (*sequi debent*) from the necessity of the divine nature." Its very infinity and perfection require its self-differentiation, first into infinite attributes and then within each attribute into infinite modes, the modes in each attribute being identical in substance with the corresponding modes in every other.

How to proceed from infinite mode to finite modes is more difficult to see, not because Spinoza provides us with no clues, but because his argument is so condensed and brief that the clues are difficult to follow; but they are there, in the Scholia to E2P13 and L7, as well as in somewhat clearer detail in the 32nd Letter. But before we turn to these, we must scotch another misapprehension, one partly invited by Spinoza's own method of expression, yet hardly worthy of Hegel's proven insight.

Neither attributes nor modes are mere appearances to the human mind. Such an interpretation of Spinoza's doctrine would be ludicrous, for he defines the human mind as the idea of the human body, which is a finite mode of Extension, as the idea is a finite mode of Thought. Spinoza could hardly suggest that modes as such, as well as the attributes under which they fall, are simply illusory products of one of their own number. But he does say that attribute is what the intellect perceives of Substance as constituting its essence. By this, however, he means the divine intellect, which is in actuality the only intellect, for it is of the nature of intellect to frame true ideas, and the human mind, when it thinks adequately, coincides with the divine.[11] The infinite intellect, however, is an infinite mode of Thought and cannot, therefore, be the source of *existence* of the attributes in general. That is Substance itself, which is the sole ground of existence of anything and everything. The truth of the matter is that attributes, the real powers of Substance, *extra intellectum*, express essence, and essence is *what* the thing is of which it is the essence; that is, it is what the intellect perceives the thing to be, of what specific nature. The attributes are the specific differentiations of the power of God (or the divine Substance) and it is the power of thought in action as intelligence that perceives the distinctions.

The infinite intellect is an infinite mode, and infinite modes, we are told,[12] follow immediately from their appropriate attribute. It is of them that Spinoza speaks in TdIE as "fixed and eternal things" in which "as in their true codes" the laws are (as it were) inscribed according to which all particular things (*singularia*) come about and are arranged. These fixed and eternal things,

> although individual, yet on account of their ubiquitous presence and wide-ranging power, will be for us as universals or genera of the definitions of mutable particulars and the proximate causes of all things.

From this statement (as from others in the TdIE) it is clear that Spinoza regarded the infinite modes as principles of systematic order actualized in the arrangement of their particulars; in short, as what Hegel conceived as concrete universals, or as self-specifying principles. The infinite intellect would thus produce the complete self-specified system of adequate knowledge, comprehending the infinite and adequate idea of God (immanent in all ideas)[13] and accordingly the ideas of his infinite attributes.

Plainly, then, neither Substance nor any of its attributes, each with its infinite modes, is to be thought of as an abstract universal (as Hegel contends), but much rather they are to be seen as concrete systems providing the principles of order and structure, and so of differences, determining the particular finite modes which follow from them. They are the principles of differentiation said to be lacking in Spinoza's Substance, and that they are so is further confirmed and illustrated by what Spinoza writes in Ep 32. Here we find the main clue to the derivation of finite modes from infinite modes, those which follow logically and directly from the concept of the attribute concerned. This is the transition from *Natura naturans*, the dynamic activity of God, to *Natura naturata*, the effects or products of that activity.

(4) What Spinoza writes in the 32nd Letter runs directly counter to Hegel's accusation that Spinoza misconceives individuality as mere juxtaposition (*Zusammenstezung*). Spinoza, in fact, rejects the notion of whole and part which represents the whole as a mere aggregate subsequent and posterior to its parts conceived as having independent reality. Substance, we must always remember, in itself and in each of its attributes, is indivisible. But by this Spinoza does not mean that it has no distinguishable modes—quite the contrary—but these modes are interdependent and inseparable. Thus whole-and-part, properly conceived, is a system in which "the laws or nature of one part adapt themselves to the laws or nature of another part so that they should be minimally at variance."[14] Things are parts of a whole (properly understood) only insofar as they fit together and are mutually adjusted, constituting an integrated system, as various organic fluids in the blood are integrated to constitute a single whole, maintaining itself as an individual fluid body by combination in constant proportions of its constituents. Such a whole, regularly transmitting among its parts constant proportions of motion and rest, is what constitutes an individual, one which may be regarded as a single complex body with persistent identity in spite of internal changes.

Bodies, we learn from this letter, as well as in E2L7S, are graded in a hierarchy of increasing complexity and integration, ranging from the simplest (mutually distinguished by no more than their velocity, or amount of Motion-and-rest) to the most comprehensive, and extending (as Spinoza says) to infinity, to constitute *facies totius universi*. This infinite whole controls and determines, as a concrete universal principle, the interrelations of its parts (their mutual adaptation) in such a way as to "compel" innumerable changes regulated so as to maintain its individual form, so that its overall structure remains constant, in spite of infinite internal change.

> For all bodies are surrounded by others and are determined by one another to exist and act on a certain determinate principle (*ratione*), always and in all of them together, that is, in the whole universe, the same proportion of motion and rest being maintained.[15]

The face of the whole universe, the total *Gestalt* of the physical world, is an infinite mode of Extension, following directly from its primary infinite mode, Motion-and-rest,[16] and it provides the principle of order, structure, and diversification constituting the variety of physical bodies and their interaction throughout the whole physical world. This explanation of the relation between attribute, infinite mode, and finite modes, although it is set out in detail only for the attribute of Extension, applies equally to all attributes. Thus it is evident that Spinoza's conception of individuality is anything but limited to *Zusammensetzung*; and it is also clear that he does provide an intelligible way of proceeding from attribute to infinite, and thence to finite, modes. The infinite modes are the immediate logical (if you like, dialectical)[17] consequence of the concept of the appropriate attribute, and they are permanent and immutable principles of order, "in which the laws are inscribed" determining the distinctive natures of, and changes among, finite modes. Such changes are inexhaustible, each producing its successor, as efficient cause producing its effect, but all conforming to laws in such a way as to maintain the constant and unchangeable configuration of the entire universe.

The actual existence of finite modes is the way in which God's power of existence expresses itself, through his attributes and their infinite modes. Nothing, Spinoza tells us, exists except Substance and its modes; that is to say, the attributes are simply the various ways in which God expresses his infinite power of existing in diverse finite modes, in whose *conatus in suo esse perseverandi* it manifests itself.

(5) As Spinoza was well aware, the systematic unity of a whole involves differentiation into mutually adapted and determining parts. But, as he insists, all determination is negation; that is, all determination *ab extra*. The absolute whole, however, is not determined *ab extra*, because there is nothing beyond, or outside, it by which it could be determined. Consequently, Spinoza maintains that God-or-Substance involves no negation. Its determination is all within itself; it is self-determined or free, *causa sui*. The determination of the parts by other parts is indeed negation, but in their mutual adaptation they are governed by the principle of order universal to the whole, which is thus immanent in each and all of them, and so, by implication, negates the negation. This also supplies what each finite element lacks—its complement—which again negates the negation. Hence Spinoza's contention that God excludes all negation amounts to the same, in principle, as what Hegel declares to be the negation of negation, and what he calls *Fürsichsein*. Hegel's complaint against Spinoza is to this extent unjustified.

FINITE MIND AND INFINITE MIND

For Hegel, however, the negation of negation, the *Aufhebung* of finitude (and contradiction), the category of being-for-self, is typified by the Ego and is the category of self-consciousness. Hegel's criticism of Spinoza follows, in considerable measure, Fichte's rejection of Spinozism as dogmatism, even if the best and most consistent form of dogmatic philosophy. This judgment of Fichte's rests upon the contention that Spinozism dogmatically postulates an objective, determinate system, in which the human mind is a subordinate part, disregarding the indispensable condition of all knowledge and experience, the original, transcendental unity of apperception in the Ego. If this assessment of Spinozism were justified in terms of Spinoza's own teaching, it would be—and intrinsically it is—of great importance, for it rests on the insight that no unified system, such as Spinoza's, is fully and explicitly realizable except as the experience of a self-conscious subject.

Any unconscious or merely material system (like, for example, the solar system) is a whole in itself, but only implicitly (in Hegel's phrase, *an sich*). Its parts affect one another blindly, and their mutual relations and interdependence can only be fully realized when brought to consciousness (i.e., in scientific theory) where they are made explicit (*für sich*). The appropriate and necessary form of absolute wholeness, therefore, and the source and immanent principle of all wholeness, is *Fürsichsein*, or self-consciousness. What, if anything, is there in Spinoza's doctrine corresponding to this principle in Hegel's?

To some extent we have already seen the answer to this question. The essence of Substance is expressed in its attributes, one of which is Thought, or ideation; and thought is inherently self-conscious, for every idea involves an idea of itself ad infinitum. God or Substance, therefore, is and must be self-conscious. He must be, in and through the divine intellect, *für sich*. Moreover, this divine thought is always and essentially adequate and true. It is determined by nothing other than the nature or essence of Substance, its own nature. It is wholly self-determined and therefore free. It is *causa sui*. Accordingly, we have in Spinoza's doctrine much the same identification of true infinity, or wholeness, with self-awareness and freedom as we find in Hegel.

It may be objected, however, that infinity and absolute wholeness in Spinoza cannot actually be identified with, as properly realized in, Thought, because Thought is only one among infinite attributes, all of which constitute the absolutely infinite totality of God. We must remember, nevertheless, that all attributes are identical in substance, all equally express the same infinite essence of Substance, and the order and connection of ideas is the same as the order and connection of things. Of every finite thing there is an idea in the divine intellect, so that everything is in some degree beminded (*animata*) and at least the germ of self-consciousness pervades every detail of the modal system.

Further, adequate thinking is directly correlated by Spinoza with organic wholeness. He explains[18] that, as there is an idea in the divine mind of every single mode (of Extension, and by implication of every other attribute), so everything is, in a sense, beminded. The "minds" of simple bodies are only rudimentary, but the more complex, more organically self-dependent, bodies have minds "capable of perceiving many things together." There is a significance, seldom noticed by commentators, in Spinoza's use of the word *simul*. It is precisely the capacity to perceive things *together* that makes self-consciousness essential to coherent knowledge. As Kant saw, the synthesis of *Vorstellungen* is indispensable to the perception of objects, and the source of all synthesis is the unity of apperception. The capacity to perceive many things together is the capacity to synthesize, and Spinoza goes on to say:

> the more the actions of one body depend solely upon itself, and the less other bodies take part (*concurrunt*) with it in its action, the more is its mind capable of understanding distinctly.[19]

In short, the more fully integrated the organic body, the more unified the idea of which it is the *ideatum*, the more capable of adequate thinking is its mind.

Now, the union of body and mind is that of *ideatum* and *idea* and both are one and the same thing, identical in substance. The unity or wholeness of both is thus very much what Hegel calls *Fürsichsein*. It is registered in the self-awareness of the body, felt in *imaginatio* and purified through *ratio* to attain adequate knowledge in *scientia intuitiva*. In such adequate thinking all things are conceived *sub specie aeternitatis*, and the idea of the body, confused in *imaginatio*, becomes likewise adequate, conceived similarly in its universal and eternal relationship to all other bodies, in fact to the entire universe, so that the human intellect coincides with the divine to the extent that it thinks adequately, and the unity of the whole is realized in such adequate knowledge.[20] Thus the human mind attains to blessedness and eternity; in such knowledge and love of the infinite (the *amor intellectualis Dei*) it is both active and free. The infinite idea of God, which corresponds in Spinoza's system to the absolute Idea in Hegel's, is thus similarly related to the human intellect as is absolute Spirit to finite spirit for Hegel; and all the characteristics of absolute Spirit as demanded by Hegel are present, at least by implication, in Spinoza's conception of Substance.

HEGEL'S ADVANCE

Hegel's advance upon Spinoza is that he sets out the absolute system as a dialectical development, for he recognized more clearly and more fully than any of his predecessors that every system is in principle dialectical in structure and must be developed, or rather must generate itself, dialectically as a scale of graduated and specifically distinct forms, progressively realizing in more adequate degrees the ultimate universal. How and why this should be are further questions discussion of which would take us too far beyond the limits of the present subject for us to embark upon it.[21]

Spinoza is seduced by the geometrical method into a different form of presentation. But the method is, as I have argued above,[22] not really geometrical, nor really essential to the development of Spinoza's theory, in which all the traces of dialectical structure are implicitly present: e.g., in the process of "improvement of the intellect" and in all the other developmental structures that have been cited earlier: the gradation of finite modes up to the infinite, the progression of human thought and behavior from imagination and passion to adequate knowledge and free action, so that Spinoza can say of Substance-or-God: "*ei non defuit materia ad omnia, ex summo nimirum ad infimum perfectionis gradum creanda.*"[23] Spinoza tends always, as we observed earlier, to think from the top down, in contrast to Hegel's procedure from the most abstract and immediate at the bottom of the scale to the most concrete and absolute at the top. For both philosophers the ultimate source of all things and all concepts, the ultimate and immanent presupposition of everything, is the absolute whole. So Spinoza declares that everything, to be rightly understood, must be related to and deduced from the idea of the most perfect being,[24] without which nothing can either be or be conceived; and he proceeds to deduce his whole system from the definitions of *causa sui,* Substance and God. Hegel, on the other hand, allows the implications of the ubiquitously presupposed Absolute to develop themselves dialectically *ex infimo nimirum ad summum perfectionis gradum.* And as, for Spinoza, Substance resolves itself into reason (the intellectual love of God by which God loves himself, and which is identical with the same intellectual love for God by human beings),[25] so, for Hegel, reason resolves itself into "substance and infinite power"—"the infinite material of all natural and spiritual life."

In sum, Hegel's critique of Spinoza fails to do justice either to his own or to Spinoza's insights. We can easily see why Hegel hailed Spinoza as the philosopher's philosopher and why he declared that when one begins to philosophize one must first immerse oneself in the aether of the One Substance—for that is the ultimately presupposed reality. But when he sees deficiencies in Spinoza's philosophy, it is because he had not sufficiently pondered over its implications, had not attended closely enough to the detail of Spinoza's exposition, and had failed to take into careful consideration some of the more important passages. His own dialectic follows through the development of the concept from being to essence, to the Concept proper, to the absolute Idea and to absolute Spirit. His categories are all, up to the last, provisional definitions of the Absolute, and en route one of these is the category of substance. But this, as presented by Hegel in his logic, is Kant's category, not Spinoza's, for whom the term corresponds much more nearly to Hegel's own when he identifies it with absolute reason.

Notes

1. G. W. F. Hegel, *Lectures on the Philosophy of World History*, Introduction, trans. H. B. Nisbet (Cambridge, Cambridge University Press, 1975), p. 27.
2. E1P16.
3. Cf. *Vorlesungen über die Geschichte der Philosophie*, Vol. III, Abs. II, K1, A2.
4. Cf. Joachim, *Study of the Ethics of Spinoza*, Bk. 1, Appendix; Caird, *Spinoza*, Ch. IV; Hubbeling, *Spinoza's Methodology*, p. 10 and passim.
5. Hegel counts Spinoza's *Explicatio* following the definition of God as the sixth definition (i.c. of Infinity), and the definition of God itself as the seventh.
6. Cf. E1P17S,P20.
7. Cf. E1P11Dem3S; E2D6; E3D2.
8. Cf. E2D3, Explanation; E2P49S.
9. Cf. Epp 32, 81; E2L7S.
10. Ep 9.
11. Cf. TdIE; E2P44Dem.
12. E1P21.
13. E2PP45,46.
14. Ep 32.
15. Ibid.
16. Cf. the conception of the physical world by modern physicists as a structure of space-time differentiating itself into energy and matter, whose existence and behavior are regulated by the physical constants and measurements determined by space-time curvature. Cf. A. Einstein, *The Meaning of Relativity* (London, Methuen, 1956); *Relativity: The Special and General Theory* (London, Methuen, 1960); Eddington, *The Expanding Universe; New Pathways in Science*; and *The Philosophy of Physical Science* (Cambridge, Cambridge University Press, 1939); Sir Edmund Whittaker, *From Euclid to*

Eddington (Cambridge, Cambridge University Press, 1949).
17. For instance, Extension in its very conception implies distinction between points and instants, the relation between which is essentially distance (or lapse), which implies motion. Hence Motion-and-rest emerges as a dialectical consequence. Cf. Hegel's *Naturphilosphie, Enzyklopädie* §§254–260.
18. E2P13S.
19. Ibid.
20. Cf. E2P40S2, E5P29.
21. See, however, Collingwood, *An Essay on Philosophical Method,* and my *Foundations of Metaphysics in Science,* Ch. 3; *Formal, Transcendental, and Dialectical Thinking,* Pt. III; *An Interpretation of the Logic of Hegel* (Lanham, Md., University Press of America, 1983); and *Cosmos and Anthropos,* Ch. 2.
22. Cf. also my *Salvation from Despair,* Ch. 2.
23. E1, App.
24. Cf. TdIE.
25. Cf. E5PP35, 36 and C.

14

Constantin Brunner's Misreading of Spinoza

The different branches of Spinoza's philosophical system are so closely interconnected and so coherently united that it is virtually impossible to discuss one of them without reference to the others. His moral theory is based upon his doctrines of the *conatus in suo esse perseverandi* and the distinction between human passion and action. The *conatus* is at once the essence of the thing concerned and the power of God working in it. The power of God is the relevant attribute. So, in order to understand clearly what Spinoza intends in his theory of morality, it is necessary to understand the whole of his metaphysics and psychology. It is not, however, necessary here to expound all these matters in detail, if only because much has already been written about them both by the present author, in earlier chapters and elsewhere, and by others more competent. My object in this chapter is to consider and to criticize the interpretation of Spinoza in all the interrelated aspects of his philosophy by an important, but much neglected, thinker, who flourished early in this century, but who, apart from a few ardent devotees, has been largely overlooked, having been overshadowed by some of his own contemporaries (like Husserl and Heidegger, whom in many ways he anticipated).

Constantin Brunner, by his own confession and emphatic assertion, was strongly influenced by Spinoza. In fact, he claimed to model the whole of his own philosophy on Spinoza's. I shall try to show that, nevertheless, his understanding of Spinoza was faulty, and in order to do this, it will first be necessary to give some brief account of Brunner's own position.

Human consciousness, according to Brunner, has three inseparable aspects: feeling, knowing and willing (*Fühlen, Wissen, und Wollen*). This is the familiar psychologist's assertion that all experience is at once emotive, cognitive, and conative. The triad is reflected in all Brunner's further classification of experience, which, for him, falls into three grades, or "faculties." The first is what he calls practical understanding, embracing basic experience (*Grunderfahrung*) and scientific abstraction. Basic experience is sense-perception and common sense, and scientific abstraction includes the formal and empirical sciences, all of which, he maintains, give us only relative knowledge, useful for practical purposes, but ultimately unintelligible and unsustainable.

Practical understanding offers a conception of the world as consisting solely of matter (or things) in motion, including ourselves; and things, when closely investigated and analyzed, themselves reduce to motion, so that the ultimate scientific abstraction is the reduction of everything to one universal movement, but without anything that moves. So Brunner contends that science, and with it practical understanding, finally becomes incoherent, and what it offers in the last resort is inconceivable.

Although it is not directly relevant to my present subject, it is interesting to notice, in passing, that this idea is very close to that suggested by contemporary physics and in particular by the late Professor David Bohm, who described the physical matrix of the world as a universal "holomovement." Nowadays physicists equate matter with energy, and particles with wave motion; but what it is exactly that moves is unclear, since the theory of relativity has abolished the luciferous ether and offers no medium in which waves can occur.

Brunner, however, concludes that, mainly for this very reason, the practical understanding offers no intelligible conception of reality, and can give only relative truth. This is the cognitive aspect of this level of experience, but, as it has purely practical relevance, it participates also in willing, and, being sensuous at base, it is essentially felt and has emotive tone. We perceive ourselves as "things" (our bodies), and our consciousness is no more than the inner aspect of the motion that constitutes our bodily activity.

Brunner does not explicitly state that practical understanding corresponds to what Spinoza called *imaginatio*, but it is fairly obvious that *Grunderfahrung* does. Yet he assigns empirical science with its abstractions to the category of relative knowledge. Spinoza also includes abstract generalization under *imaginatio*; but Brunner holds that science deals with "common notions" and identifies these with that to which Spinoza applies the same phrase and attributes to *ratio*. There is here some confusion, and I shall return to it presently.

The second level of experience is spiritual thinking (*Geist oder Denken*). Here the full truth is attained, again in three forms: Art (the felt absolute), Philosophy (absolute knowing), and Love (the willed absolute). Philosophy consists in the recognition that practical understanding is merely relative knowing, and that, therefore, there is an intuitive form of mystical cognition that grasps the true nature of the real. This essential nature of reality he identifies as *Denken*. Even practical understanding is nothing really other than thought. Our sensation is a phase of consciousness, so is our perception, and all science is conceptual abstraction; thus our entire view of the thingly world is ideal—an ideal construction created solely for practical purposes. Once the relative character of this construction is recognized, we are able if we think spiritually to realize that the true nature of the real is spiritual thinking.

Few people, however, are capable of spiritual thinking. The mass of humanity (*das Volk*) cannot transcend the understanding; and, in their endeavor to grasp the ultimate truth, they absolutize the relative, and relativize the absolute, producing superstition (*Aberglauben*): religion, metaphysics, and moralism.

There is much of interest in this doctrine and also much to criticize, but it would take us too far afield from our present subject, which is to note the influence of Spinoza upon Brunner's thinking, if we were to embark upon detailed discussion of Brunner's philosophy as a whole. What is stated here is merely to provide a background for the consideration of Brunner's interpretation of Spinoza. It will, however, be immediately apparent that Brunner is expounding a form of Idealism, owing something to Schopenhauer, and with affinities to (although no evidence of direct influence from) F. H. Bradley, as well as Bergson (e.g., in its characterization of the physical world as a mere intellectual construction for practical purposes).

Like Brunner, Bradley also held that ordinary relational thinking, good enough for everyday practical purposes, provides no acceptable account of reality as such, but only constitutes an appearance of the real, even (or especially) in the form of exact and empirical science. The objects and theories of such thinking he calls "ideal constructions," as does Brunner, and he contends that Reality itself can be grasped only in some form of experience that transcends relational thinking, although, for Bradley, such experience lies beyond the limits of the human understanding, and we can know what it is only in general terms and never in detail. In this respect he is nearer to Kant than Brunner would confess to be, for, as we shall presently see, Brunner thought that Kant, for all his reservations about metaphysics, adhered to a metaphysical position that is no less and no better than superstition.

In Brunner's system, the influence of Spinoza is evident through-out, as he acknowledges, maintaining that Spinoza cannot be faulted, either in detail or in general.[1] But, as I hope presently to show, it is a Spinoza in many respects misconceived and misunderstood. Brunner believed that his own philosophy was in complete agreement with Spinoza's, which he considered to be the true, in fact the only true, philosophy; but his first and perhaps most far-reaching error of inter-pretation (shared with many other Spinoza commentators) is his un-derstanding of the fourth definition in Part 1 of the *Ethics*, where Spinoza defines attribute as that which the intellect perceives of substance as constituting its essence, as referring to the human intellect. This can-not be right, because the human intellect is a finite mode in the at-tribute of Thought and could not, therefore, be the "cause" of the attribute itself, which is prior to it both logically and ontologically. Spinoza, here, is clearly referring to the infinite intellect in act (*intellectus infinitus actu*). An attribute is what God perceives as constituting His own essence, as *what* substance actually is; and what God perceives as constituting His essence is His power of action, which is the same as His power of existing. Attributes, therefore, are God's powers, and sub-stance is no crass substratum, but is a dynamic principle of creation. This misconception of Brunner's has far-reaching consequences both for his own theory and for his subsequent interpretation of Spinoza.

Brunner's next mistake is to identify Spinoza's *ratio* with abstract science, and *notiones communes* with *universalia*, which is quite contrary to Spinoza's teaching. For him, scientific abstractions (*universalia*) are no more than aids to the imagination, while the *notiones communes*, on the other hand, are the "eternal things" of which he writes in the TdIE, where he says they are *singularia*, and in them "the laws are inscribed (so to speak) . . . as in their true codes, according to which all particular things take place and are arranged." For Brunner, science is the product of the practical understanding, so even Spinoza's *ratio* becomes "relative," and morality, in consequence, is reduced to super-stition. Needless to say, Brunner's view of superstition is not Spinoza's, which is the combined result of the passions of hope and fear, and does not depend, as it does for Brunner, on the spurious absolutization of what is merely relative.

For Brunner, the human understanding cannot grasp the ultimate truth. Its knowledge is only relative. Consequently, what it perceives as constituting the essence of Substance is merely relative to its limited purposes and outlook. For those of us who understand Spinoza aright, this cannot be what he means by an attribute of God. Be that as it may, the consequence for Brunner's theory of morality is profound.

The human intellect is a feature of human nature, which Brunner ranks as one of innumerable genera, ranged in a scale of degrees corresponding to the complexities of the bodies of which they are the consciousnesses. Bodies and minds, as Spinoza teaches, are identical in substance, and *omnia animata sunt*. The human mind is thus simply the inner aspect of the motion to which its body (like all bodies), according to Brunner, reduces. This motion (he holds) is experienced as the *conatus in suo esse perseverandi*. Accordingly, the paramount human motive is self-preservation, and all human practice is self-seeking. Common morality, therefore, is nothing other than a mask and a rationalization of disguised egoism. It is the absolutizing (cf. Kant's categorical imperative) of the relativism of the practical understanding. Ordinary morality is thus a form of superstition. According to Brunner, genuine morality is mystical love, which, in his view, has no rational basis (no foundation in "understanding").

Brunner takes all this to be Spinoza's doctrine, which, unfortunately for him, it is not. Spinoza does assert the identity in substance of extension and thought (body and mind), and he does hold that all things are *animata*. So far Brunner is correct, but the consequences that he draws from these assertions are not what they should be. Also, Spinoza does maintain that common opinions of good and bad are merely relative, and that the majority of people are "are led by blind desire rather than by reason." But this is only on the level of *imaginatio* and inadequate thinking. Adequate thinking, on the level of *ratio*, leads to free action, of which the true nature of men and women (the rational nature of the intellect) is the adequate cause. For Spinoza, such action is genuine virtue, and it is not irrational, or purely mystical, love (although it abjures hate and sentimental love, and espouses true concern for the welfare of others).

Brunner declares that Spinoza's ethics has nothing whatever to do with ordinary morality, which is a dubious claim. At the same time he identifies mystical love with the blessedness of which Spinoza speaks in the fifth Part of the *Ethics*. But, whatever view one takes of mysticism, Spinoza's *amor intellectualis Dei*, as the term implies, is no mere nonrational feeling. It is concomitant with *scientia intuitiva*, which differs from *ratio* only in that it is the immediate grasp of the essence of things in relation to the essence of Substance (the relevant attribute), whereas *ratio* deduces its conclusions step by step from the laws inscribed in the "eternal things." They are both adequate levels of thinking, producing true ideas such as it is of the nature of the intellect to frame.

The eternal things of the TdIE are (as I have earlier maintained) the attributes of Substance and their infinite modes. As Spinoza explains in Ep 32, the infinite modes of extension are Motion-and-rest and *facies totius universi* (the face of the whole universe). On the first, Brunner bases his own conception of the physical world as universal motion— but this, he says, is a scientific abstraction, the product of the practical understanding, which gives merely relative truth, and is ultimately unintelligible—whereas, for Spinoza, it is an eternal truth, following immediately from the nature of Substance. From this again, the second infinite mode follows directly, the face of the whole universe, of which Spinoza says that it "compels" the changes which occur among the finite modes of extension (cf. Ep 32). It is an eternal principle of order determining the structure of the physical world, both spatially and temporally. But Brunner seems altogether to have overlooked the significance of this second infinite mode.

Further, Spinoza explains, both in this letter and in E2P13S and L7S, that all things are beminded, though in differing degrees (a doctrine that Brunner takes very seriously), and that minds are more capable of adequate thinking as their bodies are more complex and are more capable of doing and suffering many things at the same time. Bodies, moreover, are ranged in a scale of degrees of complexity from the simplest (distinguished one from another only by Motion-and-rest and velocity of motion) right up to the face of the whole universe. Again, Brunner adopts this schema, and he identifies the various grades of bodies and their ideas as genera, each of which, he says, at its own level, has its own conception of the nature of substance. There are an infinite number of such levels, and each perceives the essence of substance in its own way. These, he avers, are the infinite attributes of Substance, what the various "intellects" perceive as constituting the essence of Substance.

Ingenious though this interpretation may be, it cannot be accepted. The differing genera are all types of finite modes, and the corresponding ideas will, therefore, all be finite modes of thought. They cannot be attributes of Substance, which are eternal and each infinite in its own kind. Moreover, the finite modes of thought are logically and ontologically consequent (and not prior) to the attribute of Thought, as are likewise the finite bodies, modes of extension, posterior to the attribute of Extension.

What Spinoza actually says is that everything must be conceived under some attribute or other, and the more "perfection," or reality, anything has, the more attributes it must possess; accordingly, what is absolutely infinite and perfect must have infinite attributes (cf. E1P10S and Ep 9). Of these we know two (only), Extension and Thought, because we are bodies, the ideas of which constitute our minds. The attributes express the essence of Substance, and there is only one absolutely infinite Substance, God. But the essence of God is identical with his power, *Natura naturans* (cf. E29S), so the attributes are the powers of God. Much the same is true of finite modes, for we are told (E3P7) that the *conatus* is nothing but the actual essence of the thing itself. And it is at the same time a definite and determinate way in which the power of God expresses itself (E3P6Dem). The endeavor to persist in its own being is, in the human body, as in every other finite mode, the urge to preserve, and by the same token to increase, its power of action; for, Spinoza tells us, action, as opposed to passion, is activity of which our own nature (or essence) is the adequate cause (whereas passive affects involve external causes, and the essence of man is only an inadequate cause of the behavior associated with them). The *conatus*, therefore, being identical with essence, is an endeavor to preserve that which is the adequate cause of action, and thus to increase one's power of action.

Further, Spinoza says that it operates in the human mind both insofar as it has inadequate and insofar as it has adequate ideas (E3P9). It will follow that the endeavor of the *conatus* is to progress from *imaginatio* to more adequate ideas—to increase its power of action. Human consciousness, moreover, is self-reflective, because of every idea there is an idea (*idea ideae*), so the human mind is capable of reflecting upon its own activity and of improving its intellectual performance, progressing from *imaginatio* to *ratio* and *scientia intuitiva*. Accordingly, it can emerge, by its own effort, from what Spinoza calls a state of bondage, in which it is subject to the passions and tossed hither and thither, like the waves of the sea by contrary winds, to one of freedom, in which it acts from its own nature alone. In the first condition it is subject to all the strictures that Brunner pronounces against moralism, but in the second it is virtuous and free. This second condition, however, is no mystical ecstasy, but is the consequence of adequate, rational, thinking. Indeed, Spinoza declares that "even if we did not know that our mind is eternal, we should still regard as being of prime importance piety and religion and, to sum up completely, everything which . . . we have shown to be related to courage and nobility" (E5P41, Shirley's translation).

In this doctrine, Spinoza reconciles egoism with genuine altruism; for, while he admits that people seek what is to their advantage, it is only while they think inadequately that they misunderstand what their true advantage is, whereas, if they think adequately, they come to know for certain what is their true good; and then "the good which every man who pursues virtue aims at for himself he will also desire for the rest of mankind . . ." (E4P37). Genuine morality, therefore, is neither mere hypocritical egoism, nor simply mystical love.

Having reduced scientific theory to relative knowledge of no more than appearances (phenomena), Brunner nevertheless repudiates all allegiance to Kant, whose doctrine he classifies as metaphysics and therefore as superstition.[2] Failing to notice his own unconscious debt, as an idealist, to Kant, Brunner castigates Kantianism, in quite extreme terms, regarding the transcendental ego as a purely metaphysical concept. He likewise rejects as superstition the theory of evolution, presumably considering it metaphysical as expounded by Bergson, again apparently ignoring his own affinity to Bergson in his account of physical science and the human understanding.

In adopting these views and attitudes toward other philosophers, Brunner considers that he is faithfully following Spinoza, but we may question the justice of this assumption. Certainly Spinoza does not from surface appearances seem to espouse an evolutionary doctrine; nevertheless, there are traces of it in the passages cited above. For instance, in his account of the physical hierarchy, Spinoza more than suggests that bodies increase their power of action and degree of perfection by becoming progressively more complex and self-dependent. The title of the *Tractatus de Intellectus Emendatione* hardly suggests a rejection of the notion of a progressive intellectual advance, and the *conatus in suo esse perseverandi* is clearly a principle of striving toward greater self-sufficiency and power, not altogether unlike Bergson's *élan vital*. Whether or not one is prepared to concede these points with regard to Spinoza, Brunner's understanding of his doctrine is not in all respects entirely sound, for in several respects he seems somewhat to have misread Spinoza, although he believed himself to be following Spinoza's doctrine implicitly; and many of his followers—in fact, all whose work I have come across—accept his interpretation without question, paying too little heed to Spinoza's own text and his explicit statements.

Notes

1. Cf. Constantin Brunner, *Spinoza gegen Kant* (Assen, van Gorcum, 1974), p. 24.
2. Cf. Brunner, *Spinoza gegen Kant.*

Bibliography

Works of Spinoza

B.D.S. *Opera postuma, quorum series post praefationem exhibitur.* O.O., Amsterdam, Jan Riewertsz, 1677.

De Nagelate Schriften van B.D.S. als Zedekunst, Staatkunde, Verbetering van 't Verstand, Breven en Antwoorden. Uit verscheide Talen in het Nederlandsche gebracht. O.O., Amsterdam, Jan Riewertsz, 1678.

Benedicti de Spinoza opera quae supersunt omnia. Iterum edenda curavit, praefationes, vitam auctoris, nec non notitias, quae ad historiam scriptorem pertinet, addidit Henr. Eberh. Gottlieb Paulus, Ph. ac Th. D. hujus Prof. Ord. Jenensis. 2 Bde. Jena, Bibliopolis academico, 1802–1803.

Benedicti de Spinoza Opera quae supersunt omnia. Ex ed. principibus denuo ed et praef. est Carolus Hermanus Bruder. 3 Bde Leipzig, Tauchnitz, 1843–1846.

Spinoza, Benedict: *Opera quotquot reperta sent.* Ed. J. van Vloten and J. P. N. Land (Latin and Nederlands). The Hague, Nÿhoff, 1882–1883, 2 vols.; 1913–1914, 4 vols.

Spinoza Opera. Im Auftrag der Heidelberger Akademie der Wissenschaften hrsg. von Carl Gebhardt. 4 Bde. Heidelberg, Winter, 1925, 1972 (kritische Ausgabe).

English Translations

Baruch Spinoza: The Ethics and Selected Letters. Trans. Samuel Shirley, ed. and introduction by Seymour Feldman. Indianapolis and Cambridge, Hackett, 1982.

Benedict de Spinoza, The Political Works. The Tractatus Theologico-Politicus in part and the *Tractatus Politicus* in full. Ed., trans., and with an introduction and notes by A. G. Wernham. Oxford, Clarendon Press, 1958.

The Chief Works of Spinoza. Trans. R. H. M. Elwes. 2 vols., London, Bell, 1883–1884: 1 vol. with introduction by Frank Sewall, New York, Tudor, 1936; rpt. New York, Dover, 1955, 1966.

The Collected Works of Spinoza. Ed. E. Curley. Princeton, Princeton University Press, 1985.

The Correspondence of Spinoza. Trans. with introduction and annotations by A. Wolf. London, Frank Cass (by arrangement with Allen and Unwin), 1928, 1966.

Early Philosphical Writings: The Cartesian Principles and Thoughts on Metaphysics. Trans. F. A. Hayes and D. Bidney. Indianapolis and New York, Liberal Arts Press, 1963.

Ethic of Benedict de Spinoza. Trans. W. Hale White and Amelia Hutchinson Stir-
ling. London, T. Fisher Unwin, 1894.
The Philosophy of Spinoza. Selected from his chief works, with a Life and an
introduction by Joseph Ratner. New York, Modern Library, Random House,
1927, 1954.
Spinoza's "Ethics" and "De Intellectus Emendatione." Trans. A. Boyle, with introduction by G. Santayana. London, J. M. Dent & Sons; New York, E. P.
Dutton, 1910.
Spinoza's Short Treatise on God, Man, and his Well-being. Trans., ed., and with
an introduction, commentary, and a short life of Spinoza by A. Wolf. New
York, Russell and Russell, 1963.
Spinoza: Works (Selections). Ed. John Wild. New York, Charles Scribner's Sons,
1930.

BIBLIOGRAPHIES

Catalogue van de Bibliotheek der Vereniging het Spinozahuis. Leiden, Vereniging
het Spinozahuis, 1965.
Oko, Adolph S. *The Spinoza Bibliography.* Boston, G. K. Hall, 1964.
van der Werf, T. and Heine Siebrand, Coen Westerveen. *A Spinoza Bibliography 1971–1983.* Mededelingen XLVI vanwege het Spinozahuis. Leiden,
E. J. Brill, 1984.
Wetlesen, J. *Spinoza Bibliography 1940–1970.* Oslo, Universitetsforlaget, 1972.

OTHER WORKS ON SPINOZA AND REFERENCES IN THE TEXT

Althusius, J. *Politica Methodica Digesta* (1603). Gröningen, 1610; Herborn, 1614;
Cambridge, Mass., Harvard University Press, 1932.
Aquinas, T. *Summa Theologica: Basic Writings of St. Thomas Aquinas.* Edited and
Annotated with Introduction by A. C. Pegis. New York, Random House,
1945. 2 vols.
Barker, H. "Notes on the Second Part of Spinoza's *Ethics.*" *Mind* 67, 1938.
Bennett, J. *A Study of Spinoza's Ethics.* Indianapolis, Hackett, 1984.
Bertalanffy, L. von. *Problems of Life.* London, Watts, 1952.
Bidney, D. *Psychology and Ethics of Spinoza.* New York, Russell and Russell, 1962.
Bohm, D. *Wholeness and the Implicate Order.* London, Routledge and Kegan
Paul, 1980; Boston, Ark Paperbacks, 1983.
Bowman, C. "Spinoza's Idea of the Body." *Idealistic Studies,* I, 1971.
Bradley, F. H. *Essays on Truth and Reality.* Oxford, Clarendon Press, 1914,
1962.
———. *Appearance and Reality.* Oxford, Clarendon Press, 1897, 1962.
Brain, R. *Mind, Perception, and Science.* Oxford, Blackwell, 1951.
Braithwaite, R. B. *Scientific Explanation.* Cambridge, Cambridge University Press,
1946.
Bratuschek, E. *Worin bestehen die unzählichigen Attribute der Substanz bei Spinoza.*
Berlin, Druk der Associations Buchdruckerei, 1871.
Brunner, Constantin, *Science, Spirit, Superstition.* Trans. Abraham Suhl, ed. Walter
Bernard. London, G. Allen and Unwin, 1968.
———. *Spinoza gegen Kant.* Assen, van Gorcum, 1974.

Buchanan, G. *De Jure Regni apud Scotos.* Edinburgh, Johannum Rosseum pro Henrico Charten's, 1579.

Caird, J. *Spinoza.* Edinburgh and London, William Blackwood and Sons, 1910.

Capra, F. *The Tao of Physics.* London, Wildwood House, 1976; rpt. London, Fontana, 1983.

Collingwood, R. G. *An Essay on Philosophical Method.* Oxford, Clarendon Press, 1933.

———. *The Idea of History.* Oxford, Clarendon Press, 1946.

———. *The Idea of Nature.* Oxford, Clarendon Press, 1945.

———. *The New Leviathan.* Oxford, Clarendon Press, 1942, 1944, 1947, 1958.

Curley, E. M. *Spinoza's Metaphysics: An Essay in Interpretation.* Cambridge, Mass., Harvard University Press, 1969.

DeDeugd, C. *The Significance of Spinoza's First Kind of Knowledge.* Atlantic Highlands, N.J., Humanities Press, 1966.

Deleuze, G. *Spinoza et le probleme de l'expression.* Paris, Les Editions de Minuit, 1968: English translation by M. Joughin, *Expressionism in Philosophy,* New York, Zone Books, 1990.

den Tex, J. *Spinoza over de Tolerantie.* Mededelingen vanwege het Spinozahuis. XXIII, Leiden, E. J. Brill, 1967.

Descartes, R. *Meditations on First Philosophy.* New York, Library of Liberal Arts, 1951.

Dunner, J. *Baruch Spinoza and Western Democracy.* New York. Philosophical Library, Random House, 1955.

Duplessis Mornay, P. *Vindiciae contra Tyrannos.* English trans., 1622, 1631, 1648, 1660, 1689.

Eddington, A. *The Expanding Universe.* Cambridge, Cambridge University Press, 1933.

———. *New Pathways in Science.* Cambridge, Cambridge University Press, 1953.

———. *The Philosophy of Physical Science.* Cambridge, Cambridge University Press, 1939.

Einstein, A. *The Meaning of Relativity.* London, Methuen, 1956.

———. *Relativity: The Special and General Theory.* London, Methuen, 1960.

Eisenstein, I. *Ein neuer Beitrag zum Verständnis Spinozas, aufgrund der Lehre Constantin Brunners.* Frankfurt-am-Main, Athenäum, 1989.

Evans, C. O. "A Parapsychological Interpretation of Freud." *Psychoenergetic Systems* 2, No. 6, 1976.

Feuer, L. S. *Spinoza and the Rise of Liberalism.* Boston, Beacon Press, 1966.

Fichte, J. G. *Darstellung der Wissenschafteslehre* (1801–1802). Herausgegeben von Reinhard Lauth. Hamburg, Felix Meiner Verlag, 1977.

———. *Grundlage der gesamten Wissenschaftslehre* (1794). Hamburg, Felix Meiner Verlag, 1961.

———. *Die Wissenschaftslehre im Allgemeinen Umriß, Nagelassene Werke* (1810).

Fischer, K. *Spinozas Leben, Werke, und Lehre.* Heidelberg, C. Winter, 1946.

Freudenthal, J. *Die Lebensgeschichte Spinozas in Quellenschriften.* Leipzig, Veit, 1899.

Friedmann, G. *Leibniz et Spinoza.* Paris, Gallimard, 1962.

Gueroult, M. *Spinoza.* Paris, Hildesheim, 1968–1974. 2 vols.

Goetz, H. *Leben ist Denken.* Frankfurt-am-Main, Athenäum, 1987.

Grier, P., ed. *Dialectic and Contemporary Science.* Lanham, Md., University Press of America, 1989.

Haldane, J. S. *The Philosophical Basis of Biology*. London and New York, Doubleday, 1931.
Hallet, H. F. *Aeternitas: A Spinozistic Study*. Oxford, Clarendon Press, 1930.
———. *Benedict de Spinoza: Elements of his Philosophy*. London, Athlone Press, 1957.
———. *Creation, Emanation, and Salvation: A Spinozistic Study*. The Hague, Martinus Nijhoff, 1962.
———. "On a Reputed Equivoque in the Philosophy of Spinoza." *Review of Metaphysics*. III, 1949.
Hampshire, S. *Spinoza*. Harmondsworth, Penguin Books, 1946, 1961.
Harris, E. E. *Atheism and Theism*. New Orleans, Tulane University Press, 1977; reprinted, Atlantic Highlands, N.J., Humanities Press, 1993.
———. *Cosmos and Anthropos*. Atlantic Highlands, N.J., Humanities Press, 1991.
———. *Cosmos and Theos*. Atlantic Highlands, N.J., Humanities Press, 1992.
———. *Formal, Transcendental, and Dialectical Thinking*. Albany, State University of New York Press, 1987.
———. *The Foundations of Metaphysics in Science*. London, G. Allen and Unwin, 1965; Reprinted, Lanham Md., University Press of America, 1983; Atlantic Highlands, N.J., Humanities Press, 1992.
———. *Hypothesis and Perception: The Roots of Scientific Method*. London, G. Allen and Unwin, 1970.
———. *An Interpretation of the Logic of Hegel*. Lanham, Md., University Press of America, 1983.
———. *Salvation from Despair: A Reappraisal of Spinoza's Philosophy*. International Archives for the History of Ideas, The Hague, Martinus Nijhoff (Kluwer Academic), 1973. Italian translation by G. Rinaldi, *Salvezza dalla disperazione: Rivalutazione della filosofia di Spinoza*, Milan, Guerini e Associati, 1991.
———. *Spinoza's Philosophy: An Outline*. Atlantic Highlands, N.J., Humanities Press, 1992.
Hegel, G. W. F. *Enzyklopädie der Philosophischen Wissenschaften*. Vols. 8–10 of *Werke in zwanzig Bänden*. Frankfurt-am-Main, Theorie Werkausgabe, Suhrkamp, Verlag, 1970.
———. *Hegel's Philosophy of Mind*. Trans. William Wallace, together with the *Zusätze* in Boumann's text (1845), trans. A. V. Miller. Oxford, Clarendon Press, 1971.
———. *Hegel's Philosophy of Nature*. Trans. A. V. Miller, with foreword by J. N. Findlay. Oxford, Clarendon Press, 1970.
———. *Lectures on the History of Philosophy*. Trans. E. S. Haldane and Frances H. Simson. London, Routledge and Kegan Paul, 1896, rpt. 1955, 1963, 1968, 3 vols.
———. *Lectures on the Philosophy of World History, Introduction*. Trans. H. B. Nisbet. Cambridge, Cambridge University Press, 1975.
———. *The Logic of Hegel*. Trans. William Wallace. Oxford, Clarendon Press, 1892. Revised with introduction by J. N. Findlay, Oxford, Clarendon Press, 1975.
———. *Vorlesungen über die Geschichte der Philosophie*. Vols. 19–20 of *Werke in zwanzig Bänden*. Frankfurt-am-Main, Theorie Werktausgabe, Suhrkamp Verlag, 1971.
Heisenberg, W. *Philosophical Problems of Nuclear Science*. London, Faber and Faber, 1952.

——. *Physics and Philosophy.* New York, Harper, 1958, 1962.

Hobbes, T. *Leviathan.* Rpt. from the edition of 1651, with introduction by W. G. Pogson Smith. Oxford, Clarendon Press, 1909, 1929, 1943.

Huan, G. *Le Dieu de Spinoza.* Arras, Schoutheer Frères, 1913.

Hubbeling, H. G. *Spinoza.* Baarn, Het Wereldvenster, 1966.

——. *Spinoza's Methodology.* Assen, van Gorcum, 1964.

Husserl, E. *Experience and Judgement.* Trans. J. S. Churchill and K. Ameriks. Evanston, Northwestern University Press, 1973.

Jaspers, K. *Spinoza.* New York and London, Harcourt Brace, 1966.

——. *A Study of the Ethics of Spinoza.* Oxford, Clarendon Press, 1901; rpt. New York, Russell and Russell, 1964.

Joachim, H. H. *Spinoza's Tractatus de Intellectus Emendatione.* Oxford, Clarendon Press, 1940.

Kant, I. *Kritik der reinen Vernunft.* Leipzig, Felix Meiner Verlag, 1926.

Leibniz, G. W. *Philosophical Letters and Papers.* Ed. L. E. Loemke. Dordrecht, D. Reidel; Atlantic Highlands, N.J., Humanities Press, 1979.

——. *Philosophische Schriften.* Berlin and Halle, Weidmann, 1875–1890.

——. *De vera methodo Philosophiae et Theologiae.* In *Opera Philosophica*, ed. J. E. Erdmann. Faksimile der Ausgabe 1640, Berlin, G. Eichlerei, 1840.

——. *Philosophical Essays.* Trans. R. Ariew and D. Garber. Indianapolis and Cambridge, Hackett, 1989.

Locke, J. *Two Treatises of Government.* Ed. P. Laslett. Cambridge, Cambridge University Press, 1960, 1963.

Lovelock, J. *Gaia: A New Look at Life on Earth.* Oxford, Oxford University Press, 1979.

Macherey, P. *Hegel ou Spinoza.* Paris, François Maspero, 1979.

McKeon, R. *The Philosophy of Spinoza: The Unity of his Thought.* New York, Longmans, Green, 1928.

McShea, R. J. *The Political Philosophy of Spinoza.* New York, Columbia University Press, 1968.

Matheron, A. *Individu et communauté chez Spinoza.* Paris, Editions de Minuit, 1969.

——. *Le Christ et le salut des ignorants chez Spinoza.* Paris, Editions de Minuit, 1971.

Mark, T. C. *Spinoza's Theory of Truth.* New York, Columbia University Press, 1972.

Martineau, J. *A Study of Spinoza.* London, Macmillan, 1883; rpt. Books for Libraries, 1971.

Meinsma, K. O. *Spinoza en zijn kring.* The Hague, Martinus Nijhoff, 1896.

Merleau-Ponty, M. *The Phenomenology of Perception.* Trans. C. Smith. London, Routledge and Kegan Paul; Atlantic Highlands, N.J., Humanities Press, 1962.

——. *The Primacy of Perception.* Evanston, Northwestern University Press, 1964.

——. *The Visible and the Invisible.* Trans. A. Lingis. Evanston, Northwestern University Press, 1964.

Meyer, H. A. *The Spinoza-Hegel Paradox.* Ithaca, Cornell University Press, 1944.

Mignini, F. *Ars Imaginandi. Apparenza e Rappresentazione in Spinoza.* Naples, 1981.

——. *Introduzione a Spinoza.* Rome, 1983.

Milton, J. *The Tenure of Kings and Magistrates.* London, pub. J. Milton, 1649.

Monod, J. *Le Hasard et la nécessité.* Paris, Edition de Seuil, 1970.

Moreau, J. *Spinoza et le spinozisme.* Paris, Presses Universitaires de France, 1971, 1977.

Naess, A. *Freedom, Emotion, and Self-subsistence: The Structure of a Central Part of Spinoza's Ethics.* Oslo, Universitetsforlaget, 1972.

Parkinson, G. H. R. *Spinoza's Theory of Knowledge.* Oxford, Clarendon Press, 1954.

Pollock, F. *Spinoza, his Life and Philosophy.* London, Duckworth, 1899; rpt. New York, Macmillan, American Scholar Publications, 1966.

Popper, K. *The Logic of Scientific Discovery.* New York and London, Basic Books, 1959.

Powell, E. E. *Spinoza and Religion.* Boston, Beacon Press, 1941.

Rousseau, J.-J. *Du Contrat social* (1762). English trans. by G. D. H. Cole. London, J. M. Dent; New York, E. P. Dutton (Everyman Library), 1913, 1946.

Roth, L. *Spinoza.* London, G. Allen and Unwin, 1929, 1954.

———. *Spinoza, Descartes and Maimonides.* Oxford, Clarendon Press, 1924; rpt. New York, Russell and Russell, 1963.

Saw, R. L. *The Vindication of Metaphysics.* London, Macmillan, 1951; rpt. New York, Russell and Russell, 1972.

Schelling, F. W. J. von. *Bruno.* Trans. M. Vater, Albany, State University of New York Press, 1984.

———. *Darstellung meines Systems der Philosophie. Sämmtliche Werke.* Vol. IV. Stuttgart, 1857.

———. *Ideen zu einer Philosophie der Natur. Sämmtliche Werke.* Vol. II. Trans. Errol E. Harris and Peter Heath as *Ideas for a Philosophy of Nature.* Cambridge, Cambridge University Press, 1988.

———. *Sämmtliche Werke.* Stuttgart, 1857.

———. *System des Transcendentalen Idealismus.* Trans. Peter Heath, with introduction by M. Vater, as *System of Transcendental Idealism (1800).* Charlottesville, University Press of Virginia, 1978.

———. *Von der Weltseele. Sämmtliche Werke.* Vol. II. Stuttgart, 1857.

Sciama, D. W. *The Unity of the Universe.* New York, Doubleday, 1961.

Strauss, L. *Persecution and the Art of Writing.* Glencoe, Ill., Free Press, 1952.

———. *Spinoza's Critique of Religion.* Translation of *Die Religionskritik Spinozas* (Berlin, Akademie Verlag, 1930) by E. M. Sinclair. New York, Schocken Books, 1965.

Suarez, F. *De Legibus, Works.* Paris, Ludovicum Vives, 1856–1866. 26 vols.

Taylor, A. E. "Some Incoherencies in Spinozism." *Mind* 66, 1937.

Thomas, L. *The Lives of a Cell.* New York, Viking Press, 1974.

van der Bend, J. G., W. Klever, M. J. Petry, J. Sperna Wieland, and F. D. Vleeskens. *Spinoza, Kernmomenten in zijn Denken.* Baarn, Het Wereldvenster, 1977.

van Leyden, W. *Seventeenth Century Metaphysics: An Examination of Some Main Concepts and Theories.* New York, Duckworth, 1968.

Vas Dias, A. M., and W. G. van der Tak. *Spinoza, Merchant and Autodidact. Studia Rosenthaliana* 16, No. 2, 1982.

Vries, T. de. *Baruch de Spinoza.* Hamburg, Rowohlt, 1970.

Walther, M. *Metaphysik als Anti-Theologie: die Philosophie Spinozas im suzammenhang der religionsphilosophischen Problematik.* Hamburg, Felix Meiner Verlag, 1971.

Watt, A. C. "The Causality of God in Spinoza's Philosophy." *Canadian Journal of Philosophy* 2, no. 2, 1972.

Wetlesen, J. *Internal Guide to the Ethics of Spinoza.* Inquiry, Blindern Oslo, Filosofisk Institutt Universitet i Oslo, 1978.

Whittaker, E. *From Euclid to Eddington.* Cambridge, Cambridge University Press, 1949.

Windelband, W. *Geschichte der Neuern Philosophie.* Breitkopf und Hartel, Leipzig, 1878.

Wisdom, J. O. *The Foundations of Inference in the Natural Sciences.* London, Methuen, 1952.

Wolfson, A. *Spinoza: A Life of Reason.* New York, Philosophical Library, 1932.

Wolfson, H. A. *The Philosophy of Spinoza.* Cambridge, Mass., Harvard University Press, 1934; rpt. New York, Meridian Books, 1965.

PERIODICALS AND ANTHOLOGIES

Chronicum Spinozanum. 5 vols. Hagae Comitis 1921–1927.

Mededelingen vanwege Het Spinozahuis. Issued annually. Leiden, E. J. Brill.

Studia Spinozana. Issued annually. Ed. W. N. A. Klever, M. Walther, and Y. Yovel. Würtzburg, Königshausen & Neumann.

Neue Hefte für Philosophie No. 12, *Spinoza 1677–1977.* Göttingen, 1977.

Curley, E. M., and P.-F. Moreau, eds. *Spinoza, Issues and Directions.* Proceedings of the Chicago Spinoza Conference. Leiden, New York, Copenhagen, and Cologne, E. J. Brill, 1990.

De Deugd, C., ed. *Spinoza's Political and Theological Thought.* International Symposium under the auspices of the Royal Netherlands Academy of Arts and Sciences, commemorating the 350th anniversary of the birth of Spinoza, Amsterdam, 24–27 November 1982. Amsterdam, Oxford, and New York, North-Holland, 1984.

Dominguez, A. *La Etica de Spinoza, Fundamentos y Significado.* Actas del Congreso Internacional, Almagro, 24–26 October, 1990. Castilla–La Mancha, Editiones de la Universidad, 1992.

Giancotti, E., ed. *Spinoza nel 350º Anniversario della Nascita.* Proceedings of the First Italian International Congress on Spinoza. Naples, Bibliopolis, 1985.

Grene, M., ed. *Spinoza: A Collection of Critical Essays.* Garden City, N.Y., Doubleday, 1973.

Hessing, S., ed. *Speculum Spinozanum 1677–1977.* London, Routledge and Kegan Paul, 1977.

Kashap, S. P., ed. *Studies in Spinoza: Critical and Interpretive Essays.* Berkeley, Los Angeles, and London, University of California Press, 1972.

Mandelbaum, M., and E. Freeman, eds. *Spinoza: Essays in Interpretation.* Lasalle, Ill., Open Court, 1975.

Olivetti, M. M., ed. *Lo Spinozismo Ieri e Oggi.* Padua, Cedam–Casa Editrice Dott. Antonio Milani, 1978.

van der Bend, J. G., ed. *Spinoza on Knowing, Being, and Freedom.* Assen, van Gorcum, 1974.

Wetlesen, J., ed. *Spinoza's Philosophy of Man.* Proceedings of the Scandinavian Spinoza Symposium, 1977. Oslo, Universitetsforlaget, 1978.

Wilbur, J., ed. *Spinoza's Metaphysics: Essays in Critical Appreciation.* Assen and Amsterdam, van Gorcum, 1976.

Index

Figures in italics indicate chapters, those in bold type indicate subsections.